CONSTRUCTIVE CONFLICT MANAGEMENT

CONSTRUCTIVE CONFLICT MANAGEMENT
ASIA-PACIFIC CASES

EDITORS
FRED E. JANDT
PAUL B. PEDERSEN

SAGE Publications
International Educational and Professional Publisher
Thousand Oaks London New Delhi

For information address:

SAGE Publications, Inc.
2455 Teller Road
Thousand Oaks, California 91320
E-mail: order@sagepub.com

SAGE Publications Ltd.
6 Bonhill Street
London EC2A 4PU
United Kingdom

SAGE Publications India Pvt. Ltd.
M-32 Market
Greater Kailash I
New Delhi 110 048 India

Printed in the United States of America

Library of Congress Cataloging-in-Publication Data

Constructive conflict management: Asia-Pacific cases / editors, Fred E. Jandt, Paul B. Pedersen.
p. cm.
Includes bibliographical references and index.
ISBN 0-8039-5948-6 (cloth). — ISBN 0-8039-5949-4 (pbk.)
1. Conflict management—Asia—Cross-cultural studies—Congresses.
2. Conflict management—Pacific Area—Cross-cultural studies—Congresses. I. Jandt, Fred Edmund. II. Pedersen, Paul, 1936- .
HM136.C69 1996
303.6′9′095—dc20 95-41816

This book is printed on acid-free paper.

96 97 98 99 10 9 8 7 6 5 4 3 2 1

Sage Production Editor: Astrid Virding
Sage Copy Editor: Joyce Kuhn
Sage Typesetter: Janelle LeMaster

Contents

Part II: Nuclear Family Conflict

Part III: Extended Family Conflict

Part IV: Land and Environmental Conflict

Conclusion

Foreword

The Asia Pacific Peace Research Association (APPRA) is the major regional organization representing academic and nonacademic peace and conflict researchers in East, South East, and South Asia and Australasia. It is one of four regional organizations within the International Peace Research Association.

As then Secretary General of APPRA, I was very pleased to join the Research and Education for Peace Unit at the Universiti Sains Malaysia and The Asia Foundation in the design and organization of the Malaysian conference at which most of the case studies included in this book were presented.

In organizing the conference it was clear that there was a fortuitous convergence of interests between the three "host" organizations and those of Fred Jandt and Paul Pedersen, the editors of this volume. All of us were concerned to spell out the extent to which the theory and practice of contemporary conflict resolution was bound to a Western cultural framework and what this might mean for theorists and practitioners from non-Occidental cultural traditions.

The conference therefore focused on facilitating dialogue with and between colleagues from the Asia-Pacific region to determine whether or not there were significant cultural differences in relation to the sources, dynamics, and resolution of dysfunctional conflicts at both the micro and macro levels of action and analysis.[1] To achieve this end, the organizers commissioned papers that traversed micro (interpersonal, local, or community based) and macro (national, regional, or international) conflicts and asked contributors to think about these conflicts in terms of the concepts of authority, nonviolence, security, and identity.[2] Although it could be argued that these concepts reflect distinctive Western concerns, they also relate to processes, which universally are both a cause and a consequence of peaceful relationships just as more violent processes flow from the arbitrary exercise of coercive power, insecurity, marginalization, and militarism.

The underlying theme of the conference was that nonviolent solutions to problems are likely to flow from processes that result in an expansion of political authority, legitimacy, and security, which create safe autonomous space for the construction and maintenance of identity and which stimulate cultures of peace and nonviolence. These processes stand in contrast to those that emphasize political and military power (involving threat, force, and coercion), insecurity (fear and anxiety), marginalization (control, isolation, and enmity), and violence. What the conference set out to explore was whether or not diverse cultures and linguistic groups would endow these processes with different meanings and then evaluate the micro- and macrosignificance of these different worldviews.

Both the micro and the macro case studies indicated very strongly that culture can generally be interpreted two ways. The first is an inertial, conservative force that reproduces the same behavior generation after generation and is generally resistant to change. (Indigenous people, for example, who appeal to some concept of traditional or mythic culture to justify repressive or nondemocratic practices are using culture in this way.) This conservative conception of culture fuels pessimism and becomes an iron cage marking the limits of the possible.

The second way of looking at culture (reflected in many of the case studies in this book) is as something that is constantly being created and reshaped by every human being, family, neighborhood, community, and nation. This orientation to culture is much more empowering. It means that individuals, groups, organizations, and social movements can learn new ways of solving problems and can transmit these new ways to others.

In this conception of culture, the enhancement of nonviolent processes for dealing with conflict requires some imaging of peaceful processes and peaceful communities and positive examples of these processes working. These case studies demonstrate a number of ways in which families, neighborhoods, interest groups, and indigenous peoples use diverse cultural traditions to promote the peaceful resolution of disputes. Each one reveals the richness of different cultural orientations to conflict and suggests the need for a little more "occidental" humility in relation to the value of Western conflict resolution theory and practice. The fact is we all have much to learn from each other, and this book is one step toward fostering a deepening of the dialogue between different cultures.

—Kevin P Clements
President, International Peace Research Association
Director, Institute for Conflict Analysis and Resolution
George Mason University
Fairfax, Virginia USA

Notes

1. Some of the macro papers from this conference have been published in a special issue of *Pacifica Review,* Vol. 6, No. 2 (1994), edited by Kevin P Clements.

2. These concepts were developed at the September 17-18, 1994 conference planning meeting in Honolulu by The Asia Foundation staff, Johan Saravanamuttu, the editors of this volume, and Kevin P Clements.

Foreword

The Asia Foundation is very pleased to have had the opportunity to join together with the Peace and Research Unit at the Universiti Sains Malaysia and the Asia Pacific Peace Research Association in organizing the historic international conference on "Conflict Resolution in the Asia Pacific Region: Culture, Problem Solving, and Peacemaking" in Penang, Malaysia, at which most of the case studies included in this volume were originally presented.

Perhaps at no time in recent history has the topic of conflict resolution been more relevant than it is today. At the international level, the end of the cold war has seen the breakdown of the once clear and predictable bipolar pattern of global and regional security relations and their replacement by a system that is far more complex and fluid. In the absence of ideological certainty and the discipline of established alliance structures, old enmities between states—some based on historical rivalries, border disputes, or religious and ethnic differences—are free to resurface and grow while new conflicts continue to emerge.

At the same time, within individual Asian countries rapid economic growth and widespread social mobilization have brought about a dramatic change from traditional patterns of personal and social interaction. People have been exposed to a wide range of new influences, ideas, and possibilities. They have moved from village and community settings characterized by long-standing and deeply internalized sets of rules and obligations to urban centers where they must deal with strangers and carve out their own identities and their own futures. They have come into contact with people who are unlike themselves and who are in competition with them to secure a better life for their children and grandchildren. With rapid economic development, even people in rural areas have entered the world of modern economic transactions and, as such, have dramatically increased the likelihood that they will be involved in disputes of one kind or another, just as expanded international commerce has inevitably increased the number of transnational commercial disputes.

Given this situation, there is a widespread sense and concern in the Asia-Pacific region that existing mechanisms for dealing with disputes, whether within individual nations or internationally, are simply not up to the task. At the national level, formal court structures are often unable to provide access to justice for the large and growing number of disputants, especially those in rural areas or those with few resources to pay court costs or lawyers' fees in circumstances when cases can sometimes drag on for years. In response to this problem, efforts are under way in many countries to develop new mechanisms for mediation and other forms of alternative dispute resolution as a way of handling the large number of disputes not being adequately addressed through formal legal systems. At the same time, a number of new institutions have emerged in the region—often university-based research centers and nongovernment citizens' organizations—that are attempting to address ethnic, religious, economic, and environmental conflicts in innovative ways.

There is also a growing belief among some Asian scholars and observers that this region may have a special contribution to make in the conflict resolution field because of its unique historical and cultural background. More specifically, there is a sense that, in addressing conflicts, what are sometimes characterized as traditional Asian proclivities and preferences for compromise and consensus building as opposed to open confrontation and an adversarial approach to issues of disagreement may lend themselves more readily to solutions reached through a process of mediation. This idea evolves in part from a view that law itself, to be truly effective in many Asian cultural contexts, must be as concerned with relationships as it is with transactions and must emphasize the preservation of social harmony as much as abstract legal notions of rights or justice that are not grounded in the political, economic, and social reality of the dispute itself. In this regard, one of the important objectives of the Penang conference was to explore the cultural dimensions of conflict and conflict resolution in Asian societies through the examination of case studies based on actual conflicts of different types that have taken place in the region in recent years.

As a private American organization with its headquarters in San Francisco and offices in 15 Asia-Pacific countries, The Asia Foundation is providing support to a number of programs in Asia to help develop new mechanisms (and strengthen existing ones) of mediation and conflict resolution in the region. These programs are being carried out by both government and nongovernment organizations and a number of academic and research centers involved in conflict resolution work in Asian countries, ranging from Sri Lanka and Malaysia to Korea and the Philippines. Among the Foundation's programs are policy research and training for the mediation of ethnic disputes, the development of community-based mediation boards to deal with local property and family disputes, the strengthening of in-country and international commercial arbitration boards, and the development of cooperative problem-solving mechanisms among business, government, and nongovernment organizations on environmental issues.

Equally important, the Foundation tries to use its network of field offices throughout the region and its extensive range of contacts within each country, to encourage information sharing and project cooperation among conflict resolution organizations in different Asian countries, and to serve as a bridge between conflict resolution professionals in Asia and their counterparts in the United States. Indeed, this kind of Asia-U.S. dialogue and cooperation is perhaps especially relevant in the conflict resolution field, given that the United States faces many of the same problems as the countries of Asia and the Pacific in dealing with the challenges of a diverse and rapidly changing society.

In closing, I would like to extend my thanks and my congratulations, on behalf of The Asia Foundation, to the editors of this volume, Fred Jandt and Paul Pedersen, and to the many contributors who have contributed so substantially to this important and, in many respects, pioneering work. The publication of this book truly represents the culmination of a unique, collaborative effort involving not just the three cosponsoring organizations of the conference but also a large and diverse group of conflict resolution professionals from many countries—academic theorists, researchers, activists, and practitioners—who came together in Penang with the common goal of seeking to advance the understanding, and thereby the effectiveness, of conflict resolution mechanisms and approaches in the Asia-Pacific region. The richness and diversity of the case studies presented in this book reflect the deliberate attempt of the conference organizers to fully explore the wide range of conflict resolution issues and topics being addressed in this most dynamic of regions and yet ground these explorations in the realm of practical application and very real human experience.

Even more important, these case studies provide clear testimony to the efforts of so many dedicated and talented individuals who are working every day to help build communities and societies characterized by social harmony, justice, and a broad, inclusive notion of political membership and citizen participation. This book, then, is in many ways a tribute to their efforts as well as representing an important intellectual contribution to the field of conflict resolution itself. The Asia Foundation is privileged to have been a partner in this endeavor.

—Gordon Hein
Vice President, The Asia Foundation
San Francisco, California USA

Foreword

The Project (now a Unit) for Peace Research and Education of the School of Social Sciences at the Universiti Sains Malaysia was particularly involved in the organization of the May 22-26, 1994 conference "Conflict Resolution in the Asia Pacific Region: Culture, Problem Solving, and Peacemaking" from the very inception of the idea. We had felt that this conference should be different from other conferences. Especially because it was focusing on conflict resolution, we felt that it was not sufficient to bring together a group of academics but also to engage academics with practitioners in the field. As chair of the Organizing Committee of Conflict Resolution Conference, I am especially gratified that this book has resulted from the conference with its emphasis on learning from case studies. The project by Professors Jandt and Pedersen is particularly useful because it attempts to look at conflict from the bottom up and especially from the perspectives of those who are intimately involved in the conflict or are socially committed to the problem at hand.

I wish to congratulate the editors and the contributors for a job well done and hope that this book will further stimulate the thinking on conflict resolution in novel ways.

Johan Saravanamuttu
Chair, Organizing Committee of Conflict Resolution Conference
Universiti Sains Malaysia, Penang

Preface

In May 1994, the international conference "Conflict Resolution in the Asia-Pacific Region: Culture, Problem Solving, and Peacemaking" was held in Penang, Malaysia. The organizers for the conference were the Universiti Sains Malaysia, Penang, The Asia Foundation, and the Asia-Pacific Peace Research Association (APPRA). The planners of the conference were Tracy Wardrop for The Asia Foundation, Kevin Clements for APPRA, Johan Saravanamuttu for the Universiti Sains Malaysia, Paul B. Pedersen of Syracuse University, and Fred E. Jandt of California State University, San Bernardino.

One purpose of the conference was to bring together those interested in the theory of mediation and those practicing mediation at both the micro (governments and nongovernment organizations, or NGOs) and macro (businesses and individuals) levels. The practicing mediators were asked to bring case studies of the mediation of multicultural conflicts. The word "mediation" can be used to refer to one style of conflict resolution. One thing that this collection of case studies illustrates is the wide range of styles in use to deal with conflicts. The title of this book reflects that diversity.

This book presents case studies developed for the conference. As much as possible, the authors' original word choice and writing style have been retained. The case studies are grouped together by the general areas of the regional/cultural context, nuclear family conflict, extended family conflict, land and environmental conflict, business conflicts, neighborhood disputes, and conflicts involving indigenous peoples. The cases are framed by an introduction and a conclusion, both by the editors.

The cases can be used for analysis and study individually or collectively to develop models for dispute resolution in the Asia-Pacific region and to demonstrate the interrelationships between culture, conflict, and dispute resolution.

In a very real sense, the conference and the ideas developed there belong to all the participants. As a product of the conference, this book represents the contributions of the participants, the Universiti Sains Malaysia as host, and The Asia Foundation as sponsor.

—Fred E. Jandt
—Paul B. Pedersen

Disclaimer

The views expressed in the case studies and analytic papers are those of the individual authors and not necessarily those of the three sponsoring agencies.

Introduction

1

Culturally Contextual Models for Creative Conflict Management

PAUL B. PEDERSEN and FRED E. JANDT

Studies of conflict management have tended to emphasize either a normative/prescriptive approach based on game theory, an individual differences approach based on personality, a structural approach based on sociology, or an information-processing approach based on cognitive judgments. At the same time, the sociocultural contextual dimension of conflict management has been minimized and marginalized to the detriment of constructive conflict management. Kramer and Messick (1995) suggest that we should reconsider the importance of the social context:

> First, we would like to suggest that a social contextualist perspective encompasses a set of core ideas about negotiation processes and outcomes. Among the most central of these ideas is the assumption that in order to understand bargaining phenomena, one needs to take into account the impact of the social and organizational environments within which such phenomena are not occasionally, but inevitably, embedded. Second, a social contextualist perspective articulates a set of values about the importance of conceptualizing individuals

> as fundamentally and essentially social decision makers. . . . Third, and significantly, research emerging from a social contextualist perspective encompasses a set of methodological convictions regarding how to approach the study of conflict behavior. (p. viii)

We know that cultural factors are important in determining the success or failure of conflict management at the macro and micro levels. We also know that mediation may succeed or fail for very different reasons, depending on the cultural context. We need a better understanding of how significant factors in the cultural context influence the conflict management process to help us explain our failures and predict success in mediating multicultural conflict.

THE CULTURAL CONTEXT

Conflict is a natural aspect of any relationship. The conflict may be positive (functional) or negative (dysfunctional). Negative conflict threatens to erode the consensus needed for growth and development. Positive conflict, when it is managed creatively, is usually about less central or fundamental issues and takes place within the context of a general consensus. Positive conflict can actually strengthen group relationships, especially if different members of the conflicting groups share common ground values.

Positive conflict between individuals or groups who share a consensus perspective may prevent those individuals or groups from polarizing against one another in an "us" versus "them" dichotomous and dangerous antipathy. Culture defines the values and interests that are at the core of conflicts, shaping perceptions, shaping alternatives, and defining outcomes as positive or negative. Communication about conflict is culturally mediated, and for that reason constructive conflict management strategies depend on cultural resources to define the common ground:

> The importance of culture and cultural symbols in facilitating or hindering cross-cultural communications dictates a need to incorporate cultural attitudes and perceptions into models and theories of conflict analysis and conflict resolution. Models that were produced by Western specialists have continued to lack the proper tools to deal with non-Western nations, and thus they have remained largely irrelevant to those people. (Rabbie, 1994, p. 37)

Conflict management strategies are different from conflict resolution. Conflict management brings conflict under control, whereas conflict resolution attempts to terminate the conflict. Conflict management recognizes the importance of positive conflict in relationships and may be a strategy to prevent conflicts from being resolved. There are two approaches to conflict resolution based on competition and cooperation. Competitive strategies are typically adversarial, presume a zero-sum relationship, sometimes rely on force, are focused on short-term victories, and can result in long-term destructive consequences. Cooperative strategies are nonadversarial, usually described in non-zero-sum perspectives and are directed toward positive long-term consequences. Unfortunately, cooperative strategies are complicated and difficult to achieve. Non-Western cultures demonstrate a variety of strategies for creative conflict management through cooperation which may be usefully applied in Western settings as well as East-West conflicts.

Most empirical research about conflict has focused on the situational rather than the cultural context (Ting-Toomey, 1985). Culture is an ambiguous and multidimensional construct that makes the isolation of research variables a complex task and introduces observer effects that complicate research. Weiss (1987) describes some of the problems for doing research on conflict and culture:

> 1. Multiple cultures—people are influenced by many different cultures, including those of the nation, the region, their ethnicity, their religious and/or other affiliations, etc. 2. Consistency versus paradox—individuals do not always behave in predictable ways according to a given style or norm. 3. Consistency versus change—some cultural markers change over time while others remain stable. Those not using up-to-date information may engineer confusion. 4. Aggregate versus individual patterns—patterns of group behavior cannot be reliably used in every situation to predict individual action. (p. 31)

Lund, Morris, and LeBaron-Duryea (1994) describe the significant and increasing research that recognizes the importance of culture in research on conflict and conflict management. All conflict involves culture and this interdisciplinary research recognizes the important relationship between conflict and the cultural context. Although the staged and linear model of conflict management popular in the Euro-American setting has proved inadequate and frequently inappropriate for non-Western cultures due to presumed third-party neutrality and an emphasis on direct face-to-face negotiation, alternative theories have not yet emerged. Lund et al. suggest that culture-centered models that incorporate culturally sensitive assessments of each conflict in its cultural context may be more appropriate than any universal intervention model. Although shared values for trust, credibility, legitimacy, and insider knowledge of the cultural context have emerged as a necessary but not sufficient condition for conflict management, the skills for creative conflict management in multicultural settings are still underdeveloped. It is difficult to describe the cultural context in such a way that individual and group differences are maintained while common group linkages are identified without oversimplifying, stereotyping, or overgeneralizing about cultures.

Lund et al. (1994) define the cultural context through a series of questions:

- When is a conflict defined as a conflict requiring intervention?
- What model of conflict management is most important?
- What kind of intervention is most appropriate?
- How should the conflict be managed or resolved?
- Should a mediator be neutral?
- How are successful outcome measures defined?
- What are the criteria of a "fair" solution?
- What are the criteria of competency in mediation?
- What special skill or knowledge is required by the mediator?
- How are the necessary competencies acquired and assessed?
- What kinds of training are available for mediators?
- What are the accountability mechanisms?

The cultural context is important throughout the process of conflict management. Different cultural groups will require uniquely different processes depending, for example, on whether property is individually owned or collectively managed. Cultural aspects go beyond superficial behaviors.

THE ASIA-PACIFIC PERSPECTIVE OF CONFLICT MANAGEMENT

Conflict is perceived and managed differently in the Asia-Pacific region. Watson-Gegeo and White (1990) discuss the need to introduce new terminology as a means of understanding the Asia-Pacific cultural context:

> We prefer the label "disentangling" over conflict resolution or dispute management because disentangling points to elements of local meaning that seem to organize and guide the activities we examine. To begin with, the notion of disentangling signals a process rather than an end product, indicating that management in moral negotiation itself may be more significant than specific decisions or outcomes. Secondly, the image of a tangled net or a knotted line suggests a blockage of purposeful activity, reminding the members of a community that the problem at hand requires attention lest it impede normal social life. It is in this sense that many of the activities examined in the following chapters are considered therapeutic for individuals and collectivi-

> ties alike. Finally, disentangling presumes a conception of an unmarked, background state-of-affairs in which the strands of people's lives do not become snarled and ineffective. Whether spoken or implied, models of "straight" or correct relations may themselves be transfigured in the disentangling process. (pp. 35-36)

Katz (1993) likewise talks about "the straight path" as a healing tradition practiced in Fiji emphasizing the spiritual dimensions of health for the individual and the community as a process of healing and honorable living.

Krauss, Rohlen, and Steinhoff (1984a, 1984b) describe Japan's unique perspective of conflict management, where the cultural ideal of harmony is more notable than in the West. Conflict is an embarrassment to be avoided as an ideal that is not always possible in Japan's conflict-permeated daily reality. The authors state,

> The question is not simply one of contrasting the real with the ideal; it is a matter of examining the rationalizations, self-explanations, copy devices, role strains and attempts to redefine conflict situations and then determining how these in turn affect the conflict process itself. (1984a, p. 11)

Duryea (1992) describes this factor in the process of face saving, face restoration, or face loss. The concept of face is Chinese in origin as a literal translation of the Chinese term *lien,* which

> represents the confidence of society in the integrity of ego's moral character, the loss of which makes it impossible for the person to function properly within the community. Lien is both a social sanction for enforcing moral standards and an internalized sanction. (Hu, 1945, p. 45)

One loses face when an individual, a group, or someone representing the group fails to meet the requirements of the socially defined role or position. Ho (1976) suggests that "face can be more important than life itself" (p. 867). The evaluations of self by others is important to the person's identity. What one thinks of oneself is less important than what one thinks others think. Ting-Toomey and Cole (1990) seek to define the concept of face in conflict management as (a) important in all communication, (b) more important in ambiguous situations, (c) particularly important in ambiguous conflict situations, (d) requiring specific face management, and (e) defined by the cultural context.

Although the notion of "face" is present in both Eastern and Western cultures, the construct is defined differently, as Augsburger (1992) points out:

> The self in most collectivistic cultures is maintained and defined through active negotiation of facework; in contrast, in Western societies the self is grounded intrapsychically in self-love, self-definition, and self-direction. In the solidarity of a collectivistic setting, the self is not free; it is bound by mutual role obligations and duties as it is structured and nurtured in an ongoing process of give-and-take in facework negotiations. In the West, there must be high consistency between public face and private self-image; in the East, the self is not an individual but a relational construct. (p. 86)

Lebra (1984) describes interpersonal conflict management in Japan as nonconfrontational: "Whether through religious conversion or secular therapies, whether through self-aggression or conflict acceptance, what is ultimately aimed at is an empty egoless, joyful and thus conflict-free self" (p. 55). Conflict and harmony are not mutually exclusive alternatives. In fact, a stronger orientation toward harmony may increase the conflict at another level. It is important to understand the relationship of conflict and harmony in each sociocultural context.

Eastern societies have typically been associated with "collectivistic" perspectives, whereas Western societies have typically been associated with "individualistic" ones (Kim, Triandis, Kâgitçibasi, Choi, & Yoon, 1994). Hofstede's (1991) definition of individualism and collectivism has been the most widely accepted standard in contemporary social science research:

> Individualism pertains to societies in which the ties between individuals are loose: everyone is expected to look after himself or herself and his or her immediate family. Collectivism as its opposite pertains to societies in which people from birth onwards are integrated into strong cohesive ingroups, which throughout people's lifetime continue to protect them in exchange for unquestioning loyalty. (p. 51)

Non-Western Asian societies have defined social obligation emphasizing collective responsibilities, whereas traditional Western psychology emphasizes the primacy of the individual (Kim et al., 1994).

Barnes (1991), writing about conflict management in the Asia-Pacific region, describes four goals of traditional community dispute resolution: "making rights effective," diverting the dispute from the court system, preserving social solidarity from social change, and resisting the centralized legal bureaucracy. The Asia-Pacific perspective of these functions is unique in several ways. A Chinese mediator, for example, described his role in a holistic perspective:

> We who engage in mediation work should use our mouths, legs and eyes more often. This means we should constantly explain the importance of living in

> harmony and dispense legal education. We should also pay frequent visits to people's houses and when we hear or see any symptoms of disputes, we should attempt to settle them before they become too serious. (Barnes, 1991, p. 26)

The traditional Chinese approach to conflict resolution is based on saving face for all parties through secret negotiations to bypass direct confrontation that would result in one or both parties' embarrassment before the audience of society (Augsburger, 1992).

LeResche (1990) describes the Korean American style of community mediation as well developed but without formal organization or sanction:

> Korean-American beliefs and practices surrounding conflict reflect Confucian teachings, even in the case of those professing other belief systems. These teachings include an emphasis on reciprocity (*shu*) and proper attitudes to be exhibited within five basic complementary relationships: loyalty between ruler and ruled, piety between father and son, duty between husband and wife, obedience and respect between elders and younger people, and mutual faith and trust between friends. Human relationships in all cases are to be built on the common good, and not for individual objectives. (p. 137)

Duryea (1992) applies this perspective to demonstrate how "insiders" are preferred to "outsiders, in most cases for help in resolving conflict" and high-status persons are preferred to lower-status persons, who function broadly as "fact-finder, thinker, educator, philosopher, diplomat, advisor, go-between, planner, social coordinator or advocate" (LeResche, 1990, p. 203).

Besides the unique aspects of mediation in the Korean American context, there is the commonly held desire for procedural "fairness." For that reason, it is important to be satisfied with mediated agreements and to comply.

Barnes (1991) points out a danger in East Asia toward building conflict resolution and management models based on the formal justice system, including the alternatives of mediation, conciliation, and minitrials developed in the Euro-American context. The danger is that traditional systems of conflict management might be overlooked, minimalized, or otherwise not incorporated in functional ways. We need to understand the difference between Asian and American conflict resolution perspectives before they are institutionalized by government-affiliated or community-based structures.

THE IMPORTANCE OF HIGH AND LOW CONTEXT

Thompson, Peterson, and Kray (1995) suggest that research has focused more on the outcomes or products of conflict management than on the process in its social context. Outcome measures are easier to measure than processes in context and therefore more convenient to research. In the research on social context, most emphasis has been placed on social cognition research to examine how the individual processes social information. Much less emphasis has been given to how the social context stimulates thinking about the conflict or, perhaps more important, socially shared cognition and the multiplier effect of individuals interacting with one another.

Context has been an important psychological construct for a long time as the background elements that stimulate, sustain and support behavior (Hull, 1943; James, 1890; Titchener, 1910). James (1890) discussed how stimuli become more distinctive when experienced in a context and modify according to changing contexts. Structuralism (Titchener, 1910) depended on context to give meaning to sensations, which derived their meaning from a particular context. Contemporary learning theories have continued the conceptual importance of context. Context becomes a superordinate concept for ordering, structuring, and interpreting behavior.

Hall (1976) researched the importance of context by separating high-context messages from low-context messages on a continuum to differentiate cultural groups:

> A "high-context" (HC) communication or message is one in which most of the information is either in the physical context or internalized in the person, while very little is in the coded, explicit transmitted part of the message. A "low-context" (LC) communication is just the opposite; i.e. the mass of the information is vested in the explicit code. (p. 91)

Typically, the more complex, technologically advanced, and multi-institutional cultures are characterized as low-context, although China provides an example of a high-context, complex, and industrialized culture.

Hall (1976) contrasts the American (low context) with the Japanese (high context) perspective regarding justice. The Japanese trial puts the accused, the court, the public, and the injured parties together to work toward settling the dispute in contrast with the protagonist-antagonist conflict in an American court. The function of the trial is to locate the crime in context so that the criminal and society see the consequences. In high-context systems persons in authority are responsible for subordinates, whereas in low-context systems, responsibility is diffused, making it difficult to fix blame. In conflict, everyone runs for cover until a low-ranking scapegoat is chosen. According to Hall (1976),

TABLE 1.1 Summary of Low-Context and High-Context Face-Negotiation Processes

Key Constructs of "Face"	*Individualistic, Low-Context Cultures*	*Collectivistic, High-Context Cultures*
Identity	Emphasis on "I" identity	Emphasis on "we" identity
Concern	Self-face concern	Other-face concern
Need	Autonomy, dissociation, negative-face need	Inclusion, association, positive-face need
Suprastrategy	Self-concern positive-face; and self-concern negative-face	Other-concern positive-face; and other-concern negative-face
Mode	Direct mode	Indirect mode
Style	Control style or confront style, and solution-oriented style	Obliging style or avoidance style affective-oriented style
Strategy	Distributive or competitive strategies	Integrative or collaborative strategies
Speech act	Direct speech acts	Indirect speech acts
Nonverbal act	Individualistic nonverbal acts, direct emotional expressions	Contextualistic (role oriented), nonverbal acts, indirect emotional expressions

SOURCE: From Ting-Toomey (1988), reprinted in Gudykunst and Ting-Toomey (1988, p. 93). Used with permission.

> Low context cultures generally refer to groups characterized by individualism, overt communication and heterogeneity. The United States, Canada and central and northern Europe are described as areas where low context cultural practices are most in evidence. High context cultures feature collective identity-focus, covert communication and homogeneity. This approach prevails in Asian countries including Japan, China and Korea as well as Latin American countries. (p. 39)

Gudykunst and Ting-Toomey (1988) associate high and low context with individualism/collectivism and the Asian concept of face in a series of 12 propositions (p. 159). They also describe the relationship between context, face, and individualistic/collectivistic tendencies (see Table 1.1).

Whereas low-context persons view indirect conflict management as weak, cowardly, or evasive, members of high-context cultures view direct conflict management as impolite and clumsy. Whereas low-context persons separate the conflict issue from the person, high-context cultures see the issue and

TABLE 1.2 Summary of Characteristics of Conflict in Low- and High-Context Cultures

Key Questions	*Low-Context Cultures*	*High-Context Cultures*
Why?	Analytic, linear logic Instrumental oriented Dichotomy between conflict and conflict parties	Synthetic, spiral logic Expressive oriented Integration of conflict and conflict parties
When?	Individual oriented Low-collective, normative expectations Violations of individual expectations create conflict potentials	Group oriented High-collective normative expectations Violations of collective expectations create conflict potentials
What?	Revealment Direct, confrontational attitude	Concealment Indirect, nonconfrontational attitude
How?	Action and solution oriented Explicit communication codes Line-logic style Rational, factual rhetoric Open, direct strategies	Face and relationship oriented Implicit communication codes Point-logic style Intuitive, affective rhetoric Ambiguous, indirect strategies

SOURCE: From Ting-Toomey (1985), reprinted in Gudykunst and Ting-Toomey (1988, p. 158). Used with permission.

person as interrelated. Whereas low-context persons seek to manage conflict toward an objective and fair solution, high-context cultures focus on the affective, relational, personal, and subjective aspects, which precludes open conflict. Whereas low-context cultures have a linear and logical worldview that is problem oriented and sensitive to individuals, high-context cultures see the conflict, event, and all actors as a package. Whereas low-context cultures value independence focused on autonomy, freedom, and personal rights, high-context cultures value inclusion, approval, and association.

Gudykunst and Ting-Toomey (1988) then summarize the characteristics of conflict in low- and high-context cultures (see Table 1.2). Low-context and high-context cultures see conflict differently. In low-context cultures, the individual is important, whereas in high-context cultures, the society is primary. In the same mode, individualistic cultures that are typically low-context prefer being direct, specific, straightforward, confrontive, and self-disclosing. Collectivistic cultures that are typically high-context prefer being indirect, ambiguous, cautious, nonconfrontational, and subtle in working through conflict. Whereas conflict in a low-context culture like the United States is seen as conflict between individual opponents, a high-context culture like China would experience conflict as part of an ongoing holistic relationship. Low-context cultures see conflict as instrumental; high-context cultures see conflict as expressive.

The Asia Foundation organized a conference on the topic "Conflict Resolution in the Asia Pacific Region: Culture, Problem-Solving, and Peacemaking," which was held May 22-26, 1994 in Penang, Malaysia. The objective was to gather scholars, policy makers, and practitioners to discuss conflict resolution in the region from a variety of perspectives to identify the key role of cultural components in mediation. Over 100 case studies and critical incidents of mediation at the macro and micro levels were presented by the 120 participants from 27 countries.

Case examples of macro- or micro-conflict in the region were discussed in small groups, followed by sessions in which a panel of rapporteurs from each group synthesized patterns of similarity and difference across cultures and disciplines at the macro and micro level. Some of the specific microconflicts presented and discussed were neighborhood governance, conflict over natural resources, conflicts involving specific cultural groups, family conflict, tribal wars, gender issues, spirituality, role conflicts, copyright disputes, insurance claims, legal arbitration, culture-specific mediation strategies, community mediation, communalism, child labor disputes, development issues, reconciliation, economic conflict, environmental issues, and rural development. Some of the specific macroconflicts presented and discussed were nuclear issues, tribalism, public dissent, human rights, ethnic conflict, nationalism, war, cultural change, the peace process, and consensus-building activities.

One significant factor in successful mediation across the 100 case examples seemed to be the differentiation of high-context from low-context cultures. High-context cultures paid attention to historical relationships and long-term outcomes. Low-context cultures focused on conflict resolution or mediation toward immediate solutions, minimizing relationships between parties, and dealing with resolution/mediation at an abstract rather than contextual level.

From these observations, Jandt and Pedersen (1994) developed a series of 17 hypotheses about creative conflict management and mediation in the region:

H1: In low-context cultures, individual participants must first accept and acknowledge that there is a conflict before resolution/mediation can begin.

H2: In high-context cultures, traditional groups must first accept and acknowledge that there is a conflict before resolution/mediation can begin.

H3: In low-context cultures, conflict and the resolution/mediation process must often be kept private.

H4: In high-context cultures, conflict is not private and must be made public before the resolution/mediation process can begin.

H5: In low-context cultures, societal conflict management is most effective in preparing an individual's skill and teaching individuals how to negotiate/mediate or resolve conflict reactivity.

H6: In high-context cultures, social conflict management emphasizes preventive measures by monitoring or mediating stress in a more proactive manner.

H7: In low-context cultures, resolution and mediation are individually defined by the individuals involved in conflict.

H8: In high-context cultures, conflict and its resolution/mediation are defined by the group or culture.

H9: The role of internationals and the media from low-context cultures is not to intervene in conflicts in high-context cultures but to call public attention to the situation so that resolution/mediation can take place on its own.

H10: In low-context cultures, settlements are usually devoid of ritual and spirituality.

H11: In high-context cultures, settlements are most often accompanied by ritual and spirituality.

H12: New arrivals from high-context cultures will not be served best by conflict resolution/mediation strategies developed in low-context cultures.

H13: In groups combining high- and low-context cultures, the most powerful group's style of dispute resolution/mediation will predominate.

H14: Low-context organizations in high-context cultures will avoid "traditional" alternative dispute resolution strategies and prefer court settlements.

H15: Relying on courts to resolve/mediate conflict is regarded as a failure in high-context cultures.

H16: Low-context cultures prefer dispute resolution/mediation to be face-to-face.

H17: High-context cultures prefer to do dispute resolution/mediation through intermediaries.

Bringing together conflict resolution/mediation theory and practice at the macro and micro level provides an opportunity to test the contrasting models of constructive conflict management. Selected cases presented at the Penang conference are analyzed in subsequent chapters to test the applicability of understanding or explaining the conflict and its management by looking at the high- and/or low-context cultures in which the conflict occurred.

Maruyama (1992) describes the importance of complexity in contextual understanding. This contextual understanding can be cultivated in several ways:

> (a) by becoming aware of the relations among seemingly unrelated aspects of human activities such as social interaction patterns, science, aesthetics, business practices, and politics; (b) by looking at a complex situation contextually to generate fresh insights and new interpretations, without being bound by existing theories; (c) by having one's feet firmly on the details of the concrete reality of his/her daily activities; (d) by simple rules; (e) by developing the ability for cross disciplinary fertilization of concepts without falling into simplifying analogies; and (f) by being wary of reductionistic holism which tends to oversimplification, homogenization, nonempirical constructs, extrapolation, superficial analogy or wishful normativism. (p. xi)

The following chapters of this book seek to understand constructive conflict management in context, even when the persons in conflict operate from different high or low levels of contextual interpretation.

PERSONAL-CULTURAL CHARACTERISTICS OF CONTEXT

Most conflict involves persons from different cultural backgrounds, broadly defined. The theoretical and practical issues of constructive conflict management require the separation of "behaviors" by persons in conflict from the culturally learned expectations behind those behaviors. This separation makes it possible to understand how two persons may unknowingly share the same expectations or values but express themselves through culturally different behaviors.

Wall and Blum (1991) demonstrate how the Western perspective of mediation is not universally accepted. The Western perspective defines mediation as a process to help disputants reach a mutually acceptable resolution. The Chinese examples in Wall and Blum's sample define mediation quite differently—as a common, matter-of-fact routine for the Chinese people where the mediators typically have close relationships with the disputants and where neutrality is of little concern. Mediation in China is not necessarily voluntary; it may be forced. The mediators are less directed toward the satisfaction of disputing parties than toward settling the dispute in a "harmonious accord." The goal of social harmony is primary for constructive conflict management. In fact, the mediator is viewed as *shuo ho ti,* or "one who talks harmony" (Pruitt, 1978), who guides disputing parties toward harmony for the good of society (Cloke, 1987). Wall and Blum (1991) suggest that this Chinese perspective of mediation is useful in Western cultures:

> That is, it seems that convincing the disputants to focus upon (a) the feelings of the other, (b) the emotional payoffs of harmony, (c) respect and empathy for the other, and so on, in coordination with assessments of material benefits could prove beneficial in any mediation" (p. 19).

Janosik (1987) describes four different approaches to culture in the negotiation and mediation literature:

1. The most popular and least complicated approach is to define culture as learned behavior, focusing on what people do rather than what they think. This approach prescribes an etiquette of proper social usage for successful negotiation.
2. Defining culture as "shared value" looks for controlling concepts or values embedded in the culture, which determines negotiation behaviors such as changing the environment to fit the persons rather than changing the persons to fit the environment. This view goes beyond describing behaviors as cultural habits learned to explain behaviors as "culturally learned."
3. A more complicated "dialectical" definition of culture recognizes tensions and contradictions in cultural values within any group to explain individual differences and changes in behavior over time. This model explains apparent discrepancies as differences of interpretation.
4. The most complicated definition of culture in context builds on systems theory rather than single-cause explanations. The cultural impact of the situation as well as the individual participants is required for a multicausal explanation. Culture is broadly defined in interdependent, interactive, and complex vari-

ables. As the definitions of culture become more complex, their practical utility —and popularity—seem to decrease.

As the different definitions of culture become more complicated and less apparently practical, the areas of cultural differences are less emphasized. Goldstein (1986) suggests an approach to multicultural mediation that includes both the ways each disputing party is culturally unique and the ways in which the disputing parties share the same culture. A successful mediation then must account for both similarities across cultures and unique differences within cultures. In a similar mode, Milner and Shook (1989) point out the importance of substantive issues regarding the culture-conflict link and the role of fundamental epistemological questions to define that linkage. They describe three phases in multicultural mediation where, first, each individual's unique view is acknowledged, second, the group seeks a "lens" or shared taxonomy across differences, and third, a "prism" that allows disputing parties to maintain their differences without sacrificing the common ground they share. This prismatic orientation seeks to protect autonomy and yet identify the basis of unity for mediators. Sunoo (1990) suggests that one way to protect both cultural diversity and unity in a cultural context is by separating behaviors from expectations so that disputing parties may be similar in expectation and—at the same time—different in behaviors.

INTRAPERSONAL CULTURAL GRID

Pedersen and Pedersen (1989a, 1989b) developed a cultural grid to incorporate broadly defined social system variables on one dimension and personal behavior, expectation, or values on the other. This synthesis of personal and social system variables combines to create the individual's or group's complex and dynamic cultural identity, as indicated in Figure 1.1.

Culture controls each specific behavior or identifiable action of each individual through that person's "expectations." Expectations are the cognitive variable that includes behavior-outcome and stimulus-outcome expectancies that guide the individual's choice of behavior. Expectations, in turn, are controlled by underlying values. Values are the belief systems that explain the importance and prioritize expectations. Social system variables are the sources in society from which values were learned. An accurate understanding of culture requires that we understand how an individual's behaviors in a particular context are controlled by learned expectations and values based on or taught by broadly defined social system variables.

This framework becomes useful in understanding the high- or low-context values and expectations that control a person's behavior. In using the Intra-

Intrapersonal Cultural Grid

Social System Variables	Behavior	Expectation	Value
Ethnographic			
Nationality			
Ethnicity			
Religion			
Language			
Demographic			
Age			
Gender			
Affectional orientation			
Physical abilities			
Status			
Social			
Economic			
Political			
Educational			
Affiliation			
Formal (like family or career)			
Informal (shared idea or value)			

Figure 1.1. The Intrapersonal Cultural Grid

personal Cultural Grid, you first specify a particular behavior in a particular context. The second step is to identify the values and expectations that describe the context in which that behavior occurred using an "if (this) then (that) . . ." relationship between the behavior and expectations. The third step is to identify the values behind each expectation. Just as there are many expectations behind each behavior, there are many values behind each expectation. The fourth step is to find out where those values were learned or taught through salient social systems. The same value may have been learned or taught by many different social systems.

This Intrapersonal Cultural Grid is, of course, frozen in time and gives a glimpse of how the cultural context controls a particular behavior in that frozen moment but not how it might be controlled in subsequent moments during which the context may have changed. Culture is dynamic, and the combination of variables will change from time to time and from place to place as well as from person to person. The important point to make with this grid is that behavior is not meaningful information or data until and unless that behavior is understood in the context of culturally learned expectations and values that controlled the behavior. Approaches to multicultural mediation or conflict management that ignore the cultural context and respond to behaviors out of context—independent of their culturally learned expectations, values and social systems—are in serious danger of being inaccurate and inappropriate.

The most difficult problem in contextual analysis of multicultural conflict is the accurate identification of expectations of one or both parties. Rubin, Kim, and Peretz (1990) point out some difficulties in accurately identifying expectations in another person. First, the perceived conflict may or may not reflect the actual situation, but both parties will respond according to their perception, accurate or not. Second, there is typically a lack of reliable or complete information in making decisions, resulting in partisan expectations by both parties. Third, both parties will often rely on stereotyped expectations about one another rather than accurate data. Fourth, ongoing relations between the parties in conflict are likely to be influenced by the accuracy and appropriateness of the mediation process. Fifth, selective perception, attributional distortion, and self-fulfilling prophecies might increase the level of conflict. Finally, the mediator's skill and judgment are important factors.

Brislin (1993) shows that attributions shape behaviors even when those attributions are wrong and that the potential for disconfirmed expectancies is especially high in contact across cultures. Bandura (1986) points out that most people decide to behave in a particular way because they expect positive results as consequences. When those expectations are not fulfilled, the persons are likely to become very upset. The difference between expectations and reality are, therefore, very important. Meichenbaum (1977) and Seligman (1989) suggest "talking down" of disconfirmed expectations as a means of putting them in a more constructive perspective. More accurate attributions are likely to be less ethnocentric and result in fewer disconfirmed expectations.

Merry (1987) describes how mediation practices across cultures depend on the context where the process rather than the substance of agreement itself becomes the focus. Zubek, Pruitt, Pierce, McGillicuddy, and Syna (1992) discuss the importance of joint problem solving in successful mediation where the mediators demonstrate empathy and the ability to understand how the cultural context controls behavior and identify jointly held positive expectations, such as trust, as essential to constructive conflict management.

INTERPERSONAL CULTURAL GRID

Depending on the cultural context, similar behaviors may have different meanings, and different behaviors might have the same meaning, as indicated

		BEHAVIOR	
		Same	Different
EXPECTATION	Same or Positive	1	2
	Different or Negative	3	4

Figure 1.2. The Interpersonal Cultural Grid

on the Intrapersonal Cultural Grid. It is important to interpret behaviors accurately in terms of the intended expectations and values attached to those behaviors (Pedersen & Pedersen, 1989a, 1989b). If two persons are able to identify common-ground positive expectations such as trust, respect, and friendship that both share, then they do not always need to display the same behaviors. The two people may agree to disagree about which behavior is appropriate and still work together in harmony.

Figure 1.2 demonstrates how the Interpersonal Cultural Grid is used for matching same/different behavior with same-positive/different-negative expectations.

The interactions between two individuals are divided into four possible quadrants. In the first quadrant, two individuals have similar behaviors and similar positive expectations. There is a high level of accuracy in both individuals' interpretations of one another's behavior. This aspect of the relationship would be harmonious and typically without conflict.

In the second quadrant, two individuals have different and potentially contentious behaviors but—knowingly or unknowingly—share the same positive expectations. There is a high level of knowing or unknowing agreement in the two people's expectations for trust, friendship, or respect, for example, but there is a low level of accuracy because each person perceives and interprets the other person's behavior out of context. This relationship is typical of misattribution in multicultural conflict.

In the third quadrant, the stronger of the two persons has forced the weaker party to conform in behavior but now the conforming partner has different or negative expectations. Although their behaviors may appear similar, they no longer share the same positive expectations. Unless these two people are able to return their relationship to an earlier stage where they did perhaps share the same positive expectations of trust, respect, and friendship, for example, the conflict between them can be expected to increase.

In the fourth quadrant, the two people have different behaviors—there no longer being a need to pretend—and different or negative expectations as well. The two people are at war with one another and would rather hurt one another than find common ground. This relationship is likely to result in hostile disengagement.

Constructive conflict management in multicultural contexts depends on coaching both parties to accurately identify shared positive expectations even though the two persons' behaviors are different and potentially contentious. This condition of "common ground" is typical of the second quadrant in the grid. The Interpersonal Cultural Grid provides a conceptual road map for the mediator to interpret another person's behavior accurately in the context of that person's cultural values and learned expectations. It is not necessary for two persons to share the same behaviors as long as they share the same positive expectations.

Cross-cultural conflict is often described in terms of the culturally learned but different behaviors of the parties in conflict. When two parties misattribute the behaviors of the other, this misattribution is likely to result in the following negative sequence of events.

1. The different and apparently hostile or contentious behaviors will suggest to one or both persons that their expectations and values are also different and contentious.
2. As each person's different and apparently hostile or contentious behaviors persist, the two persons will develop negative expectations for their relationship in the future.
3. The weaker of the two persons may be forced to modify behaviors to match the stronger but his or her expectations will become more divergent and negative.
4. Eventually, the conflict is likely to become more overt as both parties attribute negative expectations to the other.
5. Neither party will be aware of his or her misattribution.

Constructive conflict management using the Interpersonal Cultural Grid depends on identifying shared positive expectations of both persons in spite of their different and potentially contentious behaviors. With the identification of shared common-ground expectations, the following sequence of events becomes more likely.

1. The different, apparently hostile, and contentious behaviors will be understood as expressions of a shared positive expectation.

2. The parties will emphasize their shared positive expectations in a joint problem-solving format and not be sabotaged by misattributions based on judging behaviors out of their cultural context.
3. One or both parties may voluntarily modify their different behaviors to match the other's, or the two persons may agree to disagree about their behaviors.
4. The common ground defined by shared positive expectations will provide a basis for harmony in their future relationships without disrespect for one another's behavior.
5. Both parties will become more accurate in interpreting the other person's behaviors within that person's cultural context.

The Interpersonal Cultural Grid is presented as a working hypothesis for constructive conflict management in multicultural settings. The practical application of this model can be accomplished in a five-step sequence for mediating multicultural conflict:

1. Identify the specific, different, and dissimilar (apparently hostile and contentious) behaviors of culturally different persons in conflict.
2. Identify positive expectations that both parties share, such as fairness, respect, or success, in spite of their different behaviors.
3. Identify the values behind each person's different behaviors, with particular attention paid to values that both parties share in spite of their different behaviors.
4. Identify the cultural contexts of social system variables where those values were learned or taught, with particular attention paid to shared salient values.
5. Develop constructive conflict management working strategies so that neither party needs to compromise one's values but where both parties seek the most promising behaviors to represent those values.

CONCLUSION

Context and meaningful communication are closely related. Hall (1983) says, "No communication is totally independent of context and all meaning has an important contextual component" (p. 60). Each culture places more or less emphasis on context than the other, making it difficult to identify the appropriate level of contexting communication: "To give people information they do not need is to 'talk down' to them; not to give them enough information is to mystify them" (Hall, 1983, p. 61). Whereas Western cultures tend to be low-context, Asian cultures are more typically high-context (Nader, 1991). In Western theories of mediation and conflict management, this has resulted in a presumption that conflict is bad and requires "resolution" or intervention of some sort to prevent or stop the conflict.

The "harmony" model of dispute resolution popular in Western cultures has tended to oversimplify the nature of conflict:

> From the evidence at hand, conciliation, harmony, and resolution have such different consequences as to merit different labels: harmony that leads to autonomy is different than harmony that leads to control or pacification; conciliation may lead to conflict as well as to resolution, and harmony as well as to justice. Disputing processes cannot be explained as a reflection of some predetermined set of social conditions; rather they reflect the processes of cultural construction that may be a response to demand, a product of ruling interests, or a result of class conflict. (Nader, 1991, p. 55)

Although the literature indicating that the cultural context is important to understanding and managing conflict, there are few guidelines on a culture-general model to incorporate culture into the process of constructive conflict management. This chapter has discussed two models. First, there is a need to adjust for the high- or low-context emphasis in the cultures of persons in conflict. Constructive conflict management assumes that a mediator would deal with the conflict differently in a high-context culture than in a low-context culture. Second, there is a need to separate culturally learned expectations from the behaviors through which those expectations are realized. Separating same/different behaviors from same/different expectations is described in a cultural grid model.

The Interpersonal Cultural Grid is presented as a conceptual scheme for mediating multicultural conflict between persons or groups whose cultural context leads them to behave differently in spite of shared positive expectations. As Western and non-Western cultures increasingly interact as equals in power it will become less acceptable for one side to impose its behaviors on the other. The differences in culturally learned behaviors by a typically high-context non-Westerner and a typically low-context Westerner need not result in nonproductive conflict. In fact, conflict between people who share the same positive expectation for trust, respect, and friendship can be constructive and productive in their relationship.

Models of mediation and conflict management developed in a low-context Western society need to be modified for typically high-context Asian settings. A review of how conflict is viewed in the Asian high-context setting suggests a reframing of conflict and constructive conflict management. Constructive conflict management and mediating multicultural conflict requires the accurate identification of behaviors in their cultural contexts defined by values and expectations learned from social systems in one or both cultures. By separating behaviors and expectations, it becomes possible to find the common ground necessary for mediation.

The chapters that follow identify 24 case examples presented at the 1994 Penang Conference of conflict in the Asia-Pacific region. Each case can be analyzed in terms of the importance of the high or low context of parties in conflict. The success and/or failure of conflict management in each case can also be also analyzed in terms of the similar and different expectations and behaviors of the parties in conflict. In this respect, the 24 cases "test" the two models based on (a) the separation of high context from low context of disputing parties and (b) the separation of behaviors from expectations in finding common ground.

REFERENCES

Augsburger, D. W. (1992). *Conflict mediation across cultures: Pathways and patterns.* Louisville, KY: Westminister/John Knox Press.

Bandura, A. (1986). *Social foundations of thought and action: A social-cognitive view.* Englewood Cliffs, NJ: Prentice Hall.

Barnes, B. (1991). *Mediation in the Pacific Pentangle* (PCR Working Paper). Honolulu: University of Hawaii at Manoa.

Brislin, R. (1993). *Understanding culture's influence on behavior.* New York: Harcourt Brace Jovanovich.

Cloke, K. (1987). Politics and values in mediation: The Chinese experience. *Mediation Quarterly, 17,* 69-82.

Duryea, M. L. B. (1992). *Conflict and culture: A literature review and bibliography.* Victoria, BC: University of Victoria Institute for Dispute Resolution.

Goldstein, S. (1986). *Cultural Issues in mediation: A literature review* (PCR Working Paper 1986-1). Honolulu: University of Hawaii at Manoa.

Gudykunst, W., & Ting-Toomey, S. (1988). *Culture and interpersonal communication.* Newbury Park, CA: Sage.

Hall, E. T. (1976). *Beyond culture.* Garden City, NY: Anchor.

Hall, E. T. (1983). *The dance of life: The other dimension of time.* New York: Anchor.

Ho, D. Y. J. (1976). On the concept of face. *American Journal of Sociology, 81*(4), 867-884.

Hofstede, G. (1991). *Cultures and organizations: Software of the mind.* London: McGraw-Hill.

Hu, H. C. (1945). The Chinese concepts of face. *American Anthropologist, 46*(January-March), 45-64.

Hull, C. L. (1943). *Principles of behavior.* New York: Appleton-Century-Crofts.

James, W. (1890). *The principles of psychology.* New York: Henry Holt.

Jandt, F., & Pedersen, P. (1994). Indigenous mediation strategies in the Asia-Pacific region. *Aspire Newsletter, 4*(1), 10-11.

Janosik, R. J. (1987, October). Rethinking the culture-negotiation link. *Negotiation Journal,* pp. 385-394.

Katz, R. (1993). *The straight path: A story of healing and transformation in Fiji.* Reading, MA: Addison-Wesley.

Kim, U., Triandis, H. C., Kâgitçibasi, C., Choi, S. C., & Yoon, G. (1994). *Individualism and collectivism.* Thousand Oaks, CA: Sage.

Kramer, R. M., & Messick, D. M. (1995). *Negotiation as a social process.* Thousand Oaks, CA: Sage.

Krauss, E. S., Rohlen, T. P., & Steinhoff, P. C. (1984a). Conflict: An approach to the study of Japan. In E. S. Krauss, T. P. Rohlen, & P. C. Steinhoff (Eds.), *Conflict in Japan* (pp. 3-15). Honolulu: University of Hawaii Press.

Krauss, E. S., Rohlen, T. R., & Steinhoff, P. C. (1984b). Conflict: Conflict and its resolution in postwar Japan. In E. S. Kruass, T. P. Rohlen, & P. C. Steinhoff (Eds.), *Conflict in Japan* (pp. 377-397). Honolulu: University of Hawaii Press.

Lebra, T. S. (1984). Nonconfrontational strategies for management of interpersonal conflicts. In E. S. Krauss, T. P. Rohlen, & P. C. Steinhoff (Eds.), *Conflict in Japan* (pp. 41-60). Honolulu: University of Hawaii Press.

LeResche, D. N. (1990). *Procedural justice of, by, and for American Ethnic Groups. A comparison of interpersonal conflict resolution procedures used by Korean-American and American community mediation centers with procedural justice theories.* Unpublished doctoral dissertation, George Mason University.

Lund, B., Morris, C., & LeBaron Duryea, M. (1994). *Conflict and culture: Report of the Multiculturalism and Dispute Resolution Project.* Victoria, BC: University of Victoria Institute of Dispute Resolution.

Maruyama, M. (1992). Introduction. In M. Maruyama (Ed.), *Context and complexity: Cultivating contextual understanding* (pp. ix-xii). New York: Springer-Verlag.

Meichenbaum, D. (1977). *Cognitive behavior modification: An integrative approach.* New York: Plenum.

Merry, S. E. (1987). The culture and practice of mediation in parent-child conflicts. *Negotiation Journal 3*(4), 411-422.

Milner, N., & Shook, V. (1989, April). Thinking about interdisciplinary inquiry on culture and disputing. *Negotiation Journal,* pp. 133-147.

Nader, L. (1991). Harmony models and the construction of law. In K. Avruch, P. W. Black, & J. A. Scimecca (Eds.), *Conflict resolution: Cross cultural perspectives* (pp. 41-59). Westport, CT: Greenwood.

Pedersen, A., & Pedersen, P. (1989a). The Cultural Grid: A complicated and dynamic approach to multicultural counseling. *Counseling Psychology Quarterly, 2,* 133-141.

Pedersen, P., & Pedersen, A. (1989b). The Cultural Grid: A framework for multicultural counseling. *International Journal for the Advancement of Counseling, 12*(4), 299-307.

Pruitt, I. (1978). *China childhood.* San Francisco: Chinese Materials Center.

Rabbie, M. (1994). *Conflict resolution and ethnicity.* Westport, CT: Praeger.

Rubin, J. Z., Kim, S. H., & Peretz, N. M. (1990). Expectancy effects and negotiation. *Journal of Social Issues, 46*(2), 125-139.

Seligman, M. (1989). Research in clinical psychology: Why is there so much depression today? In I. Cohen (Ed.), *The G. Stanley Hall Lecture Series* (Vol. 9). Washington, DC: American Psychological Association.

Sunoo, J. J. M. (1990, October). Some guidelines for mediators of intercultural disputes. *Negotiation Journal,* pp. 383-389.

Thompson, L., Peterson, E., & Kray, L. (1995). Social context in negotiation: An information-processing perspective. In R. M. Kramer & D. M. Messick (Eds.), *Negotiation as a social process* (pp. 5-36). Thousand Oaks, CA: Sage.

Ting-Toomey, S. (1985). Toward a theory of conflict and culture. In W. Gudykunst, L. P. Stewart, & S. Ting-Toomey (Eds.), *Communication, culture, and organizational processes* (pp. 71-86). Beverly Hills, CA: Sage.

Ting-Toomey, S. (1988). Intercultural conflict styles: A face-negotiation theory. In Y. Kim & W. Gudykunst (Eds.), *Theories in intercultural communication* (pp. 213-235). Newbury Park, CA: Sage.

Ting-Toomey, S., & Cole, M. (1990). Intergroup diplomatic communication: A face-negotiation perspective. In F. Korsenny & S. Ting-Toomey (Eds.), *Communicating for peace: Diplomacy and negotiation* (pp. 77-95). Newbury Park, CA: Sage.

Titchener, E. B. (1910). *A textbook of psychology.* New York: Macmillan.

Wall, J. A., & Blum, M. (1991). Community mediation in the People's Republic of China. *Journal of Conflict Resolution, 35*(1), 3-20.

Watson-Gegeo, K., & White, G. (Eds.). (1990). *The discourse of disentangling: Conflict discourse in Pacific societies.* Palo Alto, CA: Stanford University Press.

Weiss, S. E. (1987, September). Negotiation and culture: Some thoughts on models, ghosts and options, *Dispute Resolution Forum,* pp. 3-5.

Zubek, J. M., Pruitt, D. G., Pierce, R. S., McGillicuddy, N. B., & Syna, H. (1992). Disputant and mediator behaviors affecting short-term success in mediation. *Journal of Conflict Resolution, 36*(3), 546-572.

PART I

The Regional/Cultural Context

2

Community Mediation in Malaysia

A PILOT PROGRAM FOR THE DEPARTMENT OF NATIONAL UNITY

WAN HALIM OTHMAN
Centre for Policy Research, Universiti Sains Malaysia

Malaysia is one of the world's most heterogenous countries. To deal with its diversity, Malaysia established the Department of National Unity. Within that department, the Social Relations Management System was established. Among its objectives are the training of mediators to handle crisis and conflict situations.

Wan Halim Othman describes the limitations of the family, the community, the judiciary, politicians, nongovernmental organizations, and government agencies in Malaysia in resolving conflicts. He then describes a mediation training program as another method for conflict resolution based in Malaysian value systems and traditions.

Most countries in the world have heterogeneous population structures composed of peoples of different origins and cultures. Malaysia is one of the most heterogeneous polities, with a high level of ethnic or racial, language, and religious diversities. Several writers have commented that, although many countries exhibit pluralism, Malaysia stands out as one of the most ethnically divisive societies that offers an ideal laboratory for a student of contemporary national-building techniques.

Malaysia is situated in the central part of Southeast Asia, to the south of Burma, Thailand, Laos, Kampuchea and Vietnam, to the north of Singapore and Indonesia, and to the west of the Philippines. Malaysia is a federation of 13 states: 11 in peninsular Malaysia and 2 on the island of Borneo. Every state is divided administratively into several districts. The federal government controls such matters as education, national security, foreign policy, finance, industry, trade, and federal citizenship. Other domains, such as land, religion, and local government, are under the control of the state governments. The remaining aspects are shared between the two. Malaysia has a population of 16.5 million people. The original population of the region consisted almost wholly of numerous indigenous groups, or *bumiputera* ("sons of the soil") as they are called. The British colonial rule in the 19th century, however, drastically altered the population structure of the region by encouraging an uncontrolled influx of immigrants from China and India. The indigenous groups were reduced dramatically to the status of a minority group; in 1931, in peninsular Malaysia they made up only 41.6% of the total population. The percentage of the indigenous groups improved somewhat when immigration was more restricted by the colonial authorities due to protests from the *bumiputeras*. Of the estimated 14.3 million population in 1989 for peninsular Malaysia, 57.9% were bumiputeras and the remainder mainly Chinese and Indians. Although the indigenous people currently have regained their majority status, the numerical, economic, and political strength of the other groups is such that political coalition is necessary and that their interests cannot be totally ignored before a major policy or action is taken by the government, which has always been a political coalition of ethnic political parties.

During the colonial period, the three major ethnic groups existed in their own different, separate, social and cultural worlds although coexisting within a single political polity, and the members interacted superficially in the marketplace. There was a clear differentiation of labor along ethnic lines, with the Chinese mainly employed in the mining and commercial sectors, the Indians employed on the rubber estates and as colonial government servants, and the indigenous Malays mainly earning their living as traditional farmers, with a small number of aristocratic Malays being absorbed in the lower ranks of colonial government service. Even after attaining independence in 1957, the various ethnic groups continued to concentrate in particular states and areas, although social and physical mobility had reduced the extent of this segregation. For example, the major cities and towns now consist of more indigenous populations instead of being almost solely inhabited by the immigrant groups. Since each ethnic group is relatively large in number, it is easy for its members to maintain their original customs, habits, and cultures, and restrict their sphere of interaction to the members of their own ethnic group.

GOVERNMENT EFFORTS IN MALAYSIA

The Malaysian government views the problem of ethnic relations as a real threat to the social stability of the country. Pleas for national unity and a spirit of cooperation and compromise among ethnic groups appear almost daily in the mass media. The government itself has always been a coalition government involving political parties representing all the major ethnic groups in the country. Several major policies and legislation are undertaken to help promote better ethnic relations, although they do not always gain full support from all ethnic groups. What is supported by one ethnic group may be viewed with suspicion by other groups.

Malaysia is one of the few countries that tried to handle the ethnic problem by setting up a specific agency, the Ministry of National Unity, which was established in 1971 as a response to the traumatic experience of the 1969 May riots, still fresh in everyone's memory. The ministerial status of the agency meant that it was potentially capable of exerting some influence over the activities of other ministries that might affect ethnic relations in the country. However, due to a lack of a clear conception of the exact role of the agency, and as the memory of the riots receded, the agency's status was subsequently reduced to that of a National Unity Board and later to that of an ordinary Department of National Unity. Probably indicating a new awareness of the need to promote national unity, the department's status vis-à-vis other agencies was somewhat enhanced when it was incorporated with several organizations under a new ministry named the Ministry of National Unity and Social Development in 1992.

Although only one major interethnic riot had occurred since the attainment of Malaysian independence in 1957 (the 1969 May riots), interethnic tension tended to surface when issues affecting particular ethnic interests were raised. As the number of multiethnic neighborhoods, schools, and organizations increased, the frequency of interethnic contact also increased, which also increased the possibility of conflict. The major problem faced by the newly formed department was to develop its blueprint for promoting "national unity." Theoretically speaking, anything and everything could be considered relevant to national unity. Any activity whatsoever could be seen as having some potential implications for the society. One of the problems encountered when the main function of an agency is too vague and all-encompassing is the lack of guidelines for identifying a clear priority for the use of its limited resources and manpower. Activities of peripheral significance may be given priority because they tend to be noncontroversial, easier to accomplish, use familiar administrative expertise, and the results are highly visible and easily measurable. The activities might be seen as an end in themselves instead of a means toward achieving a more significant goal. The lack of a clear direction in terms of what constituted "national unity" work was not surprising. There were no other countries that had similar agencies with whom experience and expertise could be shared.

THE SOCIAL RELATIONS MANAGEMENT SYSTEM (SRMS)

As the then Director of the Centre for Policy Research, based at the Universiti Sains Malaysia in Penang, and also as an ex-officer of the department before joining the university, I was asked to make suggestions toward integrating and rationalizing the overall functions of the Department in a more coherent and theoretically sound framework. A system that I proposed to the department was named the Social Relations Management System (SRMS), or *Sistem Pengurusan Perhubungan Sosial* (SPPS) in Malay. Among its objectives were the following:

1. Monitor the level of social relations and social tensions and conflicts in specific localities and changes that occur over time
2. Predict and manage as far as possible the outbreak of open physical conflicts and violence between social groups
3. Groom mediators and conflict intervention teams who have considerable expertise to handle crisis and conflict situations
4. Encourage nonviolent alternatives to problem solving, resulting in "win-win" outcomes as far as possible
5. Provide the Department of National Unity with a more clear and effective role and framework to guide and integrate its activities

The system that I proposed to the department used the term "social relations" instead of "ethnic relations." Intraethnic and regional relations are also important aspects of the Malaysian society, which were covered by the wider concept of social relations. Tension and conflict generated in these relations would easily spill over into interethnic relations or vice versa. The term "management" was used instead of "monitoring" because it encompassed many more processes than just that of monitoring. Management could be seen as the process of planning, organizing, actuating, and controlling in a social system in order to achieve a coordination of the human and material resources essential in the effective and efficient attainment of objectives. The four basic resources that were needed to attain the objectives were financial, physical, information, and human resources. The term "system" was used to denote the existence of clear and interdependent linkages and network between the various components that would bring about a holistic approach as opposed to an ad hoc and unsystematic approach.

The SRMS deals with four different categories of activities: promotion, prevention, conflict intervention, and rehabilitation. Promotional activities are aimed at providing opportunities for interethnic contact at all levels of the society through a variety of recreational and leisure activities or social gatherings to celebrate certain festivities. Prevention activities are aimed at high-risk target groups in high-risk areas. The approach tends to be more structured. Its activities are more intensive than promotional activities because of a high level of resistance and ethnic barriers that may already be present. Conflict intervention involves active intervention in a situation where open conflict is occurring. A special conflict management team may be involved to reduce and prevent the level of tension from escalating. Only when this level has been reduced can efforts at finding solutions be fruitful. Rehabilitation involves attempts to reestablish a new trust and relationship after a conflict has subsided but where a residue of tension still remains. Without rehabilitation efforts, the level of tension may escalate into a new outbreak of conflict.

THE NEED FOR COMMUNITY MEDIATION

Conflict is a normal component of social living. Every social system learns to live and cope with conflict. The basic root of conflict is the fact that individuals in society are separate thinking and feeling organisms capable of making choices and decisions that may not be acceptable to others. As living organisms, individuals' preoccupation with survival may make them react negatively to whatever they perceive is a threat either now or in the future. Also, limited resources place individuals in a potentially competitive relationship with one another. As a result, every society creates channels for conflict resolution, some of which more effective than others. A number of channels exist in the Malaysian society.

The Family

In precolonial traditional societies, the family played the main role in conflict resolution, usually accomplished by an elderly member of the extended family. The conflicts might involve members of the same family or members of different families related by marriage and kinship. The family was recognized by traditional societies as the main instrument of social control throughout an individual's lifespan. This meant that every individual in the society was placed under the responsibility of one's own family, even after attaining adulthood. Should the individual be involved in a conflict, it was the responsibility of family elders to resolve it. The family elder was also given the role of both police and judge, whereby powers of judgment and punishment could be made without interference from the wider society. Family elders who physically punished their members even to the point of death were considered responsible and exemplary members of the society.

Limitations. In present-day society, the family is no longer capable of playing the main role in resolving all conflicts involving its members. The society feels that the power of the family itself needs to be limited because the family is also likely to abuse this power and is often partial in dealing with its own members. The family elders, such as grandparents, granduncles, and uncles and aunts, play small roles as extended families give way to nuclear families, leaving only parents to deal with family conflicts. At the same time, society demands that parents spend increasingly more time outside the home. Children thus spend more time in schools and less with the family. Also, the family elders' role is greatly reduced as children become adults, leading their own separate lives with their own families of procreation, often physically separated from their family of orientation. Also, when family members are involved in a conflict, other members are too close emotionally to one another to effectively deal with the situation. Often, there is the tendency for one parent to align oneself with particular children, thus creating rivalry and favoritism within the family. Generally, a conflict among siblings is partially handled by Malaysian parents by being protective toward the younger sibling even though that child may be equally responsible for the conflict. Many Malaysians feel that, in many situations, a family member may be the least helpful person in a conflict situation. In these instances, a nonfamily mediator may be more helpful in resolving the conflict.

The Community

Village elders or appointed leaders are often called on to resolve conflicts that cannot be solved by the family elders. Generally speaking, village elders and leaders employ their own personal styles of resolving conflict, from using threats and warnings to more subtle counseling and mediation techniques. Often, they play the role of arbitrators and judges, deciding on who is right and wrong in a particular conflict situation. Losers may react by keeping their distance from other villagers or decide to emigrate to other communities. Open expression of dissatisfaction with the decision of the village elders and leaders is generally avoided, since that is considered as signs of rudeness, or *kurang ajar.* Rare cases of *amuk,* an outburst of hysteria, suicide, or homicide, related to dissatisfaction with the decision of village leaders, have been reported.

Limitations. Present-day village leaders are often nominated or appointed by the authorities and are not necessarily those who are held in high esteem by the villagers. They often lack credibility, experience, and emotional maturity to deal with complex conflict situations. Sometimes, the appointed leader is an outsider to the village and often associated with a particular political party. Partisan interests in politics and other personal interests may make some village leaders ineffective as mediators. Members of the community would rather handle their problems themselves or bring their grievances to the courts rather than letting the village leader handle it.

The Judiciary

As in other developing countries, the Western model of judication is firmly and widely used to resolve many forms of interpersonal conflicts in the Malaysian society. "Report it to the police" or "bring it to court" is normally seen as the most appropriate action to take when faced with a conflict. Free legal aid service is provided for those who cannot afford the costs. Syariah or Islamic religious courts are set up to deal with certain conflicts involving Muslims.

Limitations. Those who hope that reporting their cases to the police and bringing their cases to the courts to be settled soon realize that the court system is often not very efficient. Inaction on the part of the police, huge costs, press coverage and publicity, and long delays in court hearings can be highly frustrating. Instead of resolving a particular conflict, new problems and conflicts may emerge. The courts may be more suitable for cases where one does not have to continue interacting and living with the disputing party. They are less helpful in settling cases where the conflicting parties must continue a relationship—say, between neighbors or between members of a family—following their court appearance.

Politicians

In Malaysia, some politicians play the role of mediator when the need arises. This may happen when certain conflicts taking place in their constituencies failed to be resolved by the community leaders. Politicians may also be called on to mediate conflicts that occur at the state and national levels, including conflicts that cross ethnic lines. The Malaysian fondness for an ethnic political coalition provides a channel for resolving certain forms of interethnic conflicts.

Limitations. The credibility of politicians as mediators is often limited to the supporters of the particular political party or coalition party to which the politicians belong. Most politicians find mediation too time-consuming and prefer to refer the cases to other bodies.

Nongovernment Organizations (NGOs)

Some members of NGOs play significant roles as mediators even though they are often not trained to do so. For example, organizations dealing with family violence may from time to time need to do family mediation with their clients. Some NGOs dealing with consumer interests, youths, and religious activities have also been known to do some mediation work when the opportunity arises.

Limitations. Some NGOs are more interested in the role of advocates and as general change agents with less emphasis given to conflict resolution and mediation. Strong attachments to clients and certain causes make some members of NGOs frown on mediation as "giving in" or "selling out" to the opponents. Also, many NGOs in Malaysia do not have enough resources to train its members in new skills, such as counseling and mediation.

Government Agencies

Government agencies are in an excellent position to offer mediation services because of the huge human, financial, and infrastructural resources possessed by these agencies. They are established as problem-solving mechanisms dealing with almost every aspect of social life, and therefore conflict resolution should be one of the services they offer to the public.

Limitations. The weaknesses that are generally found in a bureaucracy may limit the effectiveness of mediation services offered by government agencies, such as emphasis on generalist skills as opposed to specialization, high rates of staff transfer between agencies, rigid working hours, delays, unnecessary paperwork, and so on.

COMMUNITY MEDIATION SKILLS FOR NATIONAL UNITY OFFICERS

My involvement in training officers of the Department of National Unity in mediation skills was an effort to introduce mediation service into the civil service. Officers of the department often found themselves dealing with all kinds of conflict situations, yet they felt ill-equipped to deal with them. Through a series of meetings and discussions, the officers constructed a list of basic skills they considered necessary to carry out their duties more effectively:

- Skills for Promotional-Preventive Activities
  Facilitation
  Public speaking
  Physical education programming
  Stage management
  Conducting meetings
  Monitoring
  Developing a neighborhood information system
  General counseling

- Skills for community change agent

- Skills for Interventional-Rehabilitative Activities
  Mediation
  Crisis intervention
  Counseling
  Referrals
  Stress management
  Basic riot management

TRAINING PROGRAMS UNDERTAKEN

To prepare officers of the Department of National Unity to carry out their duties effectively, an elaborate and continuous in-service training program has been in effect since 1980. In view of the lack of basic training in the field of applied social science, social work, or community work among most of its officers, the early training programs were basic in nature. About 260 officers attended each course for an average of three to four days. To make the training more effective, the participants were divided into four groups, and four separate courses were offered in four different zones throughout the country: the East Coast, North, South, and East Malaysia. This meant that about 70 officers participated in each training program, although an ideal figure for this kind of skill training should be half that number. However, for advanced mediation courses, a smaller group of about 40 officers participated. The courses conducted are the following:

Basic Course in Ethnic Relations

The course covers a basic introduction to the field of ethnic relations, dealing with basic concepts such as ethnicity, discrimination, ethnocentrism, stereotyping, and a brief history of the relationship between the various ethnic groups in Malaysia since the 19th century. This course was only for officers in the Research Division of the Department.

An Introduction Course to the Social Relations Management System (SRMS)

The course introduced the overall system before more specific skills were introduced. This course was attended by more than 265 officers at all levels (i.e., the headquarters, the state and district levels) and was conducted in four regional training centers throughout the country.

Interventional-Rehabilitative Activities

The course was an exposure to the basics of crisis intervention, problem solving, and postcrisis rehabilitation. This course was crucial because officers felt inadequate to deal with any conflict situation. It was attended by the more than 265 officers who took the Basic SRMS course, and it was conducted in four different regional training centers.

Promotional-Preventive Activities

This course helped the officers look more critically and systematically at the promotional and preventive activities that had been their main function. Although the officers felt it was easier to carry out promotional activities than those that involved problem and crisis intervention, the course enabled them to further identify new approaches and types of activities that might be more relevant and effective in promoting community involvement and unity than those they had traditionally carried out.

Basic Counseling Course

This course was organized when it was realized that the officers were constantly called to provide some counseling skills in dealing with members of the community or even with their own fellow officers. The counseling course also made the officers more aware of verbal and body languages and the appropriate ways to respond to their clients. This basic skill is also essential when they do mediation work. It is inadequate for mediators to try to move toward conflict resolution if they are unaware of the subtleties of interpersonal communication, such as empathic behavior, unconditionally positive regard (UPR), reflection, paraphrasing, effective listening or even constructive confrontation, which were covered in this basic counseling course. This course was conducted four times during the year and was attended by the officers who had attended the two previous basic programs.

Basic Mediation Course

This course was a more specific follow-up to the preceding courses whereby the focus was given to one particular skill, that of mediation. Based on my experience and association with the officers, I found that a simple three-step model of mediation was more confusing that helpful. As a result, a 13-step model was developed to help guide them in more complex cases of mediation. Simple hypothetical cases were used to demonstrate how the steps could be carried out.

Advanced Mediation Course

This course helped the participants apply the principles of mediation they had learned in the basic course to specific actual cases reported in the SRMS. Simulation and role-play were used extensively, beginning with simple interpersonal and family conflict situations to more complex neighborhood and community conflicts. Initially, the participants role-played as single mediators, and in the latter and more complex cases they were involved in co-mediation. The participants were mainly limited to those who had attended the basic course.

FUTURE TRAINING PROGRAMS

The following are training programs that need to be carried out to upgrade the officers' skills and confidence to deal with more complex mediation cases:

Basic Problem-Solving Course

It is clear that the participants in the advanced course in mediation still indicate inadequacies in certain specific skills and aptitude required in mediation. This is not surprising: The courses were quite brief and intensive in nature and duration, whereas what is more suitable is a more extensive and long-term training schedule involving a smaller number of participants. One of the weaknesses is in the area of problem solving, which will require a separate additional training course in the near future.

Empathy Training

This course aims at increasing the mediator's ability to empathize with the parties involved in mediation. Although empathy is not a skill that is easily imparted to others, it is possible to increase the participants' awareness of its importance through some training activities and simulation.

Periodic Mediation Case Conferences

Case conferences are essential and need to be conducted periodically to expose would-be mediators to a wide range of mediation situations and the sharing of experiences among them. The more cases that are observed, simulated, and analyzed, the more likely the mediators will feel confident and comfortable in facing real cases.

Mediation Team Training Course

This course will involve a smaller number of participants, who are selected from those who attended the advanced course to constitute a mediation team.

The team will be involved in mediation cases ineffectively dealt with by other channels. This team may be positioned in the department headquarters, but some of the members can be from the various states. They will act as resource persons for cases requiring mediation and can also, in time, become trainers in the skill of mediation, especially at the level of community leaders and nongovernment organizations (NGOs), and provide training for other government agencies since the Department of National Unity is the first agency to have embarked on mediation training in this country.

CONCLUSION

My long-term objective in being involved in this program is to contribute in a small way to the creation of an awareness of the need to seriously look at the way the Malaysian society handles and manages conflicts and to find ways of enhancing this management capacity. As in many Asian societies, there is a strong tendency for Malaysians to consider conflict as something undesirable that needs to be eliminated. Conflicts are seen as the willful creation of antisocial, immoral, and selfish individuals. Occurrence of conflict tends to be seen as a sign of personal failure and weakness, which brings shame (*malu*) and puts one's reputation at stake. A great deal of effort goes into concealing and denying that conflict exists. There is usually a strong pressure to conform, not to "rock the boat," and not to be "different." Suppression of true and real feelings sometimes appears to be one of the most important goals of socialization. Although this may help create an outward atmosphere of social harmony, it tends to mask some real problems that will not disappear or dissolve through suppression or denial. As a result, it is often only at the latter stages of a conflict, after some irreparable damage has occurred, that attempts are made to contain it.

This situation needs to be changed. Malaysians need to realize that conflicts are often unavoidable and sometimes may even be useful and functional to society. This means that conflicts need to be acknowledged and properly managed. The skills to manage conflict need to be learned to offset some of the more destructive responses to conflict learned earlier. New methods of conflict resolution need to be developed, taking into consideration Malaysian value systems and traditions. It does not matter where this process begins. In the long run, it should involve as many members of the society as possible. Conflict resolution should be seen as a basic living and social skill and as a frame of mind that needs to be possessed by all.

CASE SUMMARY

- Conflict is accepted as normal but undesirable.
- The family provides a model of absolute authority.
- Social change breaks down traditional methods perhaps moving from a high to a low context.
- Conflict is less likely to be dealt with openly and directly because of embarrassment.
- Outsiders are the option of last resort in mediation.
- Courts are only suitable for arbitrating with outsiders.
- Informal mediation networks are important.
- Coursework to prepare mediators focuses on knowing the context.
- Mediation skills depend heavily on traditional counseling skills.
- The skills focus on interpreting behaviors in terms of the culturally learned expectations.
- The emphasis is on harmony and behaviors contributing to harmony.
- Real problems are frequently masked through suppression or denial.
- New methods of managing conflict are perceived as needed.

3

The Reconciliation System of the Republic of China

SHIR-SHING HUANG
Ministry of Justice, Taipei, Taiwan

Traditionally in the Ching Dynasty and in the book Chou Etiquette, *respected local gentry mediated conflict in their villages. In 1955, mediation committees based in this cultural tradition were established by Taiwan's legislature. The mediators put emphasis on persuading disputants to accept the mediator's solution. The mediation committees have successfully handled thousands of cases.*

The case study presented by Shir-Shing Huang concerns Jim and Lily, whom Jim struck with his motorbike as she was walking home. Both parties desired reconciliation to avoid the courts. Jim accepted blame but had limited funds to pay a settlement. Lily felt she deserved more. The mediator suggested a compromise figure and even offered to loan Jim the money to pay the settlement.

The establishment of the reconciliation system in China can be traced back to the book *Chou Etiquette,* which described the duty of "mediators" in local offices to reconcile hatred and complaints among people. In the

Ching Dynasty, there was a system called "the agreement of co-village," which specified disputes regarding marriage, land, debts, and so forth could not be appealed to officials but had to be reconciled according to "the agreement." This was a kind of autonomy that allowed townsmen to reconcile disputes themselves and avoid serious harm. Disputes would not end up with appeals to government offices. These mediations were usually undertaken by the local gentry who kept their word, were enthusiastic about local affairs, and were respected by fellow townsmen. With their prestige and reliable comments, these mediators could make the parties in dispute willing to negotiate and accept terms of reconciliation. On the whole, the majority of civil cases in Chinese society were settled by reconciliation. The so-called government offices mainly dealt with criminal cases.

Also, consider that traditional society used to lead an agricultural life with the characteristics of simplicity, tolerance, and peace. It was believed that "peace is the best; lawsuit is the worst" so that people would avoid stirring up trouble. Experiences in daily life had taught them to believe in the motto "retreat is a gain." Therefore, when people met with a dispute they bore in mind that peaceful disposition would bring wealth and they would tolerate any unhappiness. Consequently, hostile situations could be avoided so that negotiation among people would become friendly and frequent.

RECONCILIATION SYSTEM IN VILLAGES AND TOWNS

The promulgation of the reconciliation system started from the acceptance of "Reconciliation Regulations in Villages, Towns, and Cities" in the Legislative Yuan in 1955. A mediation committee was established in each village, town, district, and city. At the beginning of the system's establishment, there were about 2,000 successful cases of reconciliation. When President Teng-Hui Lee was chairman of the Taiwan provincial government, he particularly emphasized the development of the reconciliation system. Since 1982, the relevant authority has enthusiastically suggested ways of further developing the reconciliation system. In 1982, 5,751 cases were dealt with; by 1993, the number had increased to 49,171, with the prediction being that over 50,000 cases would be dealt with in 1994. These figures suggest that our reconciliation system has made remarkable achievements.

The promotion, supervision, and management of the reconciliation system in villages, towns, and cities are as follows: The business of the reconciliation system is supervised by the central government's Ministry of Justice, with its administrative matters falling within the jurisdiction of the Ministry of Interior. In the local government, there are province-governed cities and municipalities on the top of towns or province-governed cities, which are responsible for promotion and execution of the business. The next level is reconciliation commissions set up by local villages, towns, and cities. At present, there are 368 reconciliation commissions and 3,500 volunteer mediators who engage in dispute reconciliation in Taiwan. A government regulation requires that there be at least one female mediator on each reconciliation commission. Although these mediators receive no pay, they have social prestige. As for the expenses of the commissions, they are included in the budgets of the villages, towns, and cities.

Among the many promotion services offered are the following:

- *Seminars for mediators held regularly each year.* The content covers study and introduction of cases, introduction of laws, production of documents, and so on.
- *Regular supervision and assessment.* Each year, the business of local reconciliation commissions is examined randomly by the Ministry of Justice, provinces, counties, and cities to make sure the business runs smoothly according to the law and to avoid misuse of the reconciliation system.
- *Use of television, posters, propaganda publications, and so on to introduce the advantages of the reconciliation system.* These included its being free of charge, open, convenient, and as effective as court decisions.

Since 1991, the outstanding performance of the reconciliation system has reduced causes for lawsuits. Because local reconciliation commissions were short of funds, a proposal of the subsidy budget was submitted to the parliament, the Legislative Yuan, for approval. Confirming the system's endeavor and achievements, the Legislative Yuan passed the budget without dissent. Therefore, for 1993, each successful case of reconciliation, approved by the court, will be subsidized NT$500 by the Ministry of Justice.

CHARACTERISTICS OF THE RECONCILIATION SYSTEM

Private Settlement

Mediators in Taiwan are respected and prestigious local people. Because these mediators are familiar with folkways and characters, it is easier for them to reconcile disputes. Their reconciliation shows that local people themselves can deal with local affairs.

Emotionalism

Unlike the use of civil litigation, which requires obedience with force, the reconciliation system puts emphasis on persuasion. The mediator will reconcile disputes by convincing the parties concerned with reasoning and argument and by making emotional appeals to alleviate hostility.

Convenience

Reconciliation commissions are set up in the administration offices of all villages, towns, and cities. Both parties in a dispute, if they dwell in the same area, may apply to the local reconciliation commission. If they do not dwell in the same area, they can, by agreement, apply to any reconciliation commission. The application for reconciliation is free of charge.

Enforcement

A reconciliation memorandum, agreed to by both parties and approved by the court, will have the same effect as the court's decision, and this means the court can enforce the memorandum to be executed. Moreover, after the settlement of reconciliation, the disputes concerned cannot be appealed to civil procedures, criminal procedures, or private prosecution, and such an appeal will be revoked because the reconciliation is affirmed as enforceable by the law.

THE CURRENT SITUATION

According to the "Regulations of Reconciliation in Villages, Towns, and Cities," the organization of a reconciliation commission is as follows:

- A reconciliation commission is composed of from 7 to 15 mediators. They will elect a chairman among them.
- There should be at least one female mediator in a commission.
- There will be a secretary in each commission to assist the reconciliation business. The secretary should be a worker in an administration office who is a law graduate or has graduated from other relevant departments and who is appointed by the chief of a village or town or by a mayor.
- The items of expenditure of reconciliation commissions are included in the autonomous budget by administration offices in villages, towns, and cities according to their actual need.

Mediators are nominated by chiefs of villages and towns and by mayors. Their nominations have to be approved by representatives of villages, towns, and cities. The qualifications of a mediator are as follows:

- He or she is a respected and prestigious person who has a knowledge of the law and who actually has domiciled in the village, town, or city.
- A chief of a village or town or a mayor cannot be a mediator.
- A civil servant in active service cannot be a mediator.

APPLICATION AND PROCEDURES

All cases cannot be dealt with by mediators until a formal application has been made. Reconciliation starts with the application made by the parties concerned or their agent. There is no limitation on the frequency of application for reconciliation. The parties concerned, who failed to enter into an agreement before, for instance, can reapply for reconciliation. The application process involves either completing a form and submitting it to a reconciliation commission or applying orally to the manager of a reconciliation commission who will make a written record of the application.

After an application is made, reconciliation will not start until the other party's consent is obtained for a civil case or the victim's consent is obtained for a criminal case. The other party's consent in a civil case means that both parties should obey the agreement reached by reconciliation. In criminal cases, victims and people who are eligible for filing a lawsuit can apply for reconciliation. If the victim and the party concerned are not the same person, reconciliation cannot start without the victim's consent because successful reconciliation undertaken with the victim's consent will have an effect on the victim. Without the consent of the parties concerned in both civil and criminal cases, reconciliation commissions can persuade applicants to withdraw their application or will reject their application.

After a commission accepts an application, the procedure of a reconciliation is normally made public. But if the publication of a reconciliation will affect individual reputation and privacy, the procedure of a reconciliation must not be made public. With a mild and sincere attitude, a mediator will give the parties concerned proper advice, suggest a fair and reasonable reconciliation, and seek a harmonious outcome for both parties. However, it is prohibited to punish, force, or cheat the parties concerned.

SAMPLE CASE

On May 18, 1992, when Lily was crossing a road on her way home, Jim, riding his motorbike fast, knocked her down. Lily's left leg was fractured, and this accident made it difficult for her to walk. Jim admitted that he was in a hurry and rode fast to cross the road before the green light turned red. But he argued that Lily did not pay attention to the traffic before crossing the road. Jim and Lily disputed responsibility and compensation. Therefore, Jim made an application for reconciliation to the reconciliation commission and stated that he could only make a compensation of NT$200,000 for Lily's injury. Lily, however, requested NT$300,000 for compensation and NT$50,000 for medical treatment.

On the basis of morality and justice, Jim thought he should be responsible for this accident and turned to the reconciliation commission for assistance for the following reasons:

- The mediator from a reconciliation commission would assist him in persuading the other party concerned, thus making the task of reconciliation much easier.
- He could avoid filing a lawsuit in the court and show the other party his sincerity to reconcile the dispute between them.
- Application for reconciliation was free of charge and time-saving.

After receiving the reconciliation notice, Lily, thinking of her bad luck, agreed to reconcile the dispute in the reconciliation commission on May 30, 1992 because it would be worse to file a lawsuit in the court.

THE RECONCILIATION PROCEDURE

Kim, the mediator, first studied Jim's reconciliation application and its legality. After confirming the application, Kim examined the facts and both parties' request. Kim persuaded the parties concerned to consider accepting each other's terms of reconciliation:

Jim: I can only afford a compensation of NT$200,000 and this has shown you my greatest sincerity. What else do you ask me to do?

Lily: I am very unlucky. I cannot go abroad next month. Now, I am even crippled. I still insist on NT$300,000 for compensation and NT$50,000 for medical treatment.

Kim (the mediator): Please don't be angry at each other. You two have to be blamed for this accident. If you step back and think carefully, problems can be solved when we are not arguing. Besides, we all live in the same village and there will be a lot of chances to see each other. It will be better for us to get along with each other peacefully.

Lily: It is ridiculous to ask me to bear the injury and accept his terms. If he cannot accept my terms, I will file a lawsuit in the court for justice.

Kim: You two still feel angry at each other. Please go home and think about it again. You may come back for another talk.

The next day, Kim visited Lily's home. Lily's father was at home as well. It turned out that Lily's father was one of Kim's classmates in the primary school. Kim pointed out that Jim was a nice man because he could face the accident and take responsibility. Kim persuaded Lily to appreciate Jim's sincerity and suggested NT$250,000 for compensation and medical treatment. Lily accepted Kim's suggestion because he was her father's friend.

The second talk took place on June 3, 1992. Kim suggested that Jim pay Lily NT$250,000 for compensation. If Jim could not afford it, Kim said that he could lend Jim NT$50,000 and Jim could pay back the money in installments. Jim appreciated Kim's kind assistance and accepted his suggestion to reconcile this dispute. Jim borrowed money from his father to pay Lily the compensation.

CASE SUMMARY

- Mediation is based on ancient traditions.
- Conflict is managed within the group with minimum involvement by outsiders.
- Courts deal mostly with criminal, not civil, cases.
- A separate reconciliation system is organized in villages, towns, and cities.
- Mediation is done by respected local persons, probably known personally by those in conflict.
- Harmony is the universal expectation and basis of mediation.
- Lily's case was decided on the basis of morality and justice.

- Jim and Lily both wanted to avoid the courts in their dispute.
- The mediator focused on shared expectations rather than argument.
- The mediator, Kim, established a connection with Lily's father as important to reconciliation.
- The mediator was so invested he even offered to lend Jim the NT$50,000 to pay Lily.

4

The Moral Recovery Program as a Political Tool for Social Transformation in the Philippines

MARAYA DE JESUS CHEBAT
Kabisig/Moral Recovery Program,
Makati, Metro Manila, The Philippines

In this case study, Maraya de Jesus Chebat describes the Moral Recovery Program as a tool for transformation of Filipino society. From this framework, she emphasizes that conflict represents a disharmony among parts of a society.

In its brochure, the Moral Recovery Program is described as

> a movement which aims to mobilize all Filipinos for nation-building through the practical exercise of human values in our daily lives as citizens and to awaken us all to the power of these values in achieving our individual and national goals. It seeks the empowerment of all our people, the poor, the middle class and the rich through the sustained application of human values and a code of collective existence.

President Fidel V. Ramos is quoted from his July 9, 1993 speech as saying, "Under my administration, let us make the movement serve as an instrument to strengthen the moral fiber of our people—as in our program for moral recovery."

The Moral Recovery Program in the Philippines is not a tool or a strategy for direct conflict resolution of particular issues on the micro or macro level. Rather, it is a program promulgated by the Philippine government in 1992 (Proclamation No. 62) to address the rather broader social dynamics characterizing Philippine society to understand more deeply its social situation in order to bring about a more genuine social transformation in the country. Technically, it is a political tool for social transformation, but in reality it is more of a process or a journey of a people to discover their own identity and goal, transcending political, ideological, or even religious boundaries. It should be noted at the outset that the Moral Recovery Program is presented here as a hopeful attempt to address the social issues confronting the current Philippine social situation and not as a pretentious panacea to the social ills characterizing the Filipino society.

REDEFINING CONFLICT IN THE PHILIPPINES

The definition of conflict may not necessarily be limited to opposing forces competing for power or asserting certain philosophies or ideologies. It may also mean the existence of a certain kind of disharmony among the parts or sectors of society. In the Philippines, the current major conflicts involving the different blocks of the CPP-NPA-NDF (Communist Party of the Philippines, New People's Army, National Democratic Front), the RAM-SFP-YOU (Reform the Armed Forces Movement, Soldiers of the Filipino People, Young Officers Union), and the MNLF-BMA-MILF (Moro National Liberation Front, Bangsa Moro Army, Moro Islamic Liberation Front) become insignificant when analyzed within the whole social situation characterized by poverty and underdevelopment, the exploitation and the marginalization of the poor majority, graft and corruption, inefficiency and poor public services, ecological degradation, outmigration, violence and the violation of human rights, the exploitation of women and children, unemployment, colonial mentality, and so on. In the Philippine setting, the social situation is the arena of conflict from which arise social disharmony and unrest including the conflicts mentioned earlier. Without considering this whole social situation, any effect or strategy for resolving conflicts would only tend to be palliative or anesthetic and short-lived.

Yet even the whole social situation is only symptomatic of a yet deeper issue underlying the range of social issues confronting Philippine society today. One would wonder, for example, why in a country rich in natural resources as the Philippines is there so much poverty and underdevelopment?

Or why is there so much graft and corruption or inefficiency in the delivery of public services? Why the exploitation of women and children? Or why the continuous degradation of the environment?

MATERIALISM: THE OTHER SIDE OF THE ANALYSIS

It has become conventional to explain the country's social predicament as the product of its colonial past. Colonialism, and neocolonialism, characterized by social inequality, oppression, and injustice, had produced a passive, apathetic, and fatalistic Filipino. The long centuries of colonization had conditioned the people in general to be passive and apathetic regarding the development of events in the country so that governance was left more to the ruling masters. The colonial feudal structure of domination and control had given way to a form of patronage politics in which the ruling masters, because of their control of the country's land and wealth, were able to co-opt the people into the perpetuation of their political power and consequently of their economic interests, which further perpetuated social inequality and underdevelopment.

A historical analysis emphasizing colonialism shows the kind of damage that colonialism wrought in the country as in the other countries of the world that had undergone colonization. Yet what is often neglected by social analysts is the kind of worldview with which the Filipino mind operates. The colonial masters had brought with them a certain worldview that had pervaded the West since Descartes and Newton in the 17th century. This is the materialistic worldview that dichotomized reality into mind and matter, successfully asserting that the mind could know matter objectively and that the only reality is hard fact that can be measured by mathematics and science. This particular worldview gave rise to technology and the industrial era, led by Europe and later North America, which gave birth to the systematic drive for acquisition and competition for the plunder of the earth.

The Filipino had imbibed the materialistic mentality that by the turn of the 20th century had become a global phenomenon. The two competing ideological systems of liberal capitalism and Marxist socialism, which have shaped contemporary world history, were propelled by this materialistic perspective. In fact, most if not all of the conflicts that have happened or are still happening around the world are in one way or another a struggle for material power, which ultimately is a struggle for the control of resources. Economics or the politics of acquisition determine how societies are organized. In a capitalist country such as the Philippines, where the very system had institutionalized greed and self-interest, the continuous drive for acquisition by whatever means is unabated, which wreaks great damage, namely, degradation of the environment, graft and corruption, and especially moral decadence.

THE MORAL RECOVERY PROGRAM: A SPIRITUAL REVOLUTION

Realizing that the problem behind the failure of the country's politics and the underdevelopment of its economy is basically one of values or a poverty of the spirit resulting from an overemphasis on the material aspect of development, the government launched the Moral Recovery Program (MRP) to look into the Filipino character with the aim of reinforcing society's moral fiber by solving its social ills that cause social conflicts and block genuine development. In her speech during the launching of the MRP on September 30, 1992 at the Malacanang Palace, Senator Leticia Ramos Shahani, one of the prime movers of the program, emphasized that what underlies the economic problems and political instability of the Philippines is the weakness and corruption of the moral foundation of Filipino society. She stated that a moral and spiritual recovery program was an essential element in the country's economic recovery.

From the point of view of the government, the MRP is a political strategy to catalyze a social transformation process. The objectives of the program are mainly to check and to eradicate the negative characteristics in the Filipino character—apathy, passivity, lack of patriotism, graft and corruption, mendicancy, and patronage politics, among others—and to draw out the best qualities of the Filipino, especially the core values of (a) self-reflection and internalization with God as the center; (b) pride in being a Filipino; (c) love, solidarity, and teamwork; (d) integrity, accountability, and stewardship; (e) self-reliance; (f) discipline, cleanliness, and orderliness; and (g) positive thinking.

According to President Fidel V. Ramos, the Moral Recovery Program is a spiritual revolution to develop a national culture founded on a deep love for God, one's fellow human beings, the country, and the planet earth.

KABUUAN AND THE VISION OF WHOLENESS

The Moral Recovery Program as a process is initiated through a training program called *Kabuuan* (pronounced ka-bu-o-an), which is the Filipino term for wholeness. In the MRP, Kabuuan is used to describe a transformation paradigm that looks at a person as a living system conscious of a core identity and vision, interacting in solidarity with community based on relationship values that are coherent with this identity, and with the capacity to transform the self through the experience of synthesizing the opposites and elevating them to higher levels of order and being.

Used in the MRP as a values transformation program, Kabuuan addresses the value system of the individual within an organization in the context of the community it serves. It leads the individual into an experience of wholeness including *Sarili* (self), *Kapwa* (self and others), *Samahan* (the organization or community), and *Kalikasan* (environment). Kabuuan is a values recovery of a people's historical wholeness, finding expressions in contemporary needs and aspirations. The Kabuuan Training Program accomplishes its objectives by facilitating the participants' experiences in three areas: establishment of the true identity of the self, expansion of the sense of reality, and the technology of creating.

Establishment of True Identity

Kabuuan facilitates a paradigm shift from a materialistic perspective of reality to a more spiritual worldview, that is, from a material or body consciousness of the self to a spiritual or soul consciousness, thereby unifying body and mind and enabling the self to experience wholeness which facilitates the emergence of the sense of integrity of the self. It recognizes human spirituality and the identity of the self not as an isolated entity but as a related social being and even cosmic organism interconnected with the rest of the universe.

Expansion of Reality

Once the true identity of the self is recognized and established, the outlook in life changes from the narrow material goal of acquisition and self-centeredness to the more noble values of sharing and caring, or from oppression and violence to love and compassion. Establishment of the self's true identity opens up a new way of relating as one begins to discover new venues of relationships from a sense of interconnectedness with others, with the community, with the environment, and with a supreme "spiritual force or principle" governing the universe. This has implications in personal and organizational lifestyles, the use of technology and resources, and the direction of organizational policies and strategies.

Technology of Creating

Awareness of the true identity of the self in relation to one's goal or vision and the current social reality produces a certain kind of tension between the two polarities of vision and reality. Awareness of the self's true identity synthesizes the two polarities by creatively transforming the events of the current reality toward attainment of the vision, bringing the vision closer to reality and transforming reality closer to the vision. It is significant to mention in this regard the "bite-size" contributions to the Moral Recovery Program of those who have already completed the Kabuuan Training Program. Those who have already undergone this program are expected to become catalysts of social transformation, suggesting activities they can immediately implement in support of the program—for example, planting trees, becoming a vegetarian, promoting responsible parenthood, and being honest in one's job. These are creative responses directed toward synthesizing polarities, especially those of vision and reality.

CONFLICT RESOLUTION AND PEACEMAKING

The MRP is not a direct conflict resolution process but, in the context of social transformation, is, rather, a long-term program for building peace in the country. It can, however, indirectly resolve conflicts when people of different ideological orientations, given the opportunity to discover their true identity in the Kabuuan Training Program, are able to discover a common identity as interconnected beings regardless of race, creed, or culture. People are then able to see injustice without hatred in their hearts and begin to explore alternative venues for resolving conflicts with more openness and trust.

The situation just mentioned had already happened in one of the trainings conducted by the MRP staff in 1993 in Mindanao when two of the participants of that particular training program, who happened to have both personal and ideological conflicts unknown to the training's facilitators, viewed each other with suspicion and distrust. In fact, unknown to the facilitators, both antagonists had guns tucked into their waists during the entire training course. The content of the Kabuuan training course so unsettled the two that by the end of the training program they were enabled to realize their kinship as human persons that fostered their eventual reconciliation. When projected onto a massive scale, which remains a challenge that has yet to be undertaken with the full cooperation of all government, including the nongovernment and the private sectors, such a program can effect a tremendous impact on conflict resolution.

At a minimum, those who have undergone the Kabuuan training process have pledged to support the Moral Recovery Program through their bite-size contributions, which, no matter how simple, when fulfilled can regenerate the decadent moral fiber of the Filipino society toward attainment of its vision of peace and prosperity. At this point, it is important to emphasize that transforming one's value system is imperative for genuine social transformation and the attainment of peace and progress. Without this value transformation, all attempts to resolve conflicts and transform social structures are reduced to mere pragmatic strategies that can be easily dispensed with once the desired change is achieved. There is a danger that the new structures that may be created may actually be only the old structures in a new form, leaving such efforts for change as hypocritical and futile.

CONCLUSION

What has been presented here regarding the Moral Recovery Program is not yet a sufficiently proven strategy, for the program is only in the early stage of its implementation. However, an initial study of the program conducted recently by Virsely de la Cruze and Domingo Nuñez (1994) revealed that the program is beginning to effect some significant changes, among them the following: reduced complaints from the public regarding the delivery of government services, commendations from satisfied clients, improved lifestyle, fewer number of human rights violations, improved interpersonal relations, developed sportsmanship, better understanding of and respect for the rights of others, deepened appreciation for the country's heritage, more spiritual commitment, improved attendance and work performance, reduced energy consumption, and increased awareness of Filipino values.

The indicators mentioned are hopeful signs of the potential of the MRP as a new paradigm, a unique idea of approaching social transformation in the Philippines. This paradigm is actually not new but only a recapturing of the Oriental worldview of wholeness and the interconnectedness of all things, which had been submerged by the materialistic perspective of the West through long centuries of colonialism.

It is high time for Asian countries to rediscover their common identity so as to contribute to the reshaping of a new worldview that is crucial for the survival of the world in the coming 21st century. Today, there is a growing movement the world over that recognizes the supremacy of spirituality over materialism to resolve humanity's predicament of cultural alienation brought about by an overemphasis on the material aspect of existence, which results in the rise of impersonal technology, massive consumerism, ecological degradation, and even violence and war for the sake of profit and self-interest.

Arnold Toynbee, in a book titled *Choose Life* (Toynbee & Ikeda, 1976/1989), identified this problem and recognized the necessity of a spiritual renaissance two decades ago when he said,

> I agree that the sickness of modern society can be cured only by a spiritual revolution in the hearts and minds of human beings. Social maladies cannot be remedied by organizational changes; all attempts at such remedies are superficial. They either reject all organization, or they merely replace one form of organization with another. The only effective cures are spiritual. Every social organization or institution is based on a philosophy or a religion, and the organization is only as good or bad as the spiritual basis on which it is founded.
>
> I agree that mankind needs a new spiritual basis. If and when a basis is found to heal our present social sickness, a new and more satisfactory form of society can be built on this new and better spiritual foundation. Short of this, I see no possibility of a cure. (p. 138)

In working toward a genuine social transformation, the bottom line is the transformation of values, a spiritual rebirth, as social structures are created out of and are perpetrated by certain philosophical or ideological premises reflective only of the value system of the people behind particular social structures. The Moral Recovery Program is not only a political tool for effecting economic recovery, it is a movement, a process, or a journey of a people toward a spiritual renaissance of discovering its own identity and vision, thereby discovering a new politics of meaning.

On a final note, consider the words of Shri Narasimha Rao, Prime Minister of India, on the future of the organization of the world:

> In today's world there will be a race, but it will not be an arms race on who has more bombs or power. No, it will depend on who has more spiritual power. This will determine how the world will be ruled and which nation will get its leadership. The decision will not be based on which country has the most skyscrapers. But it will be awarded to that nation which has noble ideals; the country which is a benefactor to the whole of mankind. It will take some time.

CASE SUMMARY

- Conflict is defined as disharmony of the environment and not disagreement between two individuals.
- The whole social situation needs to be considered for resolving conflicts.
- The colonial emphasis on materialism separated mind from matter and emphasized objectivity.

- Reconciliation of conflict is primarily a moral problem.
- The emphasis is on kabuuan, or wholeness.
- The emphasis is on a spiritual or soul consciousness, not on acquisition or self-centeredness.
- The emphasis is on discovering a common identity.
- Future models of reconciliation require a genuine spiritual transformation of values.
- The moral recovery movement will result in economic and political development.
- The future is based on the past.

REFERENCES

de la Cruze, V., & Nuñez, D. V. (1994). *Policy research on values transformation and moral reconstruction.*

Toynbee, A. J., & Ikeda, D. (1989). *Choose life: A dialogue* (R. L. Gage, ed.). London: Oxford University Press. (Original work published 1976)

PART II

Nuclear Family Conflict

5

Culture and Conflict in Canada

TRADITION AND TRANSITION

MICHELLE LEBARON
Institute for Conflict Analysis and Resolution
George Mason University, Fairfax, Virginia USA

Michelle LeBaron reports on a study of five ethnocultural immigrant communities in Vancouver that focuses on family and transition-related conflicts resulting from varying rates of assimilation. Mediation and alternative dispute resolution services are not well used by members of any of these groups because they are perceived as less legitimate than the courts and seen by women as reproducing the patriarchal village systems in their countries of origin.

The case study reported here comes from this larger investigation of conflict-handling behavior within immigrant groups. It illustrates the clash of old and new values in a community in cultural transition. The case study illustrates the conflicts that accompany the transition from immigrant cultures with defined sex roles and extended families as the most important social unit to the more informal, individualistic, and nuclear family tradition of dominant Canadian culture.

Western Canada is a place of beauty and variety. There are striking mountains, pristine lakes, and few large cities. It is a place where diversity is a given. Before the turn of the century, Chinese and South Asian immigrants helped to build the railroad and developed the giant lumber concerns that still ply the woodlands. Aboriginal people lived on the coast and inland, harvesting the sea and tracing the well-worn paths of their ancestors in seasonal movements.

This history of the past 100 years is one of contrast and conflict. There is courage, and there is racist oppression; there is the record of people working together to build new communities, and there is the story of people doing so at the expense of those with less power and resources. You can boat along the coast of western Canada now and see the deserted aboriginal villages, with totems still marking ancient ways. You can search the law books for the passage and eventual repeal of the head tax that was levied against Chinese immigrant workers and of the ban on immigration from India that lasted for nearly 40 years.

Nestled in the southeast corner of British Columbia is the City of Vancouver surrounding one of the most beautiful natural harbors in the world. New waves of immigrants have come to Vancouver each decade for over 100 years. With them, tensions and new prejudices have arisen hand in hand with welcomes from reunited families. Conflicts, once dealt with in a known and well-rehearsed way in countries of origin, become more troublesome in Canada. The network of community and familial supports in which they would have been handled has broken down. The accepted way of being in conflict and of handling differences does not fit anymore. It does not fit with dominant-culture customs; it does not necessarily fit with Canadian law. The stress experienced by immigrants serves to magnify the conflicts and make them harder to deal with.

INTRODUCTION TO THE STUDY

From 1990 to 1994, a team of researchers at the University of Victoria studied conflict and its dynamics in five ethnocultural communities in Vancouver. The objectives of the research were to explore the identification, manifestations, and handling of conflict by individuals in visible and nonvisible minority groups. In particular, the research was designed to explore the paths of resolution taken by those in conflict. What kinds of conflicts were most commonly experienced? What role did the formal legal system play in the constellation of options perceived by the parties? What less formal options did they pursue, to whom did they look for intervention, and with which processes were they comfortable proceeding? What needs for conflict resolution services exist, and how could they best be met?

Besides these microlevel questions, the researchers sought to assess the level of intergroup tension between and among members of minority groups and the majority culture. The result was predictable: Immigrants tended to rate the level of tension as much more serious and intense than did members of the majority culture. For this reason and many others, learning more about the conflict behavior of immigrant groups in Canada is increasingly important.

THE COMMUNITIES

Community research focused on five groups: Chinese, Latin American, Polish, South Asian, and Vietnamese. These groups were selected because of their population concentration in the Vancouver area and for regional diversity. The Polish group was selected because of the unique immigration pattern of that group (post World War II and the early 1980s formed two waves of Polish immigrants) and because of the nonvisible minority status of members of that group. It is important to note that none of these groups is homogeneous and that the use of the term "community" may be misleading. Within each of the groups named above there are tremendous differences relating, among other things, to country of origin, religion, class, education, ethnicity, and worldview.

METHODOLOGY

Interviews were conducted by trained researchers with fluency in the first languages of the respondents whenever possible. Participants who were interviewed were chosen by the "snowball" method of peer referral. In this method, individuals who are interviewed are asked to suggest two other participants for the researcher to contact. This method is sometimes limited because it may result in a homogeneous group of participants. For this reason, researchers made a point of emphasizing the criteria of diversity, and participants were asked to refer individuals of different ages, backgrounds, and views than their own. In this way, 160 in-depth interviews were completed.

The interviews had both quantitative and qualitative components. Quantitative data were gathered using Susan Goldstein's (1990) Conflict Management Style Inventory. This instrument was developed and tested in Hawaii expressly to measure conflict management styles across cultures using five subscales: Confrontation, Emotional Expression, Public/Private Behavior, Conflict Avoidance, and Self-Disclosure. For each question, participants were asked to rate the degree to which a statement was true of their approach to conflict on a scale from 1 (*strongly disagree*) to 7 (*strongly agree*).

Participants were also asked to talk about their experiences of conflict. Reported conflicts in these interviews were categorized into one of four groups: between individuals and institutions, within the subject community, between the participant's community and another community, or within the family. Researchers gathered information about each individual's cultural background and values regarding conflict and conflict resolution. Data on group norms concerning conflict and degrees of openness to outside intervention in conflicts experienced within groups or families were also sought. Participants were asked to describe traditional methods of conflict resolution used in countries of origin as well as transitional and established means of resolving conflicts in Canada. Finally, interviewers asked about programming and intervention needs relating to conflict and conflict resolution.

Institutional interviews were also conducted with representatives or employees of various organizations in Vancouver. These ranged from government bureaucracies at the provincial and local level to the largest television network. Informants were asked about the state of relations between their institution and members of the interview groups and also about the general state of preparedness of their institution for effectively serving a multicultural clientele. Care was taken to elicit both the views of frontline workers and those responsible for policy development within the institutions.

SUMMARY OF RESEARCH FINDINGS

The research findings included a clear theme of family and transition-related conflicts. Generation conflicts were frequently described, as different family members adjusted and integrated into Canadian society at varying rates. One surprising finding was that mediation and conflict resolution programs were mistrusted even by those who had come from societies with a tradition of mediation.

There were many reasons for this difference. Mediation as practiced in traditional societies may look very different from the approach now becoming widely used in North America. This North American model tends to be low context,[1] focused, time-limited, and agreement driven. Mediators are trained to keep parties "on point" and future focused and to use consensus-building tools to bring parties to closure. Parties tend to be narrowly defined (to exclude, for example, extended family members), and mediators are trained to be neutral or impartial.

Quite a different model is found in traditional societies. In China, for example, mediation may involve cajoling, persuasion, and even third-party pressure to "do the right thing," defined in a traditional setting as the right action for the community rather than the optimal outcome from a purely individual perspective. This approach in some traditional settings, such as South Asia, may be associated with a male elder-dominated process, which is unacceptable given gender roles in contemporary Canadian society.

Respondents explained that their focus in many cases was to assimilate into Canadian society, and this meant using the formal judicial system rather than a "new" alternative. Recent immigrants were looking for ways to resolve conflicts that carried with them legitimacy and authority. They expressed distrust for methods of addressing conflict that involved limited enforceability, informality, and cooperativeness.

Other research findings included the following:[2]

- It was very difficult to administer the Conflict Management Style Inventory to research participants. Difficulties with language and shades of meaning were particularly experienced by recent immigrants to Canada. Students at the University of Hawaii on whom the instrument was tested were probably much more familiar with colloquial usage than the diverse group of respondents in this study. The results therefore should be generalized with caution. It is interesting, however, that the results obtained in this study paralleled Goldstein's (1990) results in her initial testing of the instrument. In both cases, significant differences were found between groups in the area of confrontation only. Latin American and Polish participants were significantly higher in their willingness to confront than were participants from the Chinese community.
- Desirable characteristics in intervenors tended to be quite similar across communities. Ability in community languages, cultural sensitivity, experience and credibility in the community, training, empathy, confidentiality, and informality were mentioned in each group as important.
- Many individuals identified media stereotyping as an important factor leading to negative intergroup relations in Vancouver. Education and alternative approaches to reporting were identified as important in changing this dynamic.

A CONFLICT CASE STUDY

Several case studies form part of the Multiculturalism and Dispute Resolution Project.[3] In them, conflicts experienced by members of the Project communities are identified and traced through attempts at management and resolution. I have woven together two stories dealing with family conflict. They illustrate the conflicts that exist for individuals and communities in cultural transition when old and new values clash.

Background

The first South Asian immigrants to British Columbia arrived about 1900. Early immigrants were primarily Sikh men who came to earn money. Most found work in the newly developing timber industry. In 1909, there was a ban on South Asian immigration, although the ban was modified in 1919 to allow families to join husbands and fathers already in Canada. Substantial numbers of South Asians came to Canada after 1961 from many parts of the world (India, Pakistan, Fiji, and East Africa) when immigration rules were changed.

Diversity in beliefs, practices, and experiences characterizes cultural and social aspects of South Asians' lives in Canada. In South Asian cultures, the extended family is the most important social unit. Traditionally, the extended family lives together in one household and interdependence is valued. In a grandfather's house, for example, all unmarried daughters and all of his sons and their families live together. This tradition has been carried on to some extent in Canada. Even when families in Canada live in nuclear units, their sentiments and behavior tend to be those of the extended family.

Earnings are often pooled in the extended family. Decisions tend to be made by the head of the household, usually the most financially established male. Sex roles are well defined in South Asian culture, with men playing the role of leader, major decision maker, provider, and head of the family. The woman is in charge of nurturing and performing household duties. Traditionally, women have not worked outside the home and have been seen as possessions of their husbands. They demonstrate submissiveness and obedience. Women do have high social status as the bearers of family honor.

Marriages for South Asians are frequently arranged, and this remains true in Canada. Many families look for marriage partners in countries other than Canada. These families may feel that those who have been raised in Canada have experienced too much freedom to accept an arranged marriage and entry into a new extended family.

Divorce is very rare in traditional South Asian culture. Women who are divorced will seldom remarry. There is strong pressure on couples, especially on wives, to stay together. A woman is brought up to believe that she should never leave her husband's home, and most of the responsibility for making or breaking a home is shouldered by the woman. If there are marital problems, the families of both husband and wife will become involved, since divorce or separation will stigmatize the whole family. In traditional society, for example, the brothers and sisters of a woman who left her husband would find it difficult to arrange marriages for themselves.

Dominant culture values in contemporary Canada concerning marriage, family, and divorce are quite different. The society is more informal, the culture is more individualistic, and divorce is common (the divorce rate is in excess of 50%). Women who are mistreated or unhappy with their marriages find community and social support for leaving, and the stigma of divorce, if any, is soon erased because most women who divorce remarry.

Procedures for Addressing Family Conflict

In Canada, there is still strong pressure for South Asian couples to stay together once married. Parents and sometimes a respected religious leader will try to resolve problems and decide who is at fault, and every attempt is made to reconcile the couple. Most men have families in the area, whereas women often do not, so intervenors are more likely to come from men's families. Traditional intervenors, according to those interviewed, tend to blame the problem on the wife and on her parents for the way they brought her up. The intervenor role tends to be directive and prescriptive. It is informal but guided by the requirements of propriety so central to traditional culture.

Expectations linger from the *panchayat,* the traditional method of mediation used in villages in India. This process might be initiated by the families of the couple. A panchayat involves convening male elders to consider the conflict, attribute blame, and determine right conduct. It could involve fact finding by the elders, but they may talk only to the husband and not to the wife. A main concern governing the process is to avoid stigmatizing the family name.

Several research participants, both male and female, indicated their strong desire not to see a panchayat-like process transported to Canada in the name of cultural sensitivity. They pointed out that it does not fit with Canadian customs or values, nor is it compatible with the value underlying North American mediation of parties taking responsibility for the outcome of their conflict. The panchayat would not be workable in Canada because the village structure has broken down and "women have power."

Conflict Example

This conflict involves Rajpal, a woman of South Asian descent who was born in Canada but raised in India. Rajpal returned to the Vancouver area at age 18 to marry Balbir, a man also raised in India whom she had never met. Rajpal, as a Canadian citizen, sponsored Balbir to immigrate from India. Rajpal is now 27 years old. She self-identifies as Punjabi and Indo-Canadian.

Rajpal's marriage to Balbir lasted for three and one half years. She spoke to her family about her concerns as the marriage continued, but she reports that "they did more damage than anything." In response to Rajpal's complaints about having no communication with her husband and no intimate relationship, her family cited their successful marriages and blamed Rajpal for failing. Her feelings were hurt by their accusations, which made her feel even worse.

Rajpal's husband, Balbir, who was raised in India, had traditional Indian expectations of the relationship. He reports that the marriage was acceptable to him. He and Rajpal did not discuss their differences at all, and he did not know she was fundamentally unhappy until more than three years had passed. When she raised her concerns, he was upset because he needed a stable family to apply to sponsor his parents to immigrate from India. He did not want to lose face with his family or his community by being involved in a divorce or separation.

Participants

This conflict was typical of many studied in the Multiculturalism and Dispute Resolution Project in that it was not addressed overtly for some time. Discomfort for Rajpal grew beneath the surface, and she made some attempts to build support among her family. Finding none, she tried to live as she was expected to. But living traditionally at home while surrounded by Canadian dominant culture values created dissonance. Her values as a woman in cultural transition brought her into conflict with her husband, her family, her community, and her family traditions. Faced with a crisis of such magnitude, it is not surprising that she did not act for some time.

Rajpal describes some of the behaviors that led to her unhappiness: "From the beginning, we had no compatibility or passion in the relationship because we were from totally different backgrounds. Our thinking never clicked." Balbir did not talk with her much at all, and there were no fights because he would dictate what should happen and she would follow through. It felt to Rajpal that she had the burden of all the responsibility for the relationship.

The action in this conflict is almost entirely submerged. The situation clearly conforms to a high-context, high-power-distance cultural profile. High-context cultures are those where hierarchy is central and the nuances of identity and status govern interpersonal transactions. High-power distance refers to a social group where members are comfortable with a relatively high degree of difference between the highest and the lowest member in terms of power. The cultural norm of not making waves is very powerful here. The value of male dominance and power was assumed by Balbir, which Rajpal found difficult to accept. Over time, this left Rajpal feeling desperate.

Intervention

Rajpal attempted to find an intervenor through talking with her family members. She did not speak with Balbir's family in India. She indicated that it would have been helpful if there were a mediator in the community of South Asian descent. This person would understand the cultural context and be able to intervene in a way that would respect the needs and values of all parties. There were no mediators of South Asian descent in the Vancouver area of whom Rajpal knew. She did not want to go to a counselor or mediator for whom the cultural context would be unknown; there would be too much explaining to do. She was afraid of using the courts.

Rajpal was typical of many who were interviewed. The horizon she could see offered nowhere to turn. Balbir did not perceive the existence of a conflict, so he was not seeking an intervenor. Rajpal was concerned that all contact could be broken off by her family if she pursued the matter further or involved someone from outside the family.

Rajpal reported that if she had tried to involve Balbir in mediation he would have expected an imposed solution, something that would have been unacceptable to her. He would have wanted to involve family members as decision makers, something that was also unacceptable to her.

Rajpal did eventually find an intervenor. When she attended the temple, she met an elderly woman who was willing to come to her home and meet with her and Balbir. The process began with the intervenor visiting the parties at home, unannounced. Protocol dictated that both of them behave with deference because of the woman's status as an elder. The intervenor steered the conversation toward the marriage and was able to weave some of the themes of concern to Rajpal into the discussion.

The main function of the intervenor was to ensure that both parties began to talk with each other and that they listened to each other. She also served as a cultural interpreter (explaining that in Canada, marriages are different than they are in India) and as an encourager. Her manner was warm, yet very strong. She spent time with the parties over several weeks, asking permission to return at the end of each visit. The end of each discussion would be marked by her encouraging the parties for their earnestness, their concern for each other, and their respect for their families. It never involved explicit or discrete agreements. This would have made the parties feel constrained and would have been too overt and obvious, according to the intervenor.

The process was reminiscent of a dance, where all parties had well understood roles and steps, but there was no explicit instruction or naming of what unfolded. Everyone understood their roles and their places, but no one identified these. The music shaping their steps was audible to them but would not have been clear to an outsider unfamiliar with the cultural context. The outsider could appreciate the balance and the symmetry of the dance but could not know the patterns to which the steps of the dancers conformed.

Outcome

Eventually, Rajpal left Balbir. Her family no longer speaks to her. She felt that the intervention was helpful but that Balbir did not want to change as much as she needed him to change.

Discussion

This conflict is typical of many family situations where traditional ways of approaching conflicts were unsuccessful or not even possible to attempt. Traditional approaches did not work in the Canadian context because the extended family were not all present and the value system that would support the use of such approaches was not intact. At the same time, new services were not accessible to parties due to cultural barriers, including lack of shared values, lack of familiarity, and the lack of trained intervenors familiar with the cultural frame of reference of the parties. Rajpal and Balbir's case was exceptional in that they did receive some help from an intervenor, and the intervenor was to some extent equipped to try to help the parties bridge the gap between them.

The interviews conducted through the Multiculturalism and Dispute Resolution Project confirm that many of the values inherent in dominant cultural mediation in North America were not shared by the parties. For example, surfacing the dispute and meeting it "head on" with all relevant information being shared was a dominant culture value that collided with the traditional values of forbearance, nonconfrontation, face saving, and deference of women toward men. Conflicts tended to be viewed negatively and even feared because they were seen as "win-lose," and it was difficult for parties to see integrative potential. Possible integrative potential was never canvassed because issues were not surfaced. This is not surprising given the consequences of surfacing issues and being seen to lose, which traditionally resulted in complete ostracism from family and community.

The metaphor of relationship as a bowl of water was one powerful image shared by a research participant. She explained that intact relationships (those not marred by the overt expression of conflict) are like water in a bowl. Once the bowl hits the floor and is broken (like a conflict rupturing a relationship), the water can never be completely retrieved and replaced in the bowl. Great effort is therefore important to ensure that the bowl remains intact.

In several of the stories related, there was a desire to "win" the conflict that was not consistent with taking a more cooperative approach. All possible ways and means of prevailing were considered. Winning for a husband in a family conflict meant maintenance of the status quo, and he had many tools at his disposal to assist him. Winning for the wife could mean anything from separation to negotiating a more equitable, open relationship.

Power was a dominant force in these family conflicts, and power was clearly constructed as "power over" rather than "power with" as feminist scholars have proposed (e.g., Gilligan, 1982). It is questionable whether North American mediation would be appropriate in such circumstances, since balancing the power would be very difficult in a situation where the deck was stacked with such social and familial power for the husband. Jagat Singh, a South Asian man who carried out a pilot project targeting the involvement of South Asians in mediation, indicates that he thinks, in some instances, power imbalance and the expectations of the parties may be best addressed through arbitration (for more information, see Roberts, 1992).

The dominant culture mediation model as used in North America is also quite optimistic. Mediation trainers emphasize the integrative potential in problems and the benefits to relationship of collaboration. There is a sense that mediation carries with it a certain magic (although it also requires hard work) that can transform a conflict. The South Asian culture is not traditionally so optimistic. Rather, it tends to be fatalistic and stoic, emphasizing the importance of acceptance over change and "right relationships" over the negotiation of new ones.

The value of neutral outside intervenors was clearly not preferable to many in the South Asian community. Those who knew the family and the traditions were consistently identified as acceptable intervenors. This stands in stark contrast to the insistence on neutrality of dominant culture mediation in North America.

Attitudes toward time were also very different. It was essential to spend time convening, exchanging pleasantries and conversation, before engaging in even this informal kind of intervention experienced by Balbir and Rajpal. The mediation that was done looked more like a conversation, involving cajoling and encouragement by the third party and the demonstration of politeness by all.

LEARNING POINTS

How mediation is understood and conducted varies among cultures, particularly as suggested by this case study among high- and low-context cultures, family-oriented and individualistic cultures, and high- and low-power-distance cultures. Among immigrant groups, individuals differ in rates of assimilation, resulting in multiple understandings of conflict and conflict resolution procedures within one country. This diversity is compounded with disputing parties of differing expectations and behaviors.

The impact of these dynamics on formal dispute resolution and on alternative dispute resolution processes suggests that conflicts may remain largely unaddressed in immigrant populations, with potentially negative consequences.

This case study suggests that when cultural dimensions enter into the dynamics of conflict, power distance may largely determine how the conflict is expressed. High-power distance may make framing the conflict as win-lose seem natural. From such a framework, the higher-power party's expectations and behaviors limit the procedures and outcomes of the conflict. Based on his traditional cultural values, Balbir saw only one cause of the conflict, Rajpal, and only one possible outcome. That outcome was not acceptable to Rajpal, who defined the conflict more broadly. In a new culture more accepting of short-term relationships, Rajpal was eventually willing to terminate the marriage.

A neutral mediator would not have been acceptable to Balbir. Rajpal herself attempted a reframing of the relationship through the use of a female intervenor. Her attempt ultimately failed. Rajpal and Balbir's case demonstrates the contradictions of a community in transition.

This scenario demonstrates how culture and conflict-related behavior are intertwined. The way in which issues are defined and thought about determines how they will be addressed, if at all. Conflicts are always colored by cultural lenses, as are all attempts at resolution.

CASE SUMMARY

- Previously accepted styles of dealing with conflict require reevaluation in the Canadian context.
- Multiple styles of conflict-related behavior coexist with one another in any cultural system.
- Immigrants experience conflict in adjusting to a new social milieu, especially as this milieu raises questions and new options when contrasted with the "cultural common sense" of the country of origin.

- Family cohesiveness is an enduring common-ground value in Canada for many immigrants.

- High-context and high-power-distance cultures may involve one party being invested with substantial power over another. This will create special problems for intervenors if a value held by the intervenor relates to helping the parties meet on a relatively level playing field.

- Disparate value sets and worldviews create difficulty in dialogue and the eventual resolution of conflict.

NOTES

1. Low context refers to the work of Edward T. Hall (1976) and means a process that is characterized by individualism, overt communication, and heterogeneity.

2. More detail about the study can be found in *Conflict and Culture: Research in Five Communities in Vancouver, British Columbia,* a 1993 publication by the University of Victoria Institute for Dispute Resolution.

3. More information about the Multiculturalism and Dispute Resolution Project can be obtained by contacting Professor Michelle LeBaron, Institute for Conflict Analysis and Resolution, George Mason University, Fairfax, VA 22030-4444, USA; telephone 703-993-1308. There are three publications available thus far from the project: *Conflict and Culture: A Literature Review and Bibliography* (1992), *Conflict and Culture: Research in Five Communities in Vancouver, British Columbia* (1993), and a set of training materials in multicultural conflict resolution published in June 1994.

REFERENCES

Gilligan, C. (1982). *In a different voice.* Cambridge, MA: Harvard University Press.

Goldstein, S. B. (1990). *Construction and validation of a Conflict Management Style Inventory: A cross-culturally oriented measure of conflict management style* (PCR Working Paper Series 1990-3). Honolulu: University of Hawaii at Manoa.

Hall, E. T. (1976). *Beyond culture.* Garden City, NY: Anchor.

Roberts, T. (1992). *Evaluation of the small claims project of Westcoast Mediation Services and the Conflict Resolution Centre.* Victoria, BC: University of Victoria Institute for Dispute Resolution.

6

Nabin and Nasima

A CLASH OF HINDU AND MUSLIM COMMUNITIES

MADARIPUR LEGAL AID ASSOCIATION
Madaripur, Bangladesh

Nabin, a young Hindu man, and Nasima, a young Muslim woman, had a relationship. Nasima became pregnant, but she opted for an abortion. However, when her pregnancy and abortion became known, the local community demanded a trial for "rape."

In the first of two mediations with influential local people, Nabin was fined. He fled the village the next day without paying. This traditional mediation relied heavily on wealthy and influential people, and many villagers felt that the fine was too meager. Nasima's father, therefore, sought out a second mediation from the Madaripur Legal Aid Association, which would insure a more neutral mediation committee. In the second mediation, a larger fine was assessed against Nabin.

The broader issue, however, is the community's feelings about the relationship between a Hindu and a Muslim. Because marriage between the two was not possible under the present legal system, a fine was assessed to help Nasima begin a new life.

This case shows mediation to be a community problem-solving mechanism whereby members of the community participated as mediators in a dispute that was representative of the larger issue of relationships between the Hindu and Muslim communities.

The relationship of Nabin, a Hindu man, and Nasima, a Muslim woman, and subsequent pregnancy is the subject of this case study. Nasima, age 18, lived in Chiraipara village of Ghatmajhi Union of Madaripur District. Her father Shawkat Ali Akon is a poor peasant who used to sell milk in Madaripur town. Nasima was the eldest of five brothers and sisters. Nabin, age 24, lived in the neighboring Sonomandi village of Baligram Union. His father Anil Chandra Mandal was a rich peasant who had 10 sons. Nabin, the sixth born, studied up to Class VII and then left school to look after family land. Nasima's cousin Wazed Ali Akon used to live near Nasima's house. Wazed was Nabin's friend, and Nabin used to come to Wazed's house to visit him.

Nabin and Nasima were introduced to each other by Wazed and later developed an attachment. Although Nasima did not readily agree to a physical relationship in the beginning, she later consented when Nabin promised to marry her. However, sexual relationships between unmarried men and women is a taboo, perceived as a crime in rural communities and censored both as socially unacceptable behavior and a grave sin.

After a year of this relationship, Nasima became pregnant. Pregnancy of an unmarried woman is perceived as a crime and, therefore, to avoid the stigma she was secretly taken to a local quack for an abortion. The local community learned of this, and some influential people of the village spontaneously arranged for a trial. Nabin was pressured to marry Nasima. Nabin did not agree to that, but promised to pay her Tk. 10,000/- instead. Local mediators informed Nasima's parents of this decision. But Nabin fled the village right after the mediation. Nasima's father then sought another mediation from the local elites for his daughter's "rape." Terming it rape helps lessen the stigma of a premarital sexual relationship and enables the "victim" to regain social acceptance, for a woman cannot be "accused" or be "guilty" of a consensual sexual relationship if she were raped.

Nabin's father was persuaded to agree to a "trial" of his son, but it could not be arranged due to Nabin's absence. Nasima's father later informed the chairman of the local Ghatmajhi Union of the incident. To resolve this dispute, he turned to the Madaripur Legal Aid Association (MLAA) in September 1992. After hearing Nasima's complaints, the MLAA fixed a date for mediation.

Both parties were sent letters to be present at the mediation on September 9, 1992, but neither appeared. On October 3, 1992, the next date for mediation, both parties requested that the mediation take place in their village for their convenience and not at the MLAA office. On the basis of their requests, mediation was held on October 20, 1992, despite Nabin's absence. In the mediation, it was decided that Nabin must pay Tk. 65,000/- as compensation to Nasima. Nasima's cousin, Wazed, was also fined Tk. 10,000/- for encouraging the relationship between Nabin and Nasima. Both sides agreed to this decision.

As both communities have a common culture (Bengali), the culture itself has no role in instigating the conflict between the Hindu and Muslim communities. However, rules of conversion from one religion to another are different for different communities. There is an established rule that no one can convert from another religion to Hinduism. But if anyone wants to be a Muslim, it is readily done. Nasima had asked Nabin to convert to Islam, but he refused. Even though Nasima wanted to abandon her religion and become a Hindu, such a conversion was not possible under Hindu law.

MEDIATION PROCESS

Background

Solving conflicts through mediation is an ancient practice. It is a system that is traditionally related to the culture and lifestyle of Bangladesh people. However, over the past few decades, the traditional mediation process has become another site for exercise of power and domination by the local elite. Rather than considering which side was good or bad, the mediator's own opinion was the determining factor in solving conflicts. Even if the opposing parties did not want to accept the solution, they were compelled to do so.

Until the past few years, village mediators and other influential community members played a big role in traditional mediation. This system was acceptable to all as the only way to resolve local conflicts. Sometimes, mediators lacked neutrality, and the parties did not get the desired solution. Nevertheless, everyone accepted this arrangement, for the only alternative was a lengthy and expensive court procedure. But due to changes in the social system and increasing lack of neutrality, the popularity of village mediations has gradually decreased. The Madaripur Legal Aid Association (MLAA) is trying to reestablish a neutral and reliable mediation system. The organization has formed village mediation committees with local people to solve conflicts legally and properly.

In every Union in the working area of the MLAA, one mediation worker is appointed. Mediation workers play a vital role of organizer in arranging these mediation meetings. On the day fixed for resolving disputes they present all documents and a legal analysis of the problem so that a proper, peaceful, and legal decision can be reached that is acceptable to the parties involved and the local community.

It is important that mediators should be persons who are well thought of in the community and have the ability to control the mediation process along with presence of mind to remove any deadlocks in a discussion.

The mediators present in the mediation of Nabin and Nasima inquired into various aspects of reports of the two sides, verified the facts, and took the conflict toward a solution. The mediators reached their decision after prolonged discussion on the conflict with the help of the workers of the organization. The decision is the outcome of openly given opinions of the opposing parties.

As stated earlier, the dispute between Nabin and Nasima was resolved locally on October 20, 1992. Of the 14 mediators present, 2 were mediation workers of the MLAA who held bachelor's degrees. All 14 had training in mediation and legal aid and also had four years' experience in resolving disputes.

Moreover, the members of the mediation committee belonged to the local community. They knew Nabin and Nasima's families and their cultural and social background. The mediators decided to demand money for Nabin's father to marry off Nasima.

Traditional Mediation

Nasima's abortion was seen as tantamount to publicizing a sexual relationship between an unmarried couple. Therefore, although Nasima did not seek justice from the local mediators, local people themselves arranged the mediation, justifying it by stating that acts of this sort are heinous crimes (in their own words) and so the society needs to be purified. Although they had no right to call a mediation and even though Nabin and Nasima had not asked for one, the local people arranged it anyway in the name of social responsibility. The people accepted Nabin's fine of Tk. 10,000/- in this mediation, although neither Nabin nor Nasima accepted it. They wanted to start a new life as husband and wife, but the local community would not accept marriage between a Hindu man and a Muslim woman unless the Hindu became a Muslim. Because Nabin and Nasima had no say in this mediation, the decision was the result of the initiative of village people themselves, which is common in traditional village mediation. The parties do not play any role in such mediation. Nasima had applied for legal assistance to the MLAA in September 1992 after Nabin had fled the area. When the organization contacted Nabin's father in Nabin's absence, he agreed to resolve the dispute.

Mediation by the MLAA

The October 20, 1992 mediation was held in Ghatmajhi Union, arranged locally by the MLAA as per both parties' pro forma. Nabin was absent on this occasion. The mediation committee consisted of 14 persons: 6 representing Nabin, another 6 representing Nasima, and 2 from the MLAA. Besides Nasima's father, her uncle, local elites, and local Union Parishad Chairman Jaker Darjee were present. On Nabin's side were two of his brothers and four other relatives. As the incident had created enough sensation in the area, about 100 observers were also present on the day of the mediation.

In the beginning segment of the mediation, Nasima's side was heard. Nasima herself said, "I was in love with Nabin. We are both responsible for what had happened. I wanted to live with Nabin as his wife. But you people did not let that happen." Before Nasima had finished, relatives on her side nudged her to keep quiet. A commotion created by the observers and relatives as well as the mediators on Nasima's side held Nabin solely responsible for the incident after listening to her statement.

Although Hindus and Muslims live side by side, the Hindus, being the minority, usually keep a low profile on such occasions, for it is perceived as a crime for a Hindu man to have a relationship with a Muslim woman. Another 25-30 villagers took Nasima's side. All of them kept blaming Nabin: "We want justice to be done for such crime." Much excitement was created in the session at this stage. The mediators intervened, and the commotion died down after some time.

Nabin's elder brother was asked for his opinion about the whole incident. He stood up with folded hands and humbly said, "You are the guardians of this village. We will be happy with whatever you decide." He spoke in such a manner as if he had committed the crime himself, not Nabin.

As per the general norm of mediation, every side and every person present on the occasion were given the opportunity to voice their views in order to discover the truth. One of the MLAA workers, Md. Shajahan Mia, told everyone present to be patient and said to Nabin's brother, "We think that neither your brother nor Nasima committed any crime, but being the elder brother of Nabin you suggest what could be the solution." In answer, Nabin's brother spoke in an impassioned voice: "Nabin is not present here. We have no objection whether he accepts Nasima or converts to a Muslim. But as he is absent, we will accept anything you decide." At this stage of the process, the mediators began to consider what would be the best solution of the dispute. Nasima's father became excited at one point and said, "My daughter is disgraced. She cannot show her face in society. What will be her future?" His outburst stirred the crowd and emotionally moved Nabin's brother. An MLAA worker then said to Nasima's father, "What harm has been done to Nasima is irreparable. It is not possible to repair the loss by any of us. Nevertheless, would you accept if all of us try to resolve the dispute together?" Nasima's father gave his assent silently and started crying like a baby.

When mediating any dispute, consent of both parties is very important, especially to those who are involved in the matter, but it was not possible in this case because of Nabin's absence. Nasima conceded to mediation due to social pressure and her relatives' perceptions, even though she did not consider Nabin a criminal.

OUTCOME

For a proper resolution by any mediation, it is necessary to have an experienced mediator who is neutral and acceptable to both parties. The relationship between Nasima and Nabin was not criminal. Nevertheless, the local people considered it a social crime. It was not legal to charge any fine in this case, but Nabin's father was fined Tk. 75,000/-.

Actually, if this conflict had been allowed to linger further, much harm would have been done to Nabin's family and other Hindus. The fine was imposed just to solve the dispute. Peaceful social coexistence was the successful outcome of the conflict. Nasima subsequently bought land with the Tk. 75,000/- and then married. She has no problem at present. Nabin never returned to the village. He has taken up permanent residence in neighboring India.

CASE SUMMARY

- Intimacy between a Hindu and a Muslim was "overlooked" by the community because it was unthinkable.
- Nabin's family took responsibility for Nabin.
- Traditional mediators were not expected to be neutral.
- Modern methods are shifting to neutral mediators.
- Mediators must be credible and powerful, with "presence of mind."
- Nabin's family was "punished" as part of the mediation.
- All persons had the chance to express their view on the conflict.
- The alternative to a successful mediation was escalation of the conflict and loss of harmony.

7

Khukumoni and Masud

LIVING HAPPILY NOW

MADARIPUR LEGAL AID ASSOCIATION
Madaripur, Bangladesh

While still students, Khukumoni and Masud married with the consent of Khukumoni's family. After a year, Masud's father accepted Khukumoni into his home. All others in Masud's family, however, did not accept the marriage and abused Khukumoni physically, perhaps harming her unborn child. As a student living in his father's home, Masud was materially dependent on his family.

Banchte Shekha, a local social welfare organization, provided shelter for Khukumoni when the relationship became stormy and tried to resolve the dispute without success. Mediation was attempted by a committee of locals, including representatives from Banchte Shekha and from both sides of the dispute. Their decision called for a divorce.

However, Khukumoni became pregnant again during the mediation. With the help of workers from Banchte Shekha and Masud's father, the couple began to live together but apart from their families.

This case illustrates the involvement of the community in both the dispute and its resolution. The mediation committee included parties with interests in the outcome of the mediation and who may have, in fact, acted to set aside the committee's decision by later actions. The community's involvement through direct action and through mediation restructured the relationships of the family members.

Khukumoni, age 18, of Rupsha in Khulna district married Masudur Rahman of Monglati, Jessore. Slim, shapely, and smart-looking, she was considered an intelligent person. Her father used to deal in coconut and betel nut in Rupsha. Khukumoni is the third of six children and second among sisters. Her father came to Jessore to start a business and had rented a house in nearby Monglati. The house he rented belonged to Masud's cousin.

Khukumoni and Masud met and gradually fell in love while still in school. Khukumoni was a student of Class VI and Masud of Class IX. When Khukumoni was in Class IX, her father decided to marry her off and had selected the bridegroom. Masud was in college by then. In the meantime, they were deeply involved with each other. Khukumoni could not even think of marrying anyone other than Masud. Under these circumstances, when her family started putting pressure on her to marry, she left for her elder sister's house in Jessore. Masud knew the reason for her leaving. After a few days with the help of her elder sister, Khukumoni and Masud's marriage was registered. Khukumoni then returned to her father's house and lived there for the next seven months. No one in either family other than Khukumoni's elder sister knew about the marriage.

Masud's father, Habibur Rahman, was a businessman in Jessore. He had three daughters and six sons; Masud was the fourth. The family was financially well-off. They had land and traded in rice. Although Khukumoni and Masud tried to keep their marriage a secret for a year, gradually a lot of people came to know about it. Neither of the families would accept the marriage, except Masud's father who formally received Khukumoni as his daughter-in-law and brought her into his house. Meanwhile, Khukumoni's father closed down his business in Jessore and went back to Rupsha. Khukumoni's mother-in-law, however, did not accept the marriage and began to mistreat her, even beating her on several occasions. Khukumoni sometimes was not allowed to eat. She was made to do all the house chores. This continued for three years.

Masud had married the girl of his choice without consulting other members of his family. Masud's father, sisters, brothers, and especially his mother could not accept the marriage. As for Khukumoni, she also did not inform any member of her family, with the exception of her elder sister, and as a result her family showed no sympathy toward her.

The dispute started when Masud's mother could not accept Khukumoni as her daughter-in-law. Because Khukumoni's family members were also angry that she had married without their approval or consent, she had to tolerate physical and mental abuse by her in-laws without any protest, knowing she had no support from members of her own family. To complicate matters, Masud was still a student and did not have any job or sufficient financial means to live with his wife independently outside his parents' home.

Khukumoni was tortured even when she became pregnant. Although Masud was totally devoted to his wife, he could not protest against his parents' treatment of her because he was still a student and did not have a job. Khukumoni gave birth to a retarded son, probably because she was not given adequate food during her pregnancy. Then, too, the torture and beatings she suffered during the pregnancy may have affected the child. Their son Nipun was unable to stand up or walk because his feet were lean and thin. Her mother-in-law continued her abuse of Khukumoni after the child's birth. She advised her son to divorce Khukumoni. Compelled by his mother's advice, Masud drove Khukumoni out of the house after beating her severely because of a petty quarrel over some family problem. Helpless, Khukumoni was crying on the street when she met Mrs. Bulu Begum, a staff member of Banchte Shekha, who provided Khukumoni shelter. This took place in August 1991. After staying with Banchte Shekha for awhile, Khukumoni went to Masud's sister's place for shelter because they liked her very much.

MEDIATION

Banchte Shekha workers tried in vain to resolve the dispute locally. It was only when Banchte Shekha workers decided to file suit on behalf of Khukumoni that Masud agreed to a mediation with the help of the local chairman. But nothing was solved in a number of mediation sessions. In the meantime, Masud tried to file suit against Khukumoni on the allegation of theft. After two months a mediation was arranged by Banchte Shekha workers, where both sides were thoroughly heard. But Masud refused to take back his wife. The local chairman also gave his opinion in favor of Masud after, probably, receiving some money from Masud's family.

Khukumoni's elder sister was present in the session. Later, with the help of Banchte Shekha workers and local elites, it was decided that their marriage would be dissolved. A sum of Tk. 55,000/- for Khukumoni's dowry, her son's 7-year maintenance, and her alimony for 3 months and 10 days was assessed to be paid by Masud to Khukumoni.

They were divorced in December 1991. Although Khukumoni was two months' pregnant at the time, she kept it a secret. Masud loved her very much, which is why he started to visit her again only 14 days after the divorce. When Khukumoni informed Banchte Shekha workers about it, they helped them arrange a remarriage. The Mohorana (the amount settled upon for the wife at the time of marriage) was fixed at Tk. 110,000/-. Khukumoni's father was also present at the occasion.

Khukumoni then had an abortion when she was three months' pregnant. Again, no one except Masud's father accepted the marriage. He arranged a separate home for them to live in, and he also gave Masud money to start a business.

ROLE OF BANCHTE SHEKHA IN THE MEDIATION

Banchte Shekha does not have local workers in Jessore to conduct mediation. In 1991, when Khukumoni was thrown out of the house after being severely beaten by Masud, she sought Banchte Shekha's help. Banchte Shekha usually tries to first resolve the dispute through coordination among local influential people and elites. Both the local people and Banchte Shekha's field workers organize the mediation sessions.

The field organizer then personally contacts both parties to be present at the session as per the advice of the organization's law official. He also calls for concerned persons and local religious leaders to be present at the session. At the session, a mediation committee is formed of persons from each party involved in the dispute, Banchte Shekha workers, and neutral locals. For this dispute, a 10-member committee was formed. This committee reached its decision only after having discussions with both parties and analyzing every aspect of the complaint and considering the legal aspects of the decision in view of the background of the dispute. The committee's decision is treated as the final one, and both parties come to mediation prepared to accept the finality of the decision.

In the mediation session to resolve the dispute between Masud and Khukumoni, Banchte Shekha law official Khijurul Begum, law support official Anwara Begum, other staff members, and 8-10 local elites were present. The Banchte Shekha law officer has a master's degree in law and is experienced in mediation procedures. The Banchte Shekha law supporting official has 18 years' experience working with nongovernmental organizations.

Many of the others present at the mediation were associated with the traditional village mediation process. They had participated in mediations at different times. Although they had no training in mediation, they had vast experience. Moreover, most of the mediators present were locals or from neighboring villages. The committee members were aware of cultural traditions and the social position of Khukumoni and Masud because the mediators also lived in the same social and cultural surroundings. Thus, the mediators could judge the mentality, or the way of thinking, of the conflicting parties very easily and were quite sympathetic to both sides.

Three mediations were held to solve the conflict of Masud and Khukumoni. The first one was arranged at the end of August 1991 by Masud's side only. No one from Khukumoni's side or Banchte Shekha was present. Three days later, another mediation was arranged with the help of the field organizers of Banchte Shekha. The mediation committee heard both sides. Masud said he would not take his wife back. He would divorce her instead. One member of the committee was the local chairman, who spoke in favor of Masud. He even said to the Banchte Shekha workers, "You have done this with one Khukumoni. How many wounds of society can you heal?" In this context, members of the Monglati social welfare women's group strongly protested, saying "We want fair judgment on the torture of Khukumoni." When Masud refused to take back his wife, the committee wanted to hear Khukumoni's opinion, and she said, "I cannot go through the same torture anymore. You [the Banchte Shekha workers] have done so much for me. You can decide what is best for me."

When Banchte Shekha workers requested that Masud take back his wife, he refused. Moreover, it was decided that it might not be a good idea to send Khukumoni back to Masud's house in view of past tortures. After prolonged discussion, the committee decided that Khukumoni and Masud could no longer stay married to each other. At that point, the workers of Banchte Shekha claimed, "If they have to divorce then it should be done legally and according to Muslim law."

The mediation committee resolved that an amount of Tk. 55,000/-, which included Khukumoni's 3-month, 10-day alimony, son Nipun's maintenance until he was 7 years old, and Khukumoni's Mohorana), must be paid by Masud. The opposition party accepted the resolution, and thus the dispute came to an end. It was also decided in the session that the amount would be paid in installments. On the day of the mediation session, Masud paid her Tk. 15,000/-.

It should be mentioned that, unknown to the mediation committee, Khukumoni was pregnant when the divorce took place. Divorce is not legal during pregnancy, so in effect they were still married.

OUTCOME

Although the divorce was settled on a payment of Tk. 55,000/-, Masud remarried Khukumoni after paying her the first installment of Tk. 15,000/-. This remarriage took place with the help of Banchte Shekha workers. Khukumoni agreed to remarry Masud when he promised to live with her outside his parents' home. Masud and Khukumoni had loved each other very much, but the members of both families had intervened and poisoned their relationship. That is why divorce did not end their conflict. Their remarriage did that.

At present, the couple and their son are leading a very happy life together. Khukumoni took the S.S.C. (secondary school certificate) exams. And Masud also continued his studies taking the bachelor of arts exam while running his business.

CASE SUMMARY

- Conflict was tolerated while living with parents.
- Masud and Khukumoni divorced, as insisted on by his family under traditional mediation.
- Both Khukumoni and Masud moved out of his parents' home to a separate place, thereby becoming more independent.
- The mediation process was more indirect and circuitous than direct.
- Khukumoni and Masud were remarried with the help of the Banchte Shekha mediators.

8

Rawshan Ara

THE VICTIM OF POLYGAMY

MADARIPUR LEGAL AID ASSOCIATION
Madaripur, Bangladesh

⌘ *Rawshan Ara was married to Yousof, who neglected many of his responsibilities to her. Abused by her in-laws and her husband who married another woman, she gave birth to a dead child.*

Rawshan sought legal aid. Yousof agreed to not beat Rawshan any more and give her a portion of land. However, he soon appealed for a second mediation, which resulted in a public divorce with payments to Rawshan Ara, who would not agree to live with another wife of her husband. Polygamy, however, is allowed in Muslim law.

The mediation committee, composed of locals familiar with local customs, were advised by the Madaripur Legal Aid Association. The committee heard statements from both parties and issued a decision based on law.

This case illustrates the importance of understanding local customs and laws, even when they may seem contradictory. The locals on the mediation committee had that knowledge. The mediation committee first reached a decision that was not accepted. After an appeal, a second decision was satisfactory to both parties.

Rawshan Ara's home is in Rajoir Thana of Madaripur district. She is the youngest of the three daughters of Abu Mollah of Shakharpara of Ilibpur Union of Rajoir Thana. She is 20 years old. Her father's main occupation was agriculture. He was also selected as a member of the Union Parishad twice. He studied up to the S.S.C. level. Rawshan Ara had studied up to Class VI, even though she lived in a village. They were not poor and owned 8-10 Bighas of land. They were somewhat influential in the village because her grandfather Fatik Mollah was also selected a member of Union Parishad twice. Her grandfather was a bit conservative. That is why her guardians were trying to marry her off as soon as her other two sisters were married. Rawshan Ara was only 15 then. She could not study further, even though she was very eager to do so, because she had to take responsibility for a family.

She was married in August 1988 to Yousof Khalifa, whose home was in Ragdi Union of Gopalganj district. Yousof had four brothers and two sisters. He had studied up to Class VII. He dealt in fruits. After marriage, Rawshan Ara spent almost a year at her father's house, as she was not yet formally handed over to her husband. Occasionally, she would go to the in-law's house for four or five days and then return to her father's house because Yousof was away from the village most of the time to look after his business.

Yousof had divorced his first wife Jharna before marrying Rawshan Ara, but Rawshan Ara's family was kept in the dark regarding this matter. Moreover, Yousof's father, Najir Khalifa, had high hopes that his son would bring a huge dowry from his in-laws' house. Rawshan Ara's father presented goods worth Tk. 8-10,000/-, but that did not satisfy her in-laws.

Although Rawshan Ara was married to Yousof, they did not seem to have developed emotional attachments. His aloofness may have been responsible for this. Yousof formally took Rawshan Ara to his house in June 1990.

After living together for six months, Yousof went off to India on a trading trip. By then, Rawshan Ara had become pregnant. In Yousof's absence, Rawshan Ara's in-laws started to abuse her, first verbally and then physically. Rawshan Ara tolerated everything for her child's sake, but when she could take the abuse no longer, she returned to her father's house.

Upon Yousof's return home, his parents advised him to get married again, saying that his wife was not good enough. No one accepted Rawshan Ara's educational qualifications; they said, "There is no need for an educated wife." Yousof tended to believe everything he was told. However, he went to Rawshan Ara's house and brought her back to his home, but the in-laws continued to abuse her, and she was not even sufficiently fed. After a few days, she again returned to her father's house. Yousof again came to fetch Rawshan Ara, but this time she refused to go with him. Yousof somewhat forcibly took Rawshan Ara to his uncle's house and even continued to beat her while she was staying there. Soon after,.Yousof married another woman —his third marriage.

Rawshan Ara returned home after Yousof's third marriage and two months later gave birth to a dead child. Yousof did not even go to see Rawshan Ara after hearing the news.

On July 7, 1991, Rawshan Ara appealed to the Madaripur Legal Aid Association (MLAA) for assistance. In her complaint, she stated that her husband had remarried without her prior approval as required by law. She demanded alimony and a settlement. In view of Rawshan Ara's appeal, MLAA mediation workers twice sent letters to Yousof, seeking to resolve the dispute in a peaceful manner, but he did not bother to respond. After repeated letters, he eventually attended the mediation and promised never to torture his wife, to give Rawshan Ara her due respect as his wife, and to let her have 10 Kathas of land. But after some days, as per his father's advice, he refused to comply with his promises and appealed for another mediation. This time, on September 20, 1991, Rawshan Ara informed the mediators that she would not live with her husband anymore as she was afraid of fur- ther abuse. A divorce was agreed to on September 30, 1991, and Yousof paid Tk. 11,000/- as alimony.

MEDIATION PROCESS

Background

Mediation to resolve conflicts created by polygamy is common in this country. In traditional mediations, polygamy is not treated as a principal problem. Although these mediations take place in the presence of influential and respected members of the community, the decisions rendered often are not agreed to by the disputing parties. The mediators often impose their decision in the name of Islamic law, leaving the two parties involved no choice but to accept the decision.

In the current mediation conducted by the MLAA's mediation workers, local mediators voiced their opinion after hearing both sides' complaints. Thus, the two parties had a say in the decision arrived at by the 8-10 mediators present. The MLAA's method is easily acceptable because all the sides to the dispute are allowed opportunities to voice their opinion, and the decision is reached on the basis of the law and the opinions offered.

As mentioned earlier, Yousof had been married once before marrying Rawshan Ara. He had divorced Jharna, his first wife, because she could not bring any dowry and also because she was not good looking. He then married

Rawshan Ara and later married once more (i.e., took a third wife). In view of his actions, it is apparent that Yousof accepted polygamy. When Rawshan tried to stop him from marrying for the third time, Yousof felt her objections were unwarranted. He also wanted to make her understand that marrying two or three times is accepted by the *Sharia* (Mohammedan ecclesiastical law).

Yousof's polygamy and his demand for dowry were the main reasons behind this dispute. Rawshan Ara could not accept this third marriage and would never agree to live with another wife. That was why Rawshan wanted to leave her husband's home.

Course of the Mediation

Four mediation sessions were held to resolve the dispute between Yousof and Rawshan Ara. These sessions were held in coordination with several mediation workers, five of whom were graduates. All had appropriate training in mediation. Each member of the MLAA of each Union is adequately trained to conduct mediation, is familiar with the local culture and its local traditional mediation system, and therefore can play a vital role in a mediation session. Other MLAA workers also help the local mediators. The MLAA always provides legal explanations of the dispute and thus plays an important role in the mediation. Because the mediators are local, their experiences are important for settling the dispute. The mediator workers exchange views with the local mediators to reach a sound conclusion.

Mediation by the family was attempted to resolve dispute between Yousof and Rawshan Ara. This, however, failed to produce acceptable results. Thereafter, upon Rawshan Ara's appeal to the MLAA, a mediation process was initiated. A letter was sent requesting both parties to be present at the session.

To resolve the dispute between Rawshan Ara and Yousof, the mediation workers of the MLAA had to send four letters of request. Yousof and his associates did not respond to initial letters, but they did show up at the third mediation meeting, during which Rawshan Ara asserted, "I want to go back to my husband's house. But first he has to divorce the one he has married." After discussions among the parties, Yousof agreed to divorce his third wife, to not abuse Rawshan Ara anymore, and to give her 10 Kathas of land. This mediation took place on September 24, 1991. But after a few days, Yousof informed the mediators that it was not possible for him to accept the decision. He could not divorce his third wife, so he appealed for another mediation to resolve the matter. The mediation workers again sent a request letter to the committee members for both parties to be present at the mediation session set for September 30, 1991. The MLAA workers talked with both sides to request them to come to a decision regarding the dispute, saying, "We shall try to find a solution to this dispute. We tried to resolve it thrice. It won't do any good to prolong this dispute." When all of those present agreed to resolve the dispute, the mediation process formally began.

The mediators asked Yousof why he could not accept the earlier decision. Yousof replied excitedly, "Don't people get married twice? What is the harm if I marry again? I agree to keep both wives. I will not divorce my other wife. Rawshan will stay, so will my other wife." People from his side agreed on this, one of them saying, "Yes, he is right. Don't people get married twice?" The mediator kept control of the situation and said, "Please don't get excited. We have come here to resolve this, not fight." The mediator in this context wished to hear Rawshan Ara's opinion. But a mediator from Yousof's side spoke up, "She is a woman. What will she say? Let her father speak." The mediator then told all present, "The dispute is between Rawshan and Yousof. It is necessary to listen to them. We have to listen to Rawshan's complaint too." Although the mediator asked her to speak, she could not gather enough courage to do so: It was difficult for her to speak in front of so many people. When the mediator requested again, she broke down in tears and said, "Send me back to my husband's place. I want to go to my husband's place. But then he will have to divorce his other wife. And all of you are here. He has to say in front of all of you that he will not beat me." Some of the mediators stated, "The girl talks too much." One mediation worker, with the help of the other mediators, requested that everyone calm down and then asked Yousof, "Think and answer how we can solve the problem." Yousof repeated, "I shall keep both wives. I shall not divorce anyone." The mediation worker in this context wished to hear Rawshan Ara's opinion again. Initially, she could not find the words, but later she said, "Maybe I am cursed. Living with my husband is not my fate. Now you do what you feel is best. I will not live with the other wife."

After listening to the statements of both parties, the mediators wanted to hear her father's opinion. Rawshan Ara's father supported his daughter. He said, "I will not send back my daughter to live with the other wife." One mediation worker said to the other mediators, "Rawshan does not want to live with the other wife. Moreover, Yousof will not divorce his other wife. In this context, what is your opinion?" After due consultations by the mediators, they proposed that the marital relationship be broken off. Both parties then agreed to a mutual divorce after having detailed discussions. All those present saw this as the only solution to the dispute, and thus the dispute was resolved at last.

OUTCOME

The mediators' decision was to dissolve the marriage in exchange for Tk. 11,000/- as alimony after reviewing the legal aspects of the dispute. Yousof was ordered to pay that amount to Rawshan Ara.

One and a half years after the divorce, Rawshan Ara remarried in April 1993. MLAA workers were present at the occasion. She and her husband are now living happily. She even has a farm of chickens and ducks.

CASE SUMMARY

- The boy's father controls his son's decisions.
- Yousof married, divorced, married, divorced, and married again, based on his father's advice.
- Polygamy is accepted by the local culture in spite of procedural restrictions imposed by recent laws.
- Mediation was done by a group of 8-10 local community members.
- The mediators, with the consent of the couple, made the decision to divorce.
- The mediation was considered a success.

PART III

Extended Family Conflict

9

Conflict Over the Role of Women in Contemporary China

PROSPECTS FOR LIBERATION AND RESOLUTION

XUE WANG
Government and Public Administration Department
University of Sydney, Sydney, NSW Australia

Professor Xue Wang reports on interviews, questionnaires, and case study data collected in 1993 in a collective enterprise and township enterprise in northeastern China.

Women's liberation has been a goal of the Chinese Communist Party (CCP) since its formation. The CCP did set up women's organizations and passed new marriage and labor insurance laws, but women's equality has not yet been achieved due to Chinese tradition and morality which supports the power of individual men. In one sense, the women's organizations established by the CCP became extensions of traditional cultural patterns. The cultural value of subordinating individual interests to national or state interests has delayed social change.

The main point of this case study is that real women's liberation has not been achieved in China, despite the efforts of the Chinese Communist Party (CCP), because the Party's methods have been wrong. I agree with the Party's premise that the most important elements of women's liberation are their economic independence and change of Chinese people's traditional ideas of women (Chinese Women's Federation, 1979; Research Institute of All China Women's Federation, 1991, hereafter cited as Research Institute; Tao & Jiang, 1993). However, in reality, as shown by the Chinese experience these cannot be achieved under a bureaucratic command economy. Political-economic structures in China have hindered women's liberation. Economic independence for women and imposed abolishment of Chinese tradition have been frustrated even further by prerevolutionary attitudes toward women—attitudes that often have been strengthened by contemporary Chinese ideology and practice. The problem of achieving women's liberation in China is greatly compounded by the political system. Civil society in China has been largely suppressed by the CCP; the organizations specifically charged with protecting and advocating for women's rights are organs of the Party and therefore of the state. Where women's interests contradict what the Party deems to be general national interests, the former are subordinated to the latter by the women's organizations.

Women's liberation in China has been a revolutionary goal of the CCP since its formation. To achieve this immediate goal, the CCP paid attention to setting up women's organizations and to passing a new marriage law and labor insurance law. However, despite the achievement of a variety of social reform, women's equality in China has been constantly postponed (Honing & Hershatter, 1988).

Since the new course of the CCP, legitimized at the Third Plenum of the Eleventh Central Committee in December 1978, shifted its priorities from broad social reconstruction to a focus on economic growth, the Party has loosened control of hiring quotas designed to ensure the increasing participation of women in the workplace. State-run agencies, institutions, universities, hospitals, and enterprises have exercised increasing flexibility in hiring practices, with a great deal of overt discrimination against women. A variety of commentators both in China and outside are recognizing that Chinese women are far from approaching equality and that the path to equality is littered with a multitude of obstacles both new and old (Honing & Hershatter, 1988). In China, women's organizations have raised vociferous protest against the new overt discrimination. However, the effects of the protest have been negligible.

How should one assess the CCP's claim that women's liberation has been achieved in China? What is the role of women's organizations in resisting discrimination in China? How does one analyze discrimination against women after 1978? What is the path now to women's equality?

My argument is that the attitudes of Chinese people toward women are shaped by Chinese tradition and morality, which also centrally affect how society is organized. A main feature of Chinese traditional bureaucracy was the power of individual men. Women hence need to break down barriers of tradition, morality, and bureaucracy. Not only has the bureaucracy since 1949 diminished the traditional role of women, but it has also strengthened its own power, characterized by highly centralized control. In such circumstances, the women's liberation project in China was carried out. Chinese women as well as men were driven by the CCP's goals of pervasive social changes; they implemented policies of women's liberation so as to meet the political demands of the CCP aimed at replacing the Chinese people's traditional ideas with Marxist ideology. In the CCP's explanation, the Chinese people were influenced by Chinese feudalism for centuries, and Chinese women were oppressed by "three mountains"—Western imperialism, Chinese feudalism, and bureaucratic capitalism. Thus, women's liberation could only be achieved by smashing the past political and economic system by political indoctrination (Chinese Women's Federation, 1979; Research Institute, 1991; Tao & Jiang, 1993). Hence, women's liberation was imposed by the CCP.

Under the dynamic of the CCP, women's organizations were established. They formulated and carried out their policies following the direction of the Party's ideological line, where the Party represented the will of the people and was the safeguard of the proletariat (Schurmann, 1968; Shink, 1992). In this rhetoric, the Party subverts women's interests. As long as they conflict with the Party, women's interests must be subordinate to the Party. Therefore, women's organizations play dual roles as both assistants of government and representatives of women, but the former role is prior to the latter.

Evidence of overt discrimination against women in employment in the state-run sector substantiates the view that the attitude of Chinese people toward women cannot be easily modified by imposed radical political and economic changes under which women have no freedom to choose. Although the new course of the CCP has loosened its direct control in economic management since 1978, the Party's political and economic base has been maintained by and large. To overcome discrimination, women must liberate themselves in a society that provides them with limited opportunities so they can pursue their own interests and make their own choices.

Although there is overt discrimination against women in the state sector, according to my interviews, many women are pursuing their own interests in the private market, where their income has increased dramatically. They are beginning to achieve economic equality with men. Using the data from

4 months' fieldwork in China recently,[1] I attempt here to explain the complex situation of Chinese women, noting various conflicts over women's role. These include the conflict between the CCP's political system and women's organizations, between women's organizations and women, between policies relating to women's liberation and the reality of women's lives, and finally, between images of women of society and women's interests and their self-images.

THE CONFLICT BETWEEN THE POLITICAL SYSTEM AND WOMEN'S ORGANIZATIONS

After 1949 when the CCP came to power, it developed a highly centralized Party leadership. Policy was directed by the Central Party Committee, under which the government conducted its administrative affairs. Under the central Party organization, Party organizations operated parallel with government from provincial, city, town, work unit, and residential committee levels to the highest level that existed. Again, as at the top level, local Party committees were the source of the legitimacy of the local government organizations. Women's organizations were agencies of the Party committee in this schema (Schurmann, 1968). Since 1978, the directive role of the Party Committee in administration at the local level has lightened, and local government has been relatively independent of Party committees, able to make decisions on administration without their having to be approved by Party committees (Deng, 1983). However, women's organizations are still organs of Party committees, which still dominate the making of policy. In addition, the Party committees from the center to the locality have never loosened their direct control on high-level personnel promotion, with crucial impacts on individual careers, social reputations, and political power of particular individuals.

There are five departments under the leadership of a Party committee at the local level and in each work unit. They are organization, propaganda, trade union, women's organization, and youth league departments. The organization department confirms high-level appointments endorsed by the Party Committee for top personnel of both government and Party organs. For employment in women's organizations, *geren zhenzi tiaojian* (personal political condition) is the key criterion: Employees must be Communist Party members or at least Party activists. In a word, they must be loyal to the Party. In this way, women's organizations are firmly controlled by their Party committee, and they must convey the Party's policies to women.

One of my informants, the head of a women's association in a village township enterprise, described her daily responsibility—to ensure that none of the female employees of the enterprise intended to break the birth planning policy, introduced by the government in 1982.[2] As the enterprise is a model national rural enterprise, its reputation affords it some favorable treatment from the government. Any woman who breaks the birth policy will damage its prestige. The head of the women's association could then be dismissed by the Party committee of the enterprise; top managers of this enterprise could be criticized by the government and the Party committee at a higher level, and the enterprise itself could be penalized. Thus, not only will the offending woman be punished, but her neighbors in the same village might not be permitted to have a child for three years, even if eligible, and they might be refused permission to build a house for five years.

Thus, women's organizations practically ensure the interests of the Party in China. Chen Muhua, president of the Chinese Women's Federation, announced at a memorial meeting on International Women's Day, March 9, 1992, that as economic development is the standpoint of the Party's policy, women's organizations should motivate and organize Chinese women to plunge into economic development.

THE CONFLICT BETWEEN WOMEN'S ORGANIZATIONS AND WOMEN

Women's organizations claim to represent women's interests. However, do they adequately do so? To answer this question, one must understand the social position of women's organizations and how they play their roles. Social position refers to social status and occupation with a work unit.

Not only its political system but also Chinese society is hierarchical in terms of age, social status, occupation, and gender, which causes complicated patterns of discrimination against women in practice. It even occurs within the same gender. Too often, older women prefer young men to young women in the workplace. In enterprises, female managers and skilled women asserted that young female employees are lazy in learning skills and not as hard-working as young men.[3] Female students from a medical university in China confirmed that they were discriminated against by female supervisors at a hospital where they were doing their practical work. Female supervisors willingly supervised male students, whom they perceived to be more capable than females of doing practical and experimental work.

The pharmacology department of the same university had refused to accept any female graduates as teachers from 1989 to 1992 because it sought male graduates. Until 1993, no male graduates were assigned by the university authorities to this department because the demand from more prestigious departments and hospitals for male medical graduates was greater. They could easily be found well-paid jobs or jobs in more desirable places.[4] The pharmacology department persisted in refusing to receive any female graduates unless they were also assigned some male ones. Those in charge of this department were female professors. In 1993, the department accepted a female student together with a male student after negotiations with the university authorities. In an interview I conducted with this female student, she complained,

> It is unfortunate to be a female. No matter how intelligent you are and how high your marks are during study, you could be rejected by many work units, as soon as they know you are a woman. I am not afraid of free competition, but afraid of competing with men, because I am a woman. Those female seniorities in this department very much favor the male student as if he could suddenly disappear one day.

In terms of social status, employees of women's organizations mark high. In general, there are five layers of social status for women in China (see Tao & Jiang, 1993):

1. Peasants
2. Industrial and service sector workers
3. Self-employed women
4. Well-educated women, women managers in companies or enterprises, and government officials with middle rank
5. Women with high official rank

Employees of women's organizations at the local government level in urban areas belong to the fourth category. Generally, they are playing a hierarchical role with regard to other women.

Some Chinese women from women's organizations asserted that the majority of women are not aware of their responsibilities to and their own value in society, unlike a few middle-class women (Hunyin Jiating Tonsuo [*Research on Marriage and the Family*], 1985; Li, 1989; Li & Tan, 1990; Tao & Jiang, 1993; J. Zhang, 1992). Needless to say, the definitions of women's responsibilities and value to society are unclear in China. For instance, my informants from a municipal women's association were critical of women seeking help with their domestic violence problems:

> They are poorly educated and accomplished. They have no self-esteem and do not look after their husbands and do not respect their mothers-in-law. It is necessary for them to be beaten by their husbands and discriminated against by their mothers-in-law because their mothers-in-law helped them in their child rearing and household; their husbands work and financially support them. Moreover, only such women ask us for help in their domestic affairs.

> Their husbands do no such thing. In addition, well-educated women never ask for help because they are independent and can solve their problems on their own.

Clearly, some employees of women's organizations do not show sympathy to women at the lower level where the majority of Chinese women are found.[5] Asked why they work for women's organizations, my informants replied that it was to satisfy their need for a social life. Working for women's organizations allows them interaction and communication with other people. None of them mentioned specifically any interest in or commitment to women's issues.

As for attitudes toward discrimination against women, my informants from both the Chinese Women's Federation and this municipal women's organization agreed that women should make a self-criticism before they criticize men because many women do not maintain their traditional virtue and have not given up Chinese feudalist ideas. Although the government has made a big effort and provided them with opportunities, they have not yet liberated themselves.

Because of their support for Party policies, women's organizations seldom recognize the difficulties caused for women by these policies. The urban housing system is an example of inequality between men and women that has gone uncriticized by women's organizations. Since 1949, the CCP has changed the national housing system from private to public ownership. But each work unit provides apartments only for its male employees, which leads female employees to experience the difficulty of both doing their job and looking after their children. Often, the location of their own family is far away from their work units, but their children are usually only allowed to attend kindergartens run by the mothers' work units. Women have to bring their children with them every day by poor transportation, often on very crowded buses. No attention has been paid to this problem by women's organizations. On the contrary, they criticize women who prefer to work in places close to their own families (Li & Tan, 1990).

THE CONFLICT BETWEEN POLICIES RELATING TO WOMEN'S LIBERATION AND THE REALITY OF WOMEN'S LIVES

A pronounced feature of women's liberation in China was that it was state initiated; that is, the state sought to enhance the role of women through economic and political reconstruction (Rai, Pilkington, & Philzacklea, 1992). The content of women's liberation in China was that women were to break with Chinese tradition, Chinese feudalism, and Chinese bureaucratic capitalism to join in Chinese socialist production and thereby gain equal participation and equal pay with men in the workplace (Chinese Women's Federation, 1979; Research Institute, 1991; Tao & Jiang, 1993). Further, the CCP passed new laws on labor insurance, medical care for employees, and marriage (P. Zhang, 1992). Nevertheless, Chinese women seem to be ambivalent about the Party's achievements on their behalf.

The collapse of polygamy in China has been considered an important achievement of women's liberation, for which the CCP strove intensively. One of my informants, a concubine of a landlord before 1949, claimed that she was encouraged by the CCP to divorce her landlord husband and was then introduced to a Communist Party member from a peasant family. But after her remarriage, she could not divorce again when she wanted to because divorce was strictly restricted after the early 1950s. From then on, getting a divorce had to be approved by the work unit or the residents' committee responsible for housewives. In principle, "free life," that is, the right to freely choose a partner, is enshrined in the Chinese constitution and the marriage law. However, in practice, sexual affairs outside marriage are prohibited by formal and informal policies.

In 1963, four lecturers (three males and one female) in the foreign language department of a university in Shenyang were penalized for their extramarital affairs. They were accused of having exercised a feudal and corrupt lifestyle. Their names and stories were spread openly by postings of criticism throughout the campus. A professor told me the affairs were also recorded in their personnel files.

Abortion before the new birth planning policy was only socially acceptable if approved by the authority of a work unit. A 44-year-old unmarried woman had an abortion 20 years ago, for which she was ill-treated by a doctor at a hospital and by the boss of her work unit. At the same time, her boyfriend broke up with her for the sake of his career. If he had maintained the relationship with her and been discovered by his work unit, he would not have been promoted. In an interview, she told me she was constantly discriminated against by her colleagues, friends, and parents and was left alone, even when she was sick.

In relation to labor insurance and social welfare in the state sector, the situation of women is once again complicated. According to the insurance law, female workers are to be prevented from working in workplaces harmful to their health, but the fact is that many women have done such work for many years. For instance, spraying paint is considered a job harmful to female biology, and women are legally prohibited from taking this job. However, in one paint spraying shop of a collective ownership enterprise in Dalian, there are 25 female workers and 1 male worker. Many of these women have worked there for more than five years. Furthermore, all retired workers from this shop are female.[6]

Conversely, this law has been one reason why the state sector is often reluctant to employ women, following the introduction of the "responsibility system"[7] (Li & Tan, 1990; Tao & Jiang, 1993). State sectors guarantee wages, welfare benefits, housing, pensions, and leave (including maternity leave) for all employees. From the viewpoint of the state sector, the cost of a female employee is higher than that of a male employee. A survey by the Chinese Women's Federation concluded that

> one male employee can produce profit 2000RMB more per year than a woman. Apart from that, because of women's biological difference to men, enterprises spend more money on women than men in providing physiological safeguards and protective conditions such as regular inspection on women's physiology, nursing rooms, and public shower rooms. (Tao, 1991)

On the whole, the experience of women's liberation in China suggests that women's equality cannot be achieved wholly by state-initiated policy, as the political and economic system stresses persistently that individual interests must be subordinate to national or state interests. Furthermore, national policies were made by men influenced by Chinese tradition and morality, and although supposedly aware of the need for eradicating tradition and morality, these policymakers have hardly escaped from traditional patterns. They behave in accordance with Chinese tradition to keep the social order that they prefer.

THE CONFLICT BETWEEN IMAGES OF WOMEN IN SOCIETY AND WOMEN'S INTERESTS AND THEIR SELF-IMAGES

Images of women in China are affected not only by the idea of women's liberation but also by the assumption of women's inferiority to men and the attitude toward women inherited from Chinese tradition. As a result, these images, to a certain degree, strengthen women's traditional role and the traditional attitude of discrimination against women in China. Overt discrimination against women has been pointed out by women's organizations. They acknowledge that women's liberation in China has a long way to go, but still they enforce those policies adversely affecting women. With the setting of flexible hiring quotas on employment, the majority of employees being fired by state-run enterprises are women; female university graduates tend to be rejected by many work units; female students, to gain university entrance, are required to achieve better scores, on average, than male students in university entrance exams; and there is now open gender discrimination in job advertisements. Moreover, with the new birth planning policy, many Chinese families strongly prefer a son to a daughter, which has resulted in much female infanticide in rural areas (Li, 1989; Li & Tan, 1990; Research Institute, 1991; Tao & Jiang, 1993).

In response to this new discrimination against women, the Chinese Women's Federation has appealed for the protection of women's rights, raising a slogan in support of the "Four Selves of Chinese Women"—self-independence, self-esteem, self-discipline, and self-confidence—and has also sought to encourage women to play well their dual role as working woman and mother (Chinese Women's Federation, 1979; Li & Tan, 1990). However, the Federation's, as well as other women's organizations' view of the warp in which Chinese women are disadvantaged compared with men is highly problematic. It is an elitist view, imbued with traditional prejudices.

First, as women's educational levels, on average, are lower than those of men, their individual capacity in accordance with need of a job is generally seen to be lower. Second, despite laws guaranteeing female equality, women have not yet developed a strong political consciousness as women and have failed to seek liberation by taking part in social activities and pursuing their own interests. Third, women are not prepared to work as hard as men. They prefer employment in relatively relaxed, well-paid white-collar jobs in cities. Fourth, it is generally believed that women are physically inferior and less competitive than men and cannot cope with the demands of economic reform. Fifth, the combined tasks of material production and human reproduction prevent women from achieving the same level in their career as do men. This is the fundamental inequality between men and women. Sixth, although the Chinese socialist system provides women equal opportunity, women themselves haven't given up those traditional ideas hindering equality. Finally, women are biologically different from men and are thus responsible for childbirth, child rearing, and housework (Chao, 1991; Dong, 1992; Hu, 1992; X. Li, 1989; Z. Li, 1992; Li & Tan, 1990). There is therefore a contradiction between the demands of women's liberation and women's traditional role. On the one hand, the Chinese Women's Federation and women's organizations work to protect women's rights, but on the other hand, they help perpetuate traditional, prejudicial views about women and their role in society.

Women in China are expected to display chastity, self-sacrifice, and tolerance. These expectations conflict with the interests of career women. They have not been accepted by men and society in general. To draw people's attention to this discrimination in order to mitigate it, women's organizations have discussed in detail how career women have worked hard without looking after their families well and how intelligent women have been discriminated against by men. Descriptions of career-oriented women in such articles as "Women Officials Are Walking on a High Wire" (Sun, 1992) point out that women have left their children at home in order to learn new skills after working hours and have sacrificed their families for the sake of their career; female officials are said to be "willful" and spend less time at home than most women. Hence, they face the difficulty of not being understood by their husbands and some other women. But they want to be both good wife and wise mother. This kind of presentation of the problems of successful women, however, does not seem to have its intended effect. Men view negatively career-oriented and intelligent women in accordance with their patriarchal attitude toward women, and women partially give up their interests in the face of such disapproval, withdrawing from society.

The results of my study show that most men acknowledge that the increase in numbers of career-oriented and successful women is the result of women's liberation and economic reform, but they still believe that career-oriented women are not capable of being good women. They lack femininity. My female informants believe that career-oriented women are independent, confident, and talented, as signified by their career success. However, there are still only two categories of Chinese women in Chinese society: the kind wife and wise mother and the career woman. As the latter is unacceptable by and large in society, she has to sacrifice herself a lot. She can choose to be only one of these two categories.[8] This problem results from the conflict between men's expectation of women and the practical realities of women's working arrangements.

A married couple I interviewed had recently experienced a crisis in their marriage because of the husband's extramarital affair. The husband resented his wife:

> She is not capable of being a wife because she does not have any sense of responsibility for our family, only for her work. She does nothing at home. My mother looks after our 3-year-old daughter and does all the housework. Relatively, my girlfriend is much better. She looks after me very well, cooking and washing clothes for me.

The wife explained,

> My husband expects too much of me and cannot understand me. I leave home for work at 6 o'clock in the morning and come back home at 7:30 in the evening every day. There is no weekend in accordance with rules of my work unit (a township enterprise), except public holidays. I cannot give up my work for the sake of cooking and washing for him. He should look after himself, because I am very busy. But I have helped him and his parents a great deal.

> He was transferred to a high school in an economic zone from that in a village as a fine art teacher by my personal connections, and his parents have received permanent residency in the economic zone. I treat his parents as my own. On every public holiday, I bought more presents for his parents than other daughters-in-law, even than his sisters, and also provide his parents with their living expenses. His parents have admitted that I am more filial than their daughters, for which reason his parents have strongly discouraged him from divorcing me.

Such difficulties caused by work have not been noticed by women's organizations.

THE RESOLUTION OF DISCRIMINATION AGAINST WOMEN

Discrimination against women stems from the attitudes of Chinese people toward women influenced by tradition, morality, and a bureaucratic system which erects barriers against women. This social structure prevents women's liberation, which can only be reached when society provides women with opportunities and compensates them for their liberating themselves by making their own choices. In the Chinese situation, women should ignore negative public attitudes to them and endure pressure from society.

At present, there is overt discrimination against women in the state sector; however, Chinese women are achieving some of their goals in the private-oriented market, as China's economy shifts from the command economy. For instance, women make up 45% of people working in the private-oriented market in Shenyang, an industrial city in northeastern China.[9] The number of female managers in non-state-directed enterprises is booming. Although most women haven't yet moved up to a higher social status, their income has increased dramatically. This should lead to women becoming economically equal with men and help liberate them from male domination and also reduce the prejudice of Chinese society toward women. Economic independence of women and equality have been main targets of women's liberation in China since 1949.

Of course, as Chinese tradition and morality maintain their important impact on the attitude of Chinese people toward Chinese women, women will face difficulties in dealing with the attitudes of patriarchy and hierarchy, but they have started to move toward economic independence, which is a significant factor in women's liberation. In the long run, women will march on the path to women's equality, and those attitudes of discrimination against women in China will decline through women's achievement.

CASE SUMMARY

- Women's interests are subordinate to the interests of the Party.
- The pretended equality of women with men is not real.
- The social values are changing rapidly.
- Women are gaining power through competing in the marketplace.
- The Party attempts to control women's organizations.
- Disobedience by a woman is considered damaging to the Party.
- Even female seniors tend to favor males over women.
- Women's liberation was state initiated and broke with Chinese traditions.
- Women's equality cannot be achieved by the state because people still follow traditions.
- Women are traditionally subject to separate rules and standards of behavior from men.

NOTES

1. From July to November 1993, I conducted fieldwork in a collective enterprise and a township enterprise in northeastern China. The data reported here are based on my case studies, interviews, and questionnaires.

2. To control the rapidly increasing birthrate, the Chinese government introduced the birth planning policy in 1982; that is, one child in urban families and two children in rural families. In the case of rural families, if their first child is a son, they are then permitted to have a second child.

3. I interviewed female managers, technicians, and skilled women in a collective enterprise and a township enterprise.

4. According to employment policy in China, graduates from medical universities are not allowed to look for a job themselves. They are assigned jobs by university authorities or the personnel department of the provincial or city government.

5. Until 1987, 36.9% of the female population lived in cities and towns, and 63.08% lived in rural areas (Research Institute, 1991). Women in rural areas are regarded as peasants. In urban

areas, there are two general types of occupations: *quanming suoyou zi* (public ownership) and *jiti suoyou zi* (collective ownership). Employees of public-owner firms have higher social status than those of collective-owner firms in terms of social reputation, higher social insurance, regular medical care, and high pension. They constitute 12.6% of female employees in urban areas (Tao & Jiang, 1993).

6. The collective enterprise where I undertook a case study.

7. The "responsibility system" is a set of policies of urban economic reform, initiated by the government in 1982. State-directed enterprises became relatively independent of the state Party organization and the government and industrial-administrative bureaucracy in terms of the production planning and employment, which previously had been finally determined by the state Party organization.

8. I distributed questionnaires on attitudes of Chinese people toward women to Chinese people with various occupations in China and received about 600 responses.

9. Oral information from an official of Shenyang Municipal Economic and Planning Commission.

REFERENCES

Chao, H. (1991). Nuxin jiaose chongtu de shehui fuxiaoying ji duice [The negative social impact on women's role and its resolution]. *Huxiang Luntan, 6.*

Chinese Women's Federation. (1979). *Zhongguo funu yundong wenxuan* [Documents of Chinese women's movement]. China: People's Publishing House Press.

Deng, X. (1983). *Deng Xiaoping wenxuan* [Selected works of Deng Xiaoping]. Beijing: People's Publishing House Press.

Dong, F. (1992). Lun funu chanzheng de zishen zangai [On the obstacle of women themselves in their political participation]. *Society, 2.*

Honing, E., & Hershatter, G. (1988). *Personal voices: Chinese women in the 1980s.* Stanford, CA: Stanford University Press.

Hu, L. (1992). Lun kefu gaige dui funu de chongji xiaoying [On the negative impact of economic reform on women]. *Social Scientific Research, 79.*

Li, X. (1989). *Huaxia funu zhimi* [The mystery of Chinese women]. Zhengzhou: Publishing House Press.

Li, X., & Tan, S. (1990). *Funu yangjiu zai zhongguo* [Women's studies in China]. Henan: People's Republishing House Press.

Li, Z. (1992). Women's value. *Women, 149.*

Rai, S., Pilkington, H., & Philzacklea, A. (Eds.). (1992). *Women in the face of change: The Soviet Union, Eastern Europe, and China.* London: Routledge.

Research Institute of All China Women's Federation. (1991). *Zhongguo funu tongji ziliao* [Statistics on Chinese women: 1949-1989]. Beijing: China Statistical Publishing House Press.

Hunyin jiating tansuo [Research on marriage and the family]. (1985). Guangzhou: Guangdong People's Publishing House Press.

Schurmann, F. (1968). *Ideology and organization in Communist China.* Berkeley: University of California Press.

Shink, S. L. (1992). The Chinese political system and the political strategy of economic reform. In K. G. Liebethal & D. M. Lampton (Eds.), *Bureaucracy, politics, and decision making in post-Mao China.* Berkeley: University of California Press.

Sun, S. (1992). Women officials are walking on a high wire. *Women, 2.*

Tao, C. (1991). Zhongguo funu zai qianjing zhong de wuxing zangai [The invisible obstacle in Chinese women's career achievement]. In *Paper collection of the Conference on Women's Issues in China and America* (pp. 106-113). Beijing: Chinese Women Publishing House Press.

Tao, C., & Jiang, Y. (1993). *Zhongguo funu shehui di wei gaiguan* [The general social status of Chinese women]. Beijing: Chinese Women Publishing House Press.

Zhang, J. (1992). Gender and political participation in rural China. In S. Rai, H. Pilkington, & A. Philzacklea (Eds.), *Women in the face of change: The Soviet Union, Eastern Europe, and China* (pp. 41-60). London: Routledge.

Zhang, P. (1992). *Kuangfu yuannu: Daling weihuntoushi* [Unmarried men and women]. Sanxi: Publishing House Press.

10

The Effects of Tribal Wars on Personal and Family Disputes in Papua New Guinea

JULIE FOSTER SMITH
Community Development and Crime Prevention Foundation
Port Moresby, Papua New Guinea

Julie Foster Smith describes the case of Norma, a career policewoman, who became suspicious that her husband was sexually abusing her daughter. As Norma's relationship with her husband deteriorated, he began to seek out a second wife. Although tribal law from the specific area that Norma and her husband come from permits and allows men to obtain additional wives, Norma turned to the court system to protect her social, economic, and personal professional interests as the "first wife" and had her husband charged with adultery.

Norma had been sent to a conflict resolution and mediation training program. Norma's colleagues in the course were placed in the position of advising her in this situation. This case illustrates the multiple layers of society and culture that can coexist in a developing country. Norma did not accept the "traditional" role of a woman. She represents the first generation of women who have been exposed to the broader perspective of "cash economies and women's rights." Her plight demonstrates the changing role of children, marriage, and family in a culture in transition.

The political system of Papua New Guinea is democratic. Christianity plays a large part in the philosophical expressions of this democracy together with the traditional values and belief systems of a diverse indigenous population, which comprises 869 different language groups. This level of diversity in cultural expression underpins the political system in the nation of Papua New Guinea.

There are four regional blocks in the country making up 20 provinces. The regional blocks are Papua, Islands, Momase, and the Highlands. These regions have distinctive features in the expression of their cultural mores.

In the Highlands, tribal fighting is an intrinsic part of their society practices toward dealing with all conflicts, from personal to national. Most conflicts often end up in violent physical confrontation to demonstrate strength, power, status, manhood, and warriorhood of a clan and that clan's ability to draw support from the tribe and neighboring tribes to assist in tribal wars.

The Highlands is made up of five larger tribal groups: Western Highlands, Eastern Highlands, Chimbu, Southern Highlands, and Enga. These groups have provincial government status within the nation of Papua New Guinea.

The impact of the people from the five regions on the Papua New Guinea diverse society as a whole and its democratic processes and the expression of cultural mores practices is significant. The migration of peoples from the Highlands who leave their tribal homelands primarily because of the tribal wars/fighting and move to the larger urban centers brings other multiple layers of problems and issues that lead to complex conflicts. These people bring with them the issues from their homelands and move to the urban centers, which often also creates problems such as the following:

- Homeless (squatting is the alternative)
- Overcrowding in the squatter settlements when they live with *wantoks* (relatives or same language tribal group)
- Illegal and criminal activities
- Unemployment
- Multiple marital relationship problems
- Compensation claims

All of the above become part of the drama in a conflict that commences often as a personal issue, moves to a clan issue, and then escalates to a tribal and then a national issue. For example, a tribal war happens, and the injured and any dead are taken to the hospital casualty area for treatment or appropriate action. Whatever medicines or services are available goes into meeting the needs of this tribal war group. Consequently, those with genuine health care needs and sicknesses are forced to endure lengthy waiting periods or are unable to obtain any medication because staff feel intimidated or have been threatened and respond only to the injured from the tribal war conflict. If there have been deaths, other ceremonial and process factors of respect for the needs of the dead are brought to the forefront. This places an added "pressure cooker situation" on the hospital and medical staff and further disadvantages the genuine needs of others requiring medical attention.

The issues of compensation are intrinsically woven into the entire fabric of these societies' expressions of their identity and self-esteem. It is with this brief background that I discuss the broader issues surrounding the case of Norma.

Norma is a career policewoman. She is married to a former army soldier whom she supported and had successfully transferred and employed by the uniformed police force. Norma is a plainclothes policewoman working with high distinction in the detective work and criminal prosecution section of the Criminal Investigation Division.

Norma is educated to Grade 10 standard, which in Papua New Guinea is considered reasonable to good. She attended a teachers' college for two years and then joined the police force to undertake training in that field. She has been on the force for 11 years and holds seniority.

NATURE OF THE CONFLICT

The conflict commenced after Norma and I first met as participants in a four-month-long conflict resolution and mediation training program, which she had been sent to by her organization.

The key players are Norma; her husband; her 3-year-old daughter; myself; two of her colleagues from the conflict resolution course; the husband's girlfriend and later second wife; the court; the police force; the community people in the Mou Mou urban settlement in Port Moresby; and members residing in Port Moresby, in particular those in Norma's home.

The conflict started with Norma during the "field research" component of the training program when she returned to her home base. During this period, she noticed a change in her daughter's behavior, and through observation and asking questions and, later, verification of her suspicions through a forensic examination conducted at the hospital, Norma learned that her daughter was being sexually abused. Norma's reaction was typical of an enraged mother. This reaction intensified when circumstances pointed to the perpetrator being the child's biological father, Norma's husband.

When Norma first realized this situation, she was cautious in her expressions of whom she suspected. She returned to the residential component of the conflict resolution program, distressed but not disclosing the problems in her household. Norma began making demands on other participants—in particular, she now wanted to bring her child to all residential programs, with the reason given as "no baby-sitter." In a conflict-raising process when other participants confronted the problems being caused by the presence of her child, Norma blurted out without any warning, "What do you expect? She is being sexually abused by someone close to me living in my house."

Apart from baby-sitting problems, no warning of the dimensions of the problem were ever given. The media were not informed because of the nature of the problem. Norma later obtained more data during and after graduating from the conflict resolution program. On one occasion, her two colleagues and I were with Norma when her husband returned with the daughter at approximately 8 p.m. According to the child's aunt and baby-sitter, the husband had taken the daughter for a 20-minute drive.

When the father and daughter returned, the child complained to her mother of pain in the "wee wee." On closer examination, Norma noticed swelling, bruising, and redness, including discharge from the child. When questioned what happened the child responded in pidgin, "Daddie fitim wee wee." The discharge was identified as sperm by Norma and later verified at the hospital.

On her return, Norma immediately confronted the husband with her suspicions in the privacy of their bedroom, whereupon he took off in the car and later returned to tell the three of us who had stayed during this incident what Norma had accused him of. Earlier, Norma had said she had a problem and needed to take the child to the doctor for an immediate examination.

Everyone present became witnesses to Norma's husband disclosing the issue that he had been accused of. Shortly after, Norma and her husband's relationship deteriorated, and he began seeking an additional wife. The conflict escalated in the following pattern:

- Child sexually abused
- Girlfriend comes into picture and becomes second wife
- Norma accused of jealousy and unable to accept second wife
- Increase in physical violence toward Norma by her husband
- Escalated physical violence, which moves from beatings to publicly tearing off her clothes and leaving her naked in a public place
- Discrediting her in the workplace because of her community voluntary work in crime prevention in the Mou Mou community
- Discrediting of her community colleagues and myself as her trainer, community worker, mediator, and friend
- Forcing the police force to remove her from their house, which is owned by the police force

- Charges of breaking all Melanesian rules and being influenced by Western values and beliefs
- Withdrawal of any financial support for the child and the costs incurred in running a household
- Constant demands of rights as legal husband from a traditional Highlands marriage based on customary law
- Threats of external violence toward her and her friends, whom she associates with professionally or socially
- Removal of personal property systematically from ironing board to larger electrical items to bedding and small personal effects to give to second wife. According to Norma, these were bought by her. Her husband did not contribute to material possessions.
- Selling of family vehicle. The vehicle was bought with financing secured by Norma.

Norma was systematically being abused emotionally, physically, and professionally. Her health is now seriously impaired. Her work performance deteriorated, and supervisors and senior officers began to raise questions of her ability to perform general duties.

The original cause of the conflict becomes secondary as the primary motive is shifted by the husband from sexual abuse to marital jealousy and change in his wife's behavior through bad influences from friends and colleagues and associates. By this he means Western and other nonindigenous and religious philosophies. Mistreatment of Melanesian cultural mores and women's true roles with their husbands are being abused, and according to her husband, lack of respect of Papua New Guinean ways is being displayed by Norma.

Norma has some options:

1. Take the matter to her tribal elders and therefore be prepared for a tribal fight, with any deaths or injuries becoming her responsibility and due compensation given to the men who take part on her behalf. (One of Norma's fears is that it is the right of the men from her clan and village to rape women—from grandmothers to girls—who belong to her husband's village and tribe.)
2. Deal with the conflict internally with her husband and use her superiors as the mediators.
3. Deal with the conflict alone and develop her own network and strategy of self-management.

ISSUES

Important differences needed to be analyzed and discussed:

- Traditional and contemporary marriages and expectations
- Role of women in developing countries and societies
- Expectations of women in professional careers
- Human rights
- Children's rights
- Traditional and Western systems of law
- Perceived and real rights of men in a patriarchal system of democracy and culture
- Role of conflict resolution and mediation in these types of complex and variable issues

It is difficult to find common ground when one key party (Norma's husband) is reluctant to give up his rights as the husband (and a law enforcer in a legitimate professional role), which is compounded by the issue of violence toward spouses within the law-enforcing agency.

THIRD-PARTY INTERVENTION

The third party used to resolve the problem was the court system. Norma charged her husband with adultery and continued to experience physical violence from her husband and remain at her paid work. As the physical injuries increased, Norma now had markings on her body. She gained credibility within her workplace as others saw the problem being her husband and not her.

This level of violence did serve her purpose of resolving the conflict without it going to a tribal war. Now that there is open evidence of the mistreatment by Norma's husband, it is being talked about as a tribal fight but without the raping of other women as a payback for the child's sexual abuse.

Thoughout this period, Norma's two colleagues from the conflict resolution program supported her. They had to be very careful in how they expressed this support because of the added dimension that they were both men and could easily be charged with being Norma's sexual partners. As it was, their lives were threatened. For myself, I maintained a supportive role emotionally as the therapeutic support arm for Norma.

LACK OF INSTITUTIONAL MECHANISMS

No mechanisms exist nationally or regionally to address these issues at this level of emotional intensity. Because of the intensity of safety and other issues in a small community like Papua New Guinea and the extent in which

I was personally involved in the mediation, facilitation, support, therapy, and as a teacher, it is difficult to identify the most appropriate institution to which Norma could have turned.

OUTCOME

Norma managed this conflict with enormous strength, courage, and determination. The focuses for Norma were a peaceful negotiation of this issue and emotional stability for herself and her child.

The key lesson learned from this conflict is the importance of discussing in depth the multiple layers of society and culture and their impact on the middle ground of the intellectual elite of a developing nation and changes to the existing cultural mores. The intellectual elite are emerging with large numbers of women who are not prepared to be a party to multiple marriages and/or lovers. Others issues are gender issues in traditional and contemporary societies and the legal issues of children, marriages, and families.

CASE SUMMARY

- Power, strength, physical force, and conflict are an important part of the tribal culture.
- Personal issues move to become clan issues and national issues.
- Sexual abuse of the child by the husband meant the conflict must be dealt with confidentially.
- When the husband is confronted, the wife is accused by the husband of breaking traditional values, and she is in turn abused physically.
- The original conflict becomes secondary to the violation of Melanesian cultural mores from the man's perspective.
- The conflict was in danger of becoming a tribal war.
- The intellectual elite are caught between traditional and contemporary cultural rules.

11

Mediation, an Effective Way of Conflict Resolution

SRI LANKA EXPERIENCE

ARIYA RUBASINGHE
Director, Government Information Department, Sri Lanka

An elaborate legal system existed in Sri Lanka centuries before the Portuguese, Dutch, or British occupations of the country. King Pandukabhaya established village boundaries for the whole island. Gamsabhawas, or village councils or courts, attempted to amicably settle such disputes as petty debts, land boundaries, and petty offenses. Although decisions were most often compromises, the Gamsabhawa had attributes of courts, such as being initiated by plaintiffs, power to summon the defendant, and its decisions being subject to review.

This case study first describes the history of dispute resolution and mediation in Sri Lanka and the existing mediation program. The case itself is over the ownership of property after the death of a family's mother. The youngest son who had cared for his mother for years forged a deed to the property to himself. The older brother and sister refused to accept the deed. In mediation, the mediation board met with the parties separately and helped them move to a resolution and to redevelop their relationships through an understanding of their mutual respect and reciprocal duties.

Persons cannot live in isolation. In community life, conflict is inevitable. Disputes and conflicts will arise when there are no behavioral norms and arrangement of resource utilization and problem solving. The ideal harmonious social life can be achieved only through facing the reality of all kinds of conflicts in group life and providing a conflict resolution system.

BACKGROUND

Long before the judicial or court system was established or employed to solve disputes in Sri Lankan social life, mediation was used as a fair reso- lution means. The history of extrajudicial dispute resolution in Sri Lanka dates back to about 425 B.C. during the reign of King Pandukabhaya. During this period, the senior or chief of the clan usually acted as the mediator to handle all kinds of daily life disputes, where cases involving petty debts, petty offenses, family disputes, boundary disputes, and so forth were dealt with. This system has been working so well that even contemporary society has maintained this practice.

MEDIATION PROCEDURES

A village tribunal, called *Gamsabhawa,* which settled disputes amicably had almost disappeared by 1871. Village Communities Ordinance No. 26 dealt with similar amicable settlements through village tribunals. The Conciliation Boards Act No. 10 of 1958 was enacted to effect settlements of petty village disputes. In 1977, all conciliation boards were dissolved, and the Judicature Act No. 2 of 1978 replaced the Conciliation Boards Act and introduced a new court system, the family court.

The family counselor, introduced by this Act, was required to make every effort to induce the parties to settle their disputes. This Act also introduced the primary court in order to attempt settlements of disputes. If the mediation or reconciliation failed, the case would be brought back to court.

The mediation system is rooted in and reflected the confusing social notion "Rule by Morality" rather than "Rule by Law." The mechanism of the judicial system alone cannot find the resolutions for the highly diversified and complex human feelings and relationships in modern society. Nevertheless, in view of the high social and personal costs of lawsuits in terms of money, time, and energy, the mediation system remains a supplementary or preliminary device of solving community disputes.

The existing mediation program in Sri Lanka was set up by the Sri Lankan government under the Ministry of Justice. An Act of Parliament (No. 78 of

1988) was passed in order to establish mediation boards in the country, and the boards were set up in 1990. At last count, 211 mediation boards have been established in divisional administrative units. The existence of a value system where the advice of elders is highly respected has contributed positively toward the successful implementation of this system. There is a need to bring about a higher public awareness of the concept of mediation as the community is accustomed to competitive dispute resolution procedures via the legal system.

The mediation panels, consisting of approximately 20 to 30 members, are appointed by the Mediation Board Commission, an autonomous body consisting of retired Supreme Court judges and retired senior administrative officers appointed by the president, who is responsible for the overall management of the mediation boards.

The members of the mediation boards are selected from the nominees of nonpolitical voluntary organizations. Members of religious institutions and government officers are also represented on these boards. All nominees selected by the Mediation Board Commission are exposed to a five-day intensive training in mediation to equip them with the necessary skills needed to perform their task effectively.

CASE STUDY NO. L/2345[1]

Background Information

The names and addresses of the complainants are Sarath Dissanayake, from Sirimalwatta, Eraminiyagalla, and Sunetra Dissanayake, from Uluwitike, Galle. The name and address of the respondent are Siripala Dissanayake, from Anuradhapura Road, Maho.

This is a land dispute in a family concerning the ownership of a property consisting of a house and a small paddy field situated in the North Western Province in Sri Lanka.

Sarath Dissanayake and Sunetra Dissanayake, children in the same family, instituted legal proceedings against their youngest brother, Siripala Dissanayake, claiming right of ownership, alleging the latter did not have a valid claim to the land. This case was filed in the law courts. It was referred to the mediation board as it entailed a land dispute among members of one family.

Case History

Siripala is the youngest of three children. The eldest in the family is Sarath, a son, and the second oldest is Sunetra, a daughter. Their father, a farmer, died when the children were very small, so the mother had to undergo immense hardship to bring up the children.

Sarath became a teacher in Eraminiyagalla, about 100 miles away from home. There he met and married another teacher. He was not in a position to give a helping hand to his mother as he had four children of his own. Sunetra eloped with a young Muslim man and also lived away from home. The family did not approve of this marriage, considering it a big calamity that had befallen the household. Siripala was left alone in the parental home. The only legacy that 21-year-old Siripala received was the responsibility of looking after his mother and the properties, which consisted primarily of a small paddy field and the ancestral home on a quarter acre of land.

Siripala had to work hard to fulfill the family obligations and maintain the family status in the village. Initially, Siripala had to face a lot of financial difficulties as he was unemployed. Later, he found employment at the village cooperative stores. The income that he received was hardly sufficient for him to keep the home fires burning.

Amid all the problems, Siripala's mother broke her hip after a bad fall while she was washing clothes at the well. She then became bedridden. When he informed his brother and sister of their mother's condition, they came to see her but couldn't afford to stay with her even for a few days; perhaps their own domestic problems did not permit them to do so. Siripala had no alternative but to marry a girl without wealth as he was more interested in looking for a person who would be willing to look after his sick mother, who by that time was in her declining years. Apart from that, he had to incur expenses on the mother's sickness.

After a few years, Siripala's mother died. Although his brother and sister attended the funeral, they did not contribute much toward the funeral expenses. Siripala had to borrow money from friends to meet the expenses. Shortly after, his sister wanted to remove the sewing machine and the wardrobe, saying they belonged to her. Siripala had a heated argument over this issue. He said, "Don't you feel ashamed to step into this house when you have done a big damage to our family?" Siripala thought she had no right whatsoever to his mother's belongings.

Siripala thought that he should be compensated adequately for the suffering he and his wife had undergone in caring for his sick and feeble mother, which was a responsibility of the other members in the family as well. He thought it was fair enough to write a deed in his name by forging the signature of the mother as she had left no last will. The brother and the sister vehemently refused to accept the deed. They added further that their mother was not in a normal mental condition in the latter part of her life.

Mediation Process

When the case was referred to the mediation board, the chief mediator explained the role of the board to the parties and said that they were not trying to impose a settlement on them. They would be an impartial third party who would assist the parties to reach their own settlement. The Board explained the negotiation process to the parties and said that they needed their full cooperation to solve this dispute.

The mediation board called all the parties, and they were asked to explain their problem. The elder brother was furious with Siripala for making a forged deed to the land, and he could not endure to see the selfish attitude of his brother. Siripala explained how he had looked after the mother when the others neglected their responsibilities. They were very angry toward each other. The board felt the tension developing as these siblings discussed the ownership of the land.

The case notes say that Sunetra, the sister, arrived a little later, timidly. The tension that she was undergoing was written on her face, and she was having trouble defining her situation. She wanted to claim the wardrobe and sewing machine, but she was afraid to tell that in the presence of the two brothers as she was feeling guilty for what she did to the family.

Siripala started calling the sister and the brother names, accusing them for not coming to see their mother when she was sick. Siripala thought his elder brother and sister were ungrateful, never cared for their mother, and did not do their duty by her. In fact, both the elder brother and the sister married on their own. The sister eloped with a Muslim man, bringing stigma to the family instead of marrying the man the mother had selected for her. Siripala said, "I wanted to be grateful to my mother who underwent enormous difficulties to bring up the children—including my brother and sister." He went on, saying the mother needed the care and protection of the daughter because she was bedridden and could not attend to very personal things on her own: "She was purging at the latter stages. My wife and I had to wash her clothes and clean her. But this woman, my sister, didn't have the gratitude to come and stay with her, even for one week. My poor wife and I had to do all the things."

Now they had come to claim the ancestral house as the eldest in the family. Siripala denied writing an illegal deed and said that it was his mother's wish to give him the house. After he had done all these things for his mother, he was not prepared to give in, even if he was asked to leave the house. Siripala was very angry, and it was difficult for him to think of problem solving when his energy was directed at attacking the brother and the sister.

The mediation board, realizing the tension between the parties had not diminished, then decided to talk with the parties separately.

Sarath, the elder brother, expressed his view that the other members of the family also had a right to inherit what the mother had left behind. He was terribly hurt over the way Siripala behaved when he had visited the mother sometime back. He thought that, being the eldest in the family and an educated person, he should be respected more by his younger brother, although he had not spent money on the mother's funeral because he was burdened with a big family. He further said he looked after the family when the children were very small. He said, "Whatever happened, Sunetra was his sister and Siripala should not have spoken to her like that."

However, in shuttle mediation the board discovered that Sarath was not interested in going to court because judicial approaches are costly and take a long time to reach finality. What he wanted was to come to a settlement, to get his share as early as possible, so that he could give that to his daughter as a dowry.

Sarath explained to the board how he obtained the teaching appointment to a school in a remote area. He never considered getting married so early, but he was compelled to marry his present wife as her parents were insisting he marry her. He had four children by that marriage, and he had to incur a lot of expenses for the education of the children. He said he had hardly any money to spend on his mother's funeral.

When talking to Siripala, the board found him to be ambivalent. On the one hand, he wanted to take revenge on his brother and sister for the suffering he'd undergone with his wife; on the other hand, he wanted the house and property.

When Sunetra was called by the board, they found that she was only interested in the wardrobe and sewing machine. She was terribly hurt over the way Siripala had spoken to her. She explained how he got involved with her husband, who was a friend of his elder brother. In tears, she talked about the suffering and humiliation she'd endured during this period.

Parties were wondering in private sessions how we board members were keeping from taking sides. We dealt with them by being as supportive as possible during the private sessions, helping the parties to identify their specific self-interests and developing the best way to present those interests. While we were engaged in this cooperative project—essentially the four of us and the three sitting outside—we were always careful to point out that we follow the same process when meeting with other parties. We try to help parties understand that impartiality is necessary to increase the negotiating efficiency of all parties and to assure the best possible final settlement from everyone's point of view.

We outlined a number of general issues, which were considered by the mediation board, to explain the settlement arrived at in respect to this dispute:

- An elder son is considered the breadwinner in a family in the absence of the father. Here, in this case, Sarath, the eldest son, being an educated person, had not lived up to the standard expected. He married on his own, lived separately, and did not bother to come and attend to his mother, especially when she was sick. He didn't even help pay for the funeral, although he had his own reasons.
- The daughter ran away with a Muslim man. In a village setting, intercultural marriages are not accepted. Although polyandry and polygamy were prevalent in traditional society, it disappeared when the Christian concept of marriage (one man, one woman) crept into the society. Muslims, however, accept polygamy. If the man marries another woman, her marriage will not be stable, and there can be religious differences that could affect the future of the children. By eloping with a Muslim, Sunetra had brought social stigma to the family. This kept her away from home. Even if she had wanted to come and see the mother, she would not have been able to do so.

  According to Sinhalese customs, a daughter has more responsibilities toward a mother than the sons, especially when the mother is old and bedridden. Because of her intercultural marriage, she was deprived of performing these duties for her mother.
- Siripala, being the youngest in the family, had sacrificed so many things, such as the wife's dowry by marrying a poor girl in order to look after their mother. He did his utmost for his mother and incurred a lot of expenses for her sickness and the funeral.
- In Sri Lankan villages, the extended family system still exists, and most people are interrelated. A person living in a village has many more social obligations than a person living in an urban area.
- Siripala had to keep up the social status of the ancestral home. According to social norms, the youngest in a family inherits the ancestral home.

The mediation board was able to convince the elder brother by asking thought-provoking questions about the duties and responsibilities of an eldest son toward his family.

The board discussed with Siripala and Sunetra separately about paying attention to their responsibilities. They were very angry with each other and yelled during the sessions. After they had calmed down, the mediation board took them into a joint session. Another point of mediation appeared during the discussion. When they discussed the sewing machine, Sunetra was very angry and frustrated and said, "Forget it, *Mallie* (brother). I don't need it. Just forget the whole thing."

The board refused to let the matter drop because we knew that in their normal relationship Siripala would have won his point simply by reducing

Sunetra to frustration and getting her to drop the matter. Certain patterns of behavior that exist between the parties will interfere with open and equal negotiations. The mediator must intervene to circumvent the normal behavior and permit the negotiations to continue.

Often, one side will have the preponderance of power only because the other side believes that an imbalance exists. In those cases, the board spends time with the parties who do not recognize their own power in the relationship to identify this power and help them use it in the negotiations.

Siripala was made to understand that although the other members of the family had not done much for their mother they had a right to enjoy whatever the mother had left behind. The board discussed the needs of all the parties and spent time with Siripala exploring this aspect of the problem. Siripala divulged that he would like to settle this matter amicably, provided he got the house. The board made him understand the harm that could be done if the others went to court and the costs he would have to bear. He agreed to give the paddy land to his elder brother Sarath and, after discussion with his wife, agreed to give the sewing machine and the wardrobe to his sister Sunetra. Considering the fact that Siripala was the youngest in the family and the sacrifice he had made to look after the mother, the elder brother and the sister agreed to give the house to Siripala. Sarath was satisfied that he got the paddy field, but he wanted Siripala to buy that and give the money to him. Siripala wanted to be careful in the way in which the value was appraised. Both came up with a proposal for each of them to appoint an appraiser and the actual value to be determined from the average of the two figures. The board felt that it would be very expensive and suggested that they write into the agreement a clause that they would appoint an appraiser who would be unknown to the parties. Both Siripala and Sarath found this acceptable. According to the current market value, the paddy field was worth approximately Rs 100,000/-. Siripala wanted to pay it within six months so that he could arrange a bank loan. His proposal was accepted by the elder brother.

Before adjourning the session, the mediation board explored the possibilities of redefining the relationship. All parties were made to understand their responsibilities, and all of them started to pay attention to mutual interests that had been forgotten in the heat of their emotions. This session helped them realize that they had much more important things they should preserve as members of the family. The elder brother came out with some stories: how he helped the mother after the father's death to look after the younger brother and sister, how he bathed them and took them to school, and how he bought their schoolbooks with his money. The board was able to observe how all of them were moved inwardly to pardon each other.

The board made them understand that mutual respect and reciprocal duties will help generate a strong relationship, and where this mutual respect and cooperation exists, there is peace and prosperity among the people. In spite of rapid social change, a strong value system prevailed in the villages. The elders always placed the interests of others before their own at all times. They sacrificed a lot for the others' sake.

These practices ceased after the advent of social change and have been replaced by the need to comply with laws based on a value system foreign to us. The traditional customs are based more on obligations and responsibilities. When you comply with your obligations and responsibilities, you are blessed with your rights. Punishment is applied to those who do not conform to the traditional values and customs, and rewards are given to those who conform to them.

The board drafted the terms of settlement as amicably arrived at by Sarath, Sunetra, and Siripala. The disputants and the chief mediator duly placed their signatures as having accepted the terms of settlement, which was also sent to the court as this case initially was referred from the court.

CASE SUMMARY

Some have said that Sri Lankan society is litigious. The Gamsabhawas (village councils) had attributes of a court. And with almost two centuries of the British adversarial system, adjudication is a prominent feature of dispute resolution in Sri Lanka.

- Traditional culture had methods of mediation that have almost disappeared.
- Modern mediation boards have been established.
- A mediation case was referred by the law courts.
- Siripala forged a will to be compensated by the mother for her terminal care.
- The conflict was between the son who cared for the mother and the elder brother who had inheritance rights to the land.
- The mediation board attempted to remain impartial but were sympathetic when meeting with any of the parties separately.

- The board emphasized mutual responsibilities of all parties as the common ground.
- With peace comes prosperity for the community, placing communal interests above individuals.
- Social change threatens the traditional systems.

NOTE

1. The names, addresses, and case number are fictitious.

PART IV

Land and Environmental Conflict

12

Ishaq Gets Back Land After 40 Years

MADARIPUR LEGAL AID ASSOCIATION
Madaripur, Bangladesh

As an orphan, Ishaq received 3 Bigha of land from his grandfather. After his father's death, Ishaq lived in his uncle's house until the age of 18 and then was forced to leave. Only after the death of his wealthy and influential uncle did Ishaq demand his land from his cousins.

Ishaq sought out mediation help to claim his land. A mediation committee of people with knowledge of the family and of local traditions and culture together with advocates for both sides was formed. The mediation committee convinced the cousins to agree to mediation as an alternative to spending money in a court. The mediation committee heard statements, examined documents, and then awarded the land to Ishaq.

This case illustrates the many forms that mediation can take. The mediation committee acted in a judicial role, yet it resolved the issue within the community without involving a court.

Ishaq Hawladar, 50, lives in Ramzanpur Union of Kalkini Thana in Madaripur district. On October 20, 1991, he filed a complaint regarding land with the mediator of Ramzanpur Union. He alleged in the complaint that his cousin Kalam Hawladar and others forcefully occupied his 3-Bigha (90-decimal) land for a long time. The Madaripur Legal Aid Association (MLAA) has recovered that land through mediation.

Ishaq is an only child. His father Golam Hawladar died when Ishaq was only 2 years old. Concerned about the future of Ishaq, his grandfather, Samsher Hawladar, registered 3 Bighas of his land to his grandson. Grandpa was a little bit worried about Ishaq's future. He used to look after Ishaq, put him in school, and even married off Ishaq's mother to his eldest son, Abdul Kader Hawladar. This was done in consideration of the future of his grandson Ishaq and daughter-in-law, even though Abdul Kader Hawladar already had a wife. After the grandfather's death in 1952, life became miserable for Ishaq. His uncle, Abdul Kader, who was now also his stepfather, took him out of school and put him to work doing house chores. His uncle then started abusing him. In 1958, when he was 18 years old, Ishaq was thrown out of the house. Later, he managed 1 Bigha of land from his neighbors. Twenty years have passed since then.

Ishaq did not have the courage to ask for the rest of his land because his uncle is an influential person in the village. Ishaq had to be content with 1 Bigha for fear of fighting and killings. Ishaq had no other choice. In 1978, his uncle died. Ishaq hoped that his cousins would return his other 2 Bighas, but when he asked for the land, they did not give it back and behaved rather badly. Some suggested that he go to court, but he could not afford to.

In 1991, when the mediation project of the Madaripur Legal Aid Association (MLAA) extended to Ramzanpur Union, Ishaq learned of their efforts to solve conflicts through mediation and appealed to get his land back. The MLAA mediators called Ishaq's cousin Kalam Hawladar and others to a peaceful settlement, but the effort fell through. Ishaq's cousins not only did not appear, they spread the word that Ishaq had no land because his father had died while the grandfather was still alive. Later, Thana mediator supervisor contacted both parties to resolve the issue. This time the cousins agreed. But on the appointed day, opponent Kalam Hawladar did not agree to a settlement. So the mediator personally talked with him to tell him that if he did not agree to settle the issue Ishaq's plea would be sent to court with legal aid from the MLAA. This time Kalam agreed to a settlement. December 14, 1992 was chosen for the mediation.

Discussions were held in the presence of the mediation workers, supervising committee, and local elites. After scrutinizing the necessary papers regarding the dispute, they decided that Ishaq was the rightful owner of the remaining two Bighas of land. After the legal issues were explained, Kalam

Hawladar accepted the decision. The dispute was ended when Ishaq got back his two Bighas of land.

THE MEDIATION PROCESS

Land disputes often lead to dangerous situations. Although village elders call the meeting, these mediations are filled with tension. Mediators often side with the wealthy party, and the outcome usually goes their way.

Agriculture is the main profession of most of the Bangladeshi. Power and wealth in rural Bangladesh are directly related to the size of land holding. Large landowners control the local society, and they determine the social rules and regulations. Generally, they play the role of mediators in solving various disputes in the villages.

They often influence the solution of mediation directly or indirectly for their own selfish reasons. For example, if the dispute is between a landlord and his working man, the landlord would try to influence the decision of the mediation. The poor opposite party, even with valid legal claims, often has to accept an unfavorable decision.

As for the legal issues involved in this mediation, if a man with children died while his father was alive, the children would not inherit the grandfather's property. Even though this rule was changed by the Muslim Family Act in 1961, most villagers are unaware of it. As such, conflicts arise regarding distribution of property of the deceased. Everyone assumed that since Ishaq's father had died before the grandfather did Ishaq would not get the property. Also, Ishaq's uncle's lengthy possession of the disputed land discouraged Ishaq from claiming his right to it.

Three meetings were held to resolve the Ishaq-Kalam conflict. Members of the mediation committee, mediation workers, and local elites supported and were present in these mediations. Their educational qualifications ranged from primary to graduation. Mediation workers and supervisors were aware of land laws and mediation resolving methods. Moreover, as they were locals, all knew Ishaq and Kalam and their culture and tradition. The members of the committee were also involved with traditional local mediations. To resolve land-related disputes, one must have knowledge of land laws as well as experience in the field; otherwise, legal issues cannot be resolved satisfactorily.

As Ishaq got a bit older, he learned of the land that was given to him by his grandfather. When he demanded the land back, his uncle told him, "Your father is dead. He had not left any property. You will not get the land. If you insist, you might not live anymore." After hearing such threats, Ishaq never spoke about his demand again. Ishaq's uncle and cousin were very influential in the village, so it may be said that Ishaq did not have any influential person on his side, and those who were on his side could not do much for him.

Once Ishaq appealed to the MLAA, they tried to resolve the dispute through mediation, but opponents Kalam Hawladar and others did not appear. Subsequently, the MLAA staff and supervisor spoke with Kalam Hawladar about the mediation to resolve the dispute. Finally, he and others agreed to do so. Accordingly, a date was fixed for mediation, but again the opponents did not appear and the dispute could not be resolved. Moreover, it took some time to collect Ishaq's land documents, as they are vital for land disputes. Kalam Hawladar could not be present on two appointed occasions as he could not get the papers ready either. Their aggressive attitude toward each other was also an important factor in whether an agreement could be reached. After the mediator and the supervisor again requested Kalam Hawladar to resolve the dispute through mediation, he was informed that "if the dispute cannot be solved through mediation, then the organization would go to the court to provide Ishaq with legal aid." Finally, he agreed to resolve the matter through mediation instead of having to spend a lot of money if Ishaq went to court.

The final mediation session was held on December 14, 1992. Eighteen persons were actively involved in the mediation: 1 MLAA mediation supervisor, 1 mediation worker, 6 members of the mediation committee, 4 persons who were on Ishaq's side, and 6 who were on Kalam's. Besides these, 24 people were present as observers.

When mediating land disputes, emphasis is placed on documents of both parties regarding landownership and on the legal basis of the dispute.

Both parties were heard and their statements taken into consideration, depositions were obtained from witnesses, and questions were asked to extract information. In solving the dispute between Kalam Hawladar and Ishaq, Ishaq's side of the story was heard first. Ishaq said, "My grandfather has given me this land in his will. I am successor of this property. You all please make arrangements for me to get back the land so that I and my children can live." The mediation supervisor then wanted to hear opponent Kalam Hawladar's comments regarding Ishaq's statement. Kalam Hawladar said, "Ishaq was brought up in our family. My father bore his food and education expenses. He has no right to demand back the land from us." The observers at this moment seemed to be a bit agitated. Elep Ali, one of the mediators on Kalam Hawladar's side, was one of the wealthy men of the village. He shouted to the onlookers, "Keep quiet. Kalam is right. Ishaq's father died when he was only a year old. He was brought up in Kalam's family. He has no right to ask for the land now." Many of the mediators supported the wealthy and influential Elep Ali's statement.

The MLAA mediation worker and the mediation supervisor then presented the legal basis of Ishaq's demand and requested that the mediators do justice by checking the documents of the land as presented to them. Although at first Kalam Hawladar and the mediators on his side tried to influence the mediation, once the legal documents of the land were presented the observers started to speak for Ishaq. In light of Ishaq's rightful demand, Kalam Hawladar and his associates told the mediators present, "All right, you do what you think is right." Afterward, they heard appeals by both sides and other opinions. They also went through the papers regarding the property and gave their judgment for Ishaq, as he was the rightful owner of the land as per the law. The dispute was settled after the uncle agreed to relinquish the land.

OUTCOME

At present, Ishaq occupies the land. There have been no further disputes over this land.

CASE SUMMARY

- Abused and disinherited, Ishaq attempted to keep land given him by his grandfather against the wishes of his family.
- Ishaq appealed to mediators to defend his interests.
- The family was threatened with legal action if they ignored mediators.
- Family traditional rules do not always regard individual rights.
- The legal documents became the common ground for settlement.
- Ishaq got his land back even though his uncle had possession for 40 years.

13

Vendetta and Buddhist Mediator in Southern Thailand

CHALIDAPORN SONGSAMPHAN
Faculty of Political Science
Thammasat University, Bangkok, Thailand

⌘ *Historically, Thai society has been described as paternalistic, with the King personally settling disputes between his subjects. At the local level particularly, people turned to village elders, monks, and other leading local figures rather than the court system. As the majority of Thai are Buddhist, monks have respect and prestige and have been respected as mediators.*

The community of Tambon Pakmark lived on rented government reservation lands in Southern Thailand. When a logging company needed land for growing replacement trees, families sold land they did not own or land that was claimed by others.

This case study describes a dispute over this issue between two families that resulted in violence. A Buddhist monk known to both families stepped in to mediate. He acted as an intermediary and got the families to meet together. The monk concluded the successful mediation with a ceremonial oath and drinking of water that had been poured over bullets, grenades, and knives.

Tambon Pakmark is a community in Chaiya district, Surathani province in the southern part of Thailand. People in this community are predominantly Buddhists, and the temple is the center of the community. The monks have provided spiritual support and helped the people develop their community by initiating and coordinating projects to build roads and schools. These monks are also active in protecting the forests in the area.

Although the people of Tambon Pakmark are quite religious, many of them like to gamble. To get money for gambling, many resorted to robbery and stealing other people's cattle. This had been a major cause of conflicts in the community, which often ended up in violence. How bloody each conflict would be depended on the wealth and influence of the parties involved. Rich villagers could afford to buy more arms to fight their enemies. The Buddhist monks in this community, especially Prakru Kasem Dhammarangsri, have attempted to change these bad habits of the people by preaching the *dhama* of Lord Buddha. This worked with some villagers, but many were still heavy gamblers who liked to settle their differences with others by violent means.

This community is in a reservation area, but villagers went in a long time ago and cut down most of the forest in order to grow rubber trees. Consequently, this area is no longer a forest but a series of villages. Like others in various communities in the rural areas around the countries, most people in Tambon Pakmark did not have legal ownership of the plots on which they lived. The government solved this problem by renting out this part of the reservation to these people. The people could live and grow trees on the plots they developed and pay rent to the government after they sold fruits and rubber, but they could not sell their land. This policy did not give much order to the chaotic issue of land ownership in the community. There were still many plots of land that did not legally belong to anyone, but people went in and planted trees anyway. Moreover, there were no clear marks to show which part of the land belonged to whom. These factors accounted for many disputes when the price of land soared and the people wanted to get rich fast by selling their plots (even though they could not do so according to the law) to profiteers and developers from outside the area.

In 1980, the government required that all the companies that had logging contracts in the reservation areas around the country had to grow trees to replace the ones they cut down. Consequently, the logging company that had a contract in Surathani province started to buy land to grow replacement trees in order to comply with the new requirement. It wanted to buy approximately 25,000 rai of land in the Pakmark community. The people tried to sell as much of their land as possible to the company. Some even sold other people's land because there was no proof of legal ownership for many plots. However, some families had already planted rubber trees on these portions of land, so they considered the plots theirs. This led to many arguments among the people of Tambon Pakmark. The bloodiest of them all was the one between the Sukmee and Cheenthai families.

The Sukmee and Cheenthai families are very influential in the communities. Both owned large pieces of land on which they grew rubber and coffee. Before this conflict occurred, they had a very good relationship. They once fought side by side when the two families quarreled with people from another community. The two families became closer because of the marriage between Kamnan Jon Cheenthai and Mrs. Chao, who was a member of the Sukmee family. All of this goodwill fell apart when they argued about a piece of land.

The Sukmee family offered to sell a big piece of land to the logging company in the area. After they reached an agreement, the company workers, with the help of the Sukmee family, went in and plowed the plot. The company did not know that a large part of the land they had bought belonged to the Cheenthai family. Actually, the Sukmee family might not have known that either, for there were no marks to show which part of land belonged to which family. By the time the company realized that they were on the Cheenthai family's property, they had already plowed about 100 rai of the Cheenthai's land on which the family grew tapioca. The cost of the land then was approximately 3,000 baht per rai. This invasion led to a major quarrel between the two families, which could not reach any agreement. Consequently, they resorted to violence to settle the conflict.

After the first fight broke out, the two families engaged in a cycle of attack and revenge that lasted for a year. A number of people in both families were injured in the gunfights; some were even killed. The police and the district officers had failed to arrest the killers and thus end the conflict because no one in the community was willing to cooperate in the investigation. The villagers were afraid that if they gave any information about the fighting to the police, they and their families might be harmed by either of the two families. Fortunately, the Buddhist monk in the community stepped in and helped both sides end this conflict.

THE MEDIATOR

Before he became a monk, Prakru Kasem Dhammarangsri used to live in the same neighborhood with both the Sukmee and Cheenthai families. His family was poor then, and Prakru Kasem worked in the orchards of both families. During that time, the owners of the orchards and rubber plantations and the villagers who worked for them were parts of a patron-client system in which the latter used their labor in return for help and favor from the former. In such a system, Prakru Kasem developed close relationships with both families. When he became a Buddhist monk, both families had supported him by bringing him food and necessary things the way Buddhists often do for the monks they respect.

Prakru Kasem had been very active in helping people in the community. After he became the abbot of the Suthavatha temple, he continued both religious and community work for the people in the same way as his predecessor had done. The previous abbot had been guiding people to develop the area by initiating projects to build roads and schools. Prakru Kasem also got the idea of forest conservation from Pra-ajarn Sudhon and Tharn Buddhadhasa who taught that people should be grateful to nature. Prakru Kasem had been successful in protecting 1,300 rai of the forest in the Chaiya district from being destroyed by villagers.

Prakru Kasem has been very successful in guiding and helping people deal with the state bureaucracy. As mentioned above, the Pakmark community was developed by people who invaded a reservation area, so these people did not have legal ownership of the land. Prakru Kasem foresaw the problems with government officials taking legal actions against these people. Officials from the Forest Department or the police could evict them at any time for breaking the law. The monk then called for a meeting with the people of the community and convinced them that they should prevent these problems from happening. He told them to apply for the rental contract with the government so that they could stay on their plots even though they would not be able to sell them.

He also helped settle the conflicts between the people and the bureaucrats. For example, in 1974 the government had a project to build a main road. When the construction started, many valuable trees that belonged to the villagers had to be cut down. Since the owners of these trees made thousands of baht each year from selling fruits from these trees, they refused to allow the workers to cut their trees. This incident halted the construction. Prakru Kasem and the community leaders tried to solve the problem by asking the villagers to sacrifice their trees for the sake of future generations who would benefit from the new road. The owners of the trees agreed to do so, and the workers were able to finish their job with no further delay. These activities brought Prakru Kasem respect and affection from the people of the Pakmark community.

His reputation and his close relationship with the two families involved in the conflict were major factors leading to his successful mediation.

THE MEDIATION PROCESS

When Prakru Kasem heard about the quarrel and the gunfight that led to the deaths of two persons—one from each family—he attempted to convince them to stop fighting. He went to the Sukmee family first. He arrived at the Sukmee compound late in the evening, but he could not get in to see the family's elders because there were armed guards in front. Even people eating in the kitchen had to carry guns so that they could fight when their enemies ambushed. The next morning he went to see both families again. He could not meet any one because both sides were still drunk and too angry. He asked both families to calm down and use reason to settle the problem.

After lunch, he went to talk to the elders of the two families. He stopped at the Sukmee compound first. While he was talking to a number of family members, he noticed that all of them were heavily armed. Some even carried M-16s. "How could you fight like this? Your families have been so close. You should have told me [about the problem] first," the monk told them. They replied that they were so angry they could not wait to consult anyone. Mr. Ung Sukmee, the eldest of the family, asked Prakru Kasem to help them. He said he had tried to stop the others in the family, but no one listened to him. Prakru Kasem said to Mr. Ung and the other members of the Sukmee family:

> I have tried to help, but I still do not know how because the situation has been worsened. The other family might misunderstand me because I come here and talk to you. They might just fire their guns into this house and I might get killed. I risked my life to come here because I am neutral. I do not take any family's side, but I came here because of love and gratitude that both families have been supporting me for years. Please understand that I who consider myself as a relative of yours will try to do my best to stay neutral. Please calm down. I will go to consult the Cheenthai family for the way out.

It seemed to Prakru Kasem that everyone in the Sukmee family believed him, so he left.

When he arrived at the Cheenthai compound, people who had gone to kill a member of the Sukmee family had already escaped. Mr. Chang Cheenthai, the leader of the family, said to Prakru Kasem with tears in his eyes, "Please help the children. They have been fighting and killing and they will do it again. I tried to stop them, but they did not listen to me. Their father, my own brother, has backed them up." Prakru Kasem replied,

> When the situation became this worse [sic], it is difficult to do anything. I came here to talk to you because I have considered myself as a relative of both families. I am what I am today because of the support of both families, so I want to do anything I can to help. But I did not know if I can do anything because there were some drunken elders who told the kids to fight. If I talked to them now, they might become more violent because they were drunk.

The next morning, Mr. Chang told his relatives, after they became more conscious, that Prakru Kasem had been concerned and asked them to listen to the reasons of the other side.

A few days after that, both families cremated the bodies of their dead relatives. The situation still did not improve. The fighting and killing continued, and the police could not arrest anyone because the people involved escaped after the incidents. In fact, it was too difficult for the police to do much of anything because no one in the community would cooperate or give them any information about the conflict and the fight. The cycle of killing and revenge went on, and more members of each family were killed. Both families mistrusted each other. They were afraid that if they did nothing, the other side would endanger their family members. Therefore, they had to prevent that from happening.

The violence started to involve another family. The Thongpraew family was related to the Sukmee family, but some of its members took the Cheenthai side and one of them was shot dead by the Sukmee family. The Sukmee family suspected that Mr. Klam Thongpraew, whose nephew was killed, might attempt revenge. The Sukmee wanted to get rid of him before he could do anything. Fortunately, Prakru Kasem found out about the plan before it was carried out. The monk then went to see Mr. Ung Sukmee and stated,

> Mr. Klam might not be like what the Sukmee family believed him to be, so think carefully before doing anything to him. You might harm an innocent man. I came here not because I wanted to interfere in your business, but I was concerned and really wanted to help. Please believe what I just said.

The Sukmee family apparently did believe him and postponed the plan to harm Mr. Klam. Prakru Kasem then went to Mr. Klam's house. Mr. Klam insisted that he did not know anything. Although his nephew was on the Cheenthai side, he himself did not get involved in the conflict between the two families. Prakru Kasem told him that he was almost killed by the people of the Sukmee family because they thought that Mr. Klam took part in the killing of their family member. He took Mr. Klam to see the people who wanted to kill him. Mr. Klam told them that he did not know anything and he did not take any side. The Sukmee family believed him.

Prakru Kasem, Pra Somnuk, and Kamnan Jon Cheenthai, who saw the conflict intensify and cause trouble to people outside the two families, were afraid that the families would keep on killing each other until there was no one left. They went to consult the district officer and the governor of Surathani. Both state officials agreed that the fight between the two families was a very serious problem and they wanted to help. So far they had not wanted to use force to solve the problem because it might worsen the situation. The police and other officials tried to deal with the conflict gently so that the situation would not get worse. However, they could not do much and the problem worsened. After discussing the situation and possible solutions, Prakru Kasem and the officials decided to arrange a meeting at the temple for the two families so they could settle their differences.

Prakru Kasem and Kamnan Jon Cheenthai pleaded with both families to talk to each other by pointing to the distress that this conflict caused them and the community. By that time, the two families had reached the point where they both wanted to end the conflict, for each had lost five relatives after the rounds of fighting and vendettas. Therefore, they agreed to join the meeting, which was set up at the Virojanaram temple.

The governor of the Surathani province, the district officer, Prakru Kasem himself, Pra Somnuk, the police officers, and teachers were among the witnesses at the meeting. The governor explained to both families why he called for the meeting and asked them to talk to each other freely. Prakru Kasem preached the Buddhist teaching that hatred could not be stopped by hatred but by forgiveness. Then the members of both families were asked to drink *nam sabarn* (literally meaning "the sworn water"). Only those who used violence against one another were asked because there were members of both families who disagreed with the fighting and tried to stop their relatives, but they were not successful in doing so. These relatives who were not involved in the conflict came to the meeting to support the attempt to end the fighting.

Water, some bullets, grenades, and knives were put in a small container. The people from both families who were asked to drink nam sabarn took an oath and then drank the water. Because the oath called for misfortune to happen to those who broke it, Prakru Kasem did not say the words himself. One police officer said the following words, which the members of both families repeated after him: "We the members of the two families will stop killing and revenging the other for the sake of happiness of both sides. If we do not stop killing, may we suffer misfortune and die because of grenades, bullets, or knives."

After taking the oath and drinking the water, they gave their weapons to the police officers, who then warned both families that any one of them who broke the law the way they had before would be arrested and receive severe punishment.

OUTCOME

The conflict and violence between the Sukmee and Cheenthai families ended after the meeting. The two families did not quarrel and fight with each other again after that.

The mediation process in this case was successful because not only did it stop the violence, it made the parties involved in the conflict settle their differences. The two sides could live together in the same community without any major problems again.

Several factors led to the success of this case:

- *The characteristics of the mediator.* Being a monk in a Buddhist community is not the only reason contributing to the achievement of Prakru Kasem in this case. He was accepted and revered by the people in the community due to his genuine concern and continuing work to improve their quality of life.
- *The relationship between the mediator and the parties in conflict.* Prakru Kasem and the two families knew one another very well. This, together with his reputation, made them trust and accept him as a neutral mediator.
- *The tactic.* Prakru Kasem had tried to deal with both families gently and patiently to show them that he did not take sides and really wanted to help. It should be noted here that he talked to each side separately before the final meeting. Both met when they were ready to talk. If they had had to confront each other before reaching the point when they were willing to end the conflict, they might not have compromised but instead tried to appear the "winner." Another reason why this scenario could worsen the situation is that in Thai culture the issue of losing face is very important. Both sides might not express their view openly or cooperate to find an acceptable solution in the meeting if they felt that doing so might ruin their images or make them lose face. Consequently, the tactic of negotiating through a mediator instead of confronting directly before both sides could reach any agreement was appropriate in this context. The parties in conflict could talk freely and openly to a mediator they trusted about their positions and their demands, so a better picture of the whole situation can appear. Whether this tactic will work depends on the image of the mediator. In this case, the mediator was trusted fully by both sides, so they felt that they could talk freely without fear of losing face.

Another interesting point about Prakru Kasem's tactic is that he used religious ("superstitious" would be a more appropriate word) beliefs of the people as a way to guarantee that they would not use violence against each other again. In a community in which people are still religious and believe in superstitions, this method may work well. However, in an urban area where the beliefs of the people have been changed by the influence of the Western-style way of life and thinking, this might not work at all.

CASE SUMMARY

- Religion is an important common ground.
- Many conflicts center on issues of gambling and land.
- Traditionally, there is no legal ownership of the land sold to developers.
- Developers bought Cheenthai land from the Sukmee family causing severe conflict between the two families.
- Villagers are uncooperative with authorities and do not want to get involved in the conflict.
- A Buddhist monk becomes a mediator supported by both families.
- Prakru Kasem (monk) convinced the community to get involved.
- Prakru Kasem could talk with both families.
- The conflict was causing trouble to people outside the family and creating disharmony in the community.
- They had to find a solution where neither side would appear to "win."
- The appeal to religion as a common ground belief and the welfare of the community.
- This approach, based on rural traditions, might not work in an urban area.

14

Tiger Saves Taiga

SAVING THE SIBERIAN ECOSYSTEM FROM HYUNDAI'S LOGGING OPERATIONS

JAE HYUN YOO
General Secretary, Citizen's Coalition for Economic Justice
Seoul, Korea

Hyundai Resources Development Company had a contract for logging operations in the old-growth boreal forests in the Russian Far East. International environmentalists planned to stop Hyundai's logging operations. A Korean nongovernment organization, the Citizen's Coalition for Economic Justice (CCEJ), was pressured by international environmentalists to intervene.

This case study reports the actions taken by the CCEJ to persuade the chairman of Hyundai, then an active candidate for the presidency of Korea, to preserve the region. The CCEJ acted as an intermediary and mediator and prevented an international boycott of Hyundai products.

The Citizens Coalition for Economic Justice (CCEJ) recently played a pivotal role in forestalling a major confrontation between international environmentalists and Hyundai Resources Development Company over the company's logging operations in the old-growth boreal forests in the Russian Far East. The boreal forests of the former USSR, which the Russians call the Taiga, perform a critical role in preserving the Earth's atmosphere. Hailed by the leaders of environmental movements worldwide as a "remarkable achievement in the history of environmental movements," CCEJ's success in the mediation efforts between the two parties marks the first time in history that a Korean nongovernment organization (NGO) played a central role in resolving an international environmental conflict outside Korea. The following is an account of CCEJ's involvement in the case.

I became aware of the approaching confrontation between the international environmentalists and the Hyundai company only after I began to receive facsimile messages from many international environmental NGOs in the summer of 1992. The first letter was from Stephen MacKay of Friends of Earth, Japan, and Yoichi Kuroda of the Japanese Tropical Action Network (JATAN). The letter informed me that many international NGOs were working together to stop Hyundai's Siberian logging operations in the area called Svetlaya on the east coast of the Russian Far East. Soon after, additional letters followed from David Gorden of the Pacific Energy Resources Centre, Patrick Anderson of Greenpeace International, and others. The small town of Svetlaya located in the area just north of Vladivostok had caught my attention immediately.

Although the Republic of Korea is the world's second largest importer of timber, no Korean NGOs have ever worked to protect forests in foreign countries. Seeing the dedication and hard work of foreign citizens groups to the issue and realizing that doing nothing about it would be considered "losing face" to Koreans, I decided to become involved in the campaign to save Taiga. Together with Rev. Kyoung-Suk Suh, Secretary General of CCEJ, I arranged to visit Hyundai Resources Development Company to uncover facts about their operations.

At the first meeting, the Hyundai representative said in an embarrassed and irritated attitude that Svetlaya Inc., a joint-venture company established in July 1990 between Hyundai and the local Russian government of the area, was engaged in logging operations that were fully legitimate according to the environmental standards of the Russian government. His explanation was that as Svetlaya Inc. was acting legally under orders and supervision of the local government, the Russian government and Svetlaya Inc., not the Hyundai group, must bear all the responsibilities for the operations. The meeting was followed by two others with experts in forest issues and other NGO leaders. Meanwhile, the international NGOs raised their voices by threatening a boycott campaign against all Hyundai products sold in their countries.

During the period of discussing the matter with foreign NGOs through fax and phone, I received an invitational letter to attend an "International Boreal

Forest Conference" to be held in Sweden September 30 to October 4. The letter urged me to attend the meeting because the Hyundai case would be dealt with and most of the people involved in the case were supposed to come. I became very anxious to meet the environmentalists in action whom I had come to know only by their names in letters. After consulting with other NGO leaders, I decided to attend the meeting.

At the conference, held in a small town called Yokkmokk in the north of Sweden around the Arctic Circle, I received a flood of questions from the participants, and I, in turn, asked many detailed questions about their activities and the local situation in Svetlaya. Dr. Alexander Gregoriev, chairman of the Russian Socio-Ecological Union, the largest environmental NGO in Russia, reported in detail about the crisis situation facing Siberian Taiga and Russian citizens' efforts to save them.

What Dr. Gregoriev worried the most about was a possible racial conflict between Koreans and Russians in the area. To Russians there was no difference whether the Koreans were from the South or from the North. The image of Koreans in Russian eyes had become extremely negative for a number of reasons. For the past 20 years, North Korea had been sending many lumberjacks into the area to carry out irresponsible and destructive logging operations. Not only was there widespread environmental degradation, but the North Koreans' actions created severe conflicts with the local residents as they engaged in reckless hunting, harassing the residents, and buying out from local markets goods that are scarce in North Korea. There were growing sentiments against Koreans.

The Svetlaya's logging operations caused soil erosion and contamination of rivers, resulting in the local fishermen's inability to continue their livelihood. This provoked local residents' protests and demonstrations demanding compensation for their loss of income. In addition, the managers from Hyundai hired many ethnic Koreans from the region or from China because they could speak Korean and paid their salaries in dollars, whereas they paid the Russian workers in rubles. As runaway inflation drastically reduced the value of rubles, the real income of Russian workers fell day by day to the point where their salaries were several times less in value than the Koreans'. This naturally caused widespread resentment against ethnic Koreans. Dr. Gregoriev's analysis was that all these resentments could erupt in racial violence against Koreans similar to that which had occurred in Los Angeles.

The leaders of the NGOs who gathered at the conference in Sweden took special note of the fact that Hyundai is one of the biggest conglomerates (*Chaebol* in Korean) and that the Siberian operations constituted only a small portion of its wide-ranging activities around the world. The environmentalists assumed readiness for actions such as blockading Svetlaya harbor with

Greenpeace's famous ship *Rainbow Warrior* to stop timber transportation, putting advertisements in major newspapers such as the *New York Times* to protest against Hyundai, and carrying out worldwide campaigns boycotting Hyundai products.

These actions would have serious repercussions on Korea-Russia economic cooperation, which started only recently after 47 years of no diplomatic relationship between both countries. It would also cause a very strong impact on Korean society and politics because, incidently, the chairman of Hyundai, a self-made billionaire named Joo Young Chung, happened to be a candidate from the United People's Party in the 1992 presidential race. Young Sam Kim, the candidate from the ruling party, and Dae Joong Kim from the major opposition party were ranked a very close tie in the public polls. Like Ross Perot in the U.S. presidential race of the same year, Chair- man Chung held a casting role in the race. Any incident or scandal related to him would be destined to change the course of Korean history. After explaining this rather sensitive situation to the participants, I requested that the NGO leaders hold their actions in waiting until I could meet with Chairman Chung and persuade him to stop. Fortunately, they all agreed to wait until my medi- ation effort would be over and to act only if I failed to reach an agreement with him.

During the 14-hour ride to the Stockholm airport and another 12-hour flight back to Seoul, I worked hard to formulate a strategy to resolve this conflict. That was not an easy job. For example, the very first thing for me to do—making an appointment with one of the presidential candidates in the middle of a fierce campaign—would be very difficult. Even if we succeeded in meeting face to face, why should he listen to me? Why should he bother to spend even a minute on this "trifle" matter during his glorious moment of dreaming to be the president of Korea? I began to sweat.

Immediately following my return, Rev. Suh and I met again with the president and the staff of Hyundai Resources Development Company. They began to understand the seriousness of the situation; however, they were very reluctant and rather afraid to bring this issue to their "Emperor." The Siberian project was the chairman's idea, and he had met with President Gorbachev and talked him into approving the project even before Korea had restored diplomatic relationships with the USSR. It was supposed to be the beginning of a longtime and mutually beneficial relationship between Korea and Russia. The staff said in fear, "The project was his baby. How could we go to him and tell him that there were some problems in Siberia and that we should stop the operations?"

Days passed. Meanwhile, Mr. Anderson of Greenpeace talked to me over the phone about their plan to blockade the Svetlaya harbor around the end of

October. "If you do not succeed before then, we will blockade the harbor and start an all-out attack on Hyundai." That was an ultimatum.

As for the problem of making an appointment with the chairman, we managed to solve that by taking advantage of an umbrella organization called the National Citizens Committee for Fair Election Campaign, consisting of 450 NGOs in various fields. CCEJ was the principal organizer of the organization, of which Rev. Suh was secretary general. Because the committee was scheduled to visit the four major candidates including Chairman Chung, Rev. Suh and I could make an appointment with him in his party chairman's office. Of course the meeting was strictly for the committee's business. The Siberian issue was not on the agenda.

Now we had to come up with a very concrete and precise strategy to persuade the chairman. After all, we were not going to have hours to explain this issue. We had to change his mind within a few minutes.

During and after the Yokkmokk conference, I hit upon the idea of bringing up the issue of the Siberian tiger and tried to form my strategy based on it. The logic went like this:

Point 1. The virgin forest alongside the Bikin River, where the joint venture company plans to harvest timber, is the protected natural habitation of Siberian tigers. The Siberian tiger is exactly the same species as the Korean tiger, which is already extinct in the Korean Peninsula.

Point 2. The tiger is the most beloved animal by Koreans throughout history. It is the symbol animal of Korea. It was no accident that the mascot animal of the 1988 Seoul Olympics was a tiger called Hodori. Incidently, Chairman Chung decided to have the Korean tiger as his party symbol. He himself was often called "tiger."

Point 3. To save the tigers, the operations along the Bikin River should stop. Posing as an environmentalist to protect the endangered species will make the chairman look good. A campaign to protect the Korean tiger would move Korean voters emotionally. The chairman may lose some monies in Siberia, but he will definitely gain much broad support and his popularity will increase. Small price to pay.

Conclusion. He will stop the Svetlaya operations around the Bikin River basin. It will take just three minutes to explain the logic. OK, I am ready.

Tiger saves Taiga!

The meeting with Chairman Chung did not go as planned. When I brought up the issue of the Svetlaya logging operations, he quickly stopped my explanation and said, "I know all about it. I started the project. But I am no longer the chairman of Hyundai. You should go to the Hyundai Resources Development Company."

After a long breath, I asked him politely, "Do you know that there are hundreds of Korean tigers living around the Bikin River basin? The tiger is your party's mascot, isn't it? If you destroy the virgin forests around the Bikin River, you are killing your symbol too. It will make all the environmentalists around the world angry—and your voters too!"

It took only 30 seconds. The chairman took the bait. He immediately corrected his posture and sat up straight. "Really?" Then I explained what had happened in Sweden and what would be the result of Greenpeace's blockade plan and worldwide boycott campaign against Hyundai products. Of course, I did not forget to mention the importance of saving old-growth forests for the benefits of mankind.

About 10 minutes had passed without further interruption. He then returned to his chairmanship not of the Party but of Hyundai, which he had denied minutes before. After all, he is the founder of Hyundai. Right after the briefing, he picked up the phone and personally ordered the president of Hyundai Resources Development Company "Do not go into the Bikin River basin!" That was it. It was over.

When I met the president of Hyundai Resources Development Company later to take follow-up measures, he told me that he was shocked by the call because it was the first time during his 18 years of service to Hyundai that he had received a phone call directly from the chairman himself.

Shortly after, Hyundai issued a statement to the international environmentalists involved in the case explaining its intention not to go into the Bikin River basin. After a couple of weeks waiting and watching the developments of the case, our friends praised the results of mediation and sent telegrams to congratulate our success.

The chairman failed to become the president of Korea. He ranked third. He had, however, succeeded at least in saving both the tiger and Taiga.

CASE SUMMARY

We see again a different definition of mediation. The environmentalists at the meeting in Sweden probably didn't see Jae Hyun Yoo as a neutral third party—nor did the former chairman of Hyundai, Joo Young Chung. It could also be reasonably argued that the chairman was not aware of any conflict with the environmentalists.

Jae Hyun Yoo made the chairman aware of the conflict and persuaded him to change the company's actions. It is worth noting, as well, that even if the conflict could be cast as between environmentalists and Hyundai,

Jae Hyun Yoo addressed his efforts to one individual and called up issues important to that one individual.

The following points are illustrated in the case study:

- A conflict existed between environmentalists and a multinational corporation.
- Doing nothing about the conflict would mean "losing face" to the Koreans by letting the corporation take over.
- Local environmentalists were very concerned about the effect of logging and environmental degradation as well local residents being harassed by North Korean outsiders.
- Koreans paid in dollars and Russians paid in devalued rubles led to more conflict among outsiders.
- Environmentalists threatened to campaign internationally against Hyundai, resulting in the company losing face.
- Conflict also endangered Russian-Korean relations.
- Chairman Chung was directly in charge of starting and running the project.
- The Siberian tiger as a national symbol and corporate trademark became the common ground.
- The mediator was not neutral, but the task was to find a working relationship to everyone's advantage.

15

Toxic Waste Management in Malaysia

GURMIT SINGH
Environmental Protection Society, Malaysia, Petaling Jaya

Gurmit Singh describes toxic waste management and conflicts between government agencies and environmentalists as an issue affecting many Asian countries. This case study describes the toxic waste management situation and its consequences in Malaysia in the conflict between the Chinese residents of Bukit Merah, environmental groups, and the government over radioactive waste, where no institutional mechanism exists to resolve such disputes. He offers specific proposals for handling environmental conflicts, such as the collection and dissemination of information to the public.

Toxic waste management has been a festering conflict in Malaysia for more than a decade. It has pitted waste generators against citizens, as in Papan and Bukit Nenas. But conflicts have also arisen between government agencies and environmentalists on issues of reduction and safe disposal. There have also been international ramifications as toxic waste has moved across the nation's boundaries.

After the 1991 tragedy at Sg. Buloh, the Malaysian community began to awaken to the chemical time bombs that have been ticking away in their midst. The bland assurances of government officials and the arrogant silence of the private sector did not sit well with ordinary but concerned Malaysians. Probably the same is happening in many other Asian countries such as Thailand and India.

SERIOUS SYMPTOMS

In a May 11, 1991 press statement, the Environmental Protection Society, Malaysia (EPSM) noted serious symptoms that had surfaced at the beginning of the 1990s. In the aftermath of the May 7, 1991 explosions at the Sg. Buloh Fireworks, the EPSM found that the factory had operated for 17 years without a certificate of fitness and that many small and medium-scale industries (SMIs) had been operating in a similar "illegal" manner for even longer periods of time with little regard for individuals' safety or the environment.

As early as January 11, 1985, the EPSM had issued a statement, titled "Avoiding Malaysian Bhopals and Other Chemical Hazards," that urged all government agencies to draft and strictly implement adequately safe regulations; ensure adequate buffer zones between plants and houses; and demand that factory owners observe the highest possible safety and environmental standards. The Sg. Buloh tragedy clearly confirmed that EPSM's concerns were ignored by all concerned.

The EPSM called for authorities and the SMI owners as well as the public to thoroughly examine why the following problems exist:

- Licenses are difficult to get or can be circumscribed.
- Regulations and guidelines drawn up by various government agencies are poorly enforced.
- Inspections, even when done, are not followed up to ensure that recommendations are implemented.
- Political and other interferences undermine public safely and the quality of the environment.
- Employees are willing to work under conditions that blatantly jeopardize their health and even lives.
- Public accountability and a willingness to assume responsibility for lapses are very weak.

A March 1991 study of 430 SMIs in the country, conducted by the Centre of Environment, Technology, and Development, Malaysia (CETDEM), identified very little concern for the environment or worker safety as well as failure on the part of most state authorities to implement effective zoning plans. Although copies of the report were made available to a number of federal administers, state governments and departments, and relevant firms and organizations, CETDEM has yet to receive substantive responses to its recommendations.

COMMUNITY VIEWS

Although there has been no comprehensive study of the Malaysian community's overall views, it is safe to state that most people are ignorant about toxic chemicals and hazardous waste. Even the small groups that are active in environmental, consumer, and public interest organizations often find themselves in the dark. This is because there is little opportunity for public participation in the safety and environmental arenas. Consequently, it is not surprising that there should be public alarm when glaring instances of failure to adequately manage chemicals or toxic waste hit the headlines. It naturally follows that the NIMBY (not in my backyard) reaction should greet any proposals for toxic waste sites.

One should not blame the public for being alarmed at discovering that highly toxic pesticides, like paraquat, are still being used in Malaysia without any legal constraints. Tons of potassium cyanide are being stored in warehouses for use by electroplating firms. Chemical laboratories are being allowed to operate in the midst of offices and restaurants. Toxic wastes are being discharged into drains or dumped behind roadside bushes or into unsanitary municipal dumps. Batteries are not being collected separately and disposed of in an environmentally sound manner. Environmental-friendly technologies hardly feature in the shopping list of trade missions or corporations, whether large or small.

There is also some public concern that dirty industries from countries with increasingly vocal environmental concerns are moving into Malaysia. In other words, Malaysia is becoming the dumping grounds for these countries' dirt. When this is coupled with the unsatisfactory implementation of an environmental impact assessment (EIA), public concern develops into fear of having to live with increased danger and pollution in the future.

The Malaysian public is also concerned that there does not seem to be a comprehensive inventory of toxic chemicals used or produced within the country. There are bits and pieces scattered among different government agencies. The Sg. Buloh fire illustrated this—explosive chemicals had been imported for years without any significant official control.

There is also great concern over the fact that the vast majority of these toxic waste generators are unwilling to assume "cradle to grave" responsibility for the wastes they churn out daily. Why won't they?

WHY PUBLIC PARTICIPATION?

The Malaysian public is quite diverse—ranging from the super-rich to the very poor (although not at the starvation level), from the highly educated to the illiterate, from the technocrats to the unskilled. There are also divisions of race, religion, and language, the presence of which is a political reality that can only be ignored at one's peril.

Although Malaysia practices a multiparty democratic system, the same coalition has been in continuous power ever since independence, and the Internal Security Act and other oppressive legislation have kept dissent on a tight leash. Consequently, there has been very little public participation or accountability.

However, public participation is important not just to avoid conflicts but for the following reasons:

- It is a basic requirement that all concerned citizens be involved in all major environmental issues in the community.
- Citizens should be sensitized and educated on the real scope of all environmental issues, especially regarding chemicals and toxic waste, so that unjustified fears are minimized if not banished completely.
- Pollution (as well as toxic chemical) management cannot be left exclusively in the hands of bureaucrats and technocrats, especially when it poses serious and long-term threats to the natural ecosystem and human health.

THE LESSONS OF THE ASIAN RARE EARTH CONTROVERSY

Without going into details of the Asian Rare Earth (ARE) controversy (one of Malaysia's most prominent environmental events), which is still simmering, the following lessons can be inferred:

- The public becomes distrustful of official explanations and actions if it is initially kept in the dark and then led on a merry-go-round after it starts asking questions.
- Insulting the public's intelligence by asserting that problems can only be understood by experts infuriates it and prevents holding any meaningful dialogue.
- Where government agencies are seen acting as spokespeople and protectors of polluters, the public is further alienated.
- When experts produce contradictory findings, the public is inclined to believe the worst, especially if the government and the polluter have compromised their credibility earlier.

- There is a tendency to see racial and religious motives when the affected people happen to be ethnically different from officials responsible for the controversy, a weakness that is often exacerbated by press reports.
- Once people realize that the risk to their immediate families is real and imminent, there is a greater willingness to take direct action, like demonstrations. They become quite emotional if the threat is seen to persist for long periods.
- The fear of the unknown silences some but fires others into desperate action.
- The paucity of readily understandable information in the public realm creates doubts and uneasiness.
- Vested interests, both local and national, can exploit public apprehension for their own benefit.

CURRENT STATUS OF CONFLICT

Despite having won a court case last year, the mainly Chinese residents of Bukit Merah were shocked when the Supreme Court allowed ARE to resume operations pending the hearing of its appeal. Now the company is closing down on the excuse that the operation is no longer viable. Yet the huge amount of radioactive waste already generated is to be left in the storage site. Naturally, the residents are concerned about the risks that this will pose to them. It is not yet clear whether the federal or state government will assume final responsibility for the safe containment of this waste.

In the case of the Bukit Nenas toxic waste site, construction work is about to occur, and once again the predominantly Chinese protesters are worried that their livelihood, which depends to a large extent on pig rearing, will be jeopardized, even forced to relocate or that their produce will be disadvantaged in the market. They have not been given assurances that the plant will operate safely and so remain fearful that toxic wastes beyond Malaysian shores will be brought to the site.

In both cases, the government sees the protesters as standing in the way of national interests, although the project operators are private entities. The environmental groups have tried to play the role of honest brokers—very often coming in on the side of residents when they have been disadvantaged by the lack of expertise—but it has been a very delicate and difficult role, especially when political parties have intervened.

No institutional mechanism exists at the national level to resolve such disputes. Even turning to the courts has proved unsatisfactory. It is neither a cheap nor a quick option. The mass media have repeatedly proved themselves unequal to the task, especially when the federal government is directly involved. Truth is often the first casualty.

WINNING PUBLIC CONFIDENCE

Winning public confidence and support is as important as finding satisfactory technical solutions. Although the Malaysian public may not be very articulate and assertive of its rights, the ARE controversy should convince the skeptics that even the most docile of people can be moved into action. There is a vital need to have much improved communication between the government and polluters/managers/professionals, on the one hand, and the affected public and public interest groups, especially the environmentalists, on the other.

This communication should not be the mere process of "telling" but should be a comprehensive consultation, which starts at the idea's inception and involves constant feedback and interaction. Once people are involved in this process, they will feel that they have a say in the final choices and directions. Even if the end result does not entirely meet their expectations, they are more likely to accept it. But it is important that there is real communication and information sharing so there are no misunderstandings and that all the public's fears and doubts are cleared.

In Malaysia, it is essential that a variety of languages or dialects are used, supplemented whenever possible, with audio-visual material. In some cases, visits to other sites and nearby residents would be useful. Many other communication tools can be found by consulting the right sources.

Still, the most important obstacle to overcome is the resistance of policy-makers and technocrats to such consultation. There seems to be an ingrained mistrust of consultation—justified under the dubious excuses that it politicizes the issue, allows financial speculation, creates unnecessary public alarm, makes the issue too complex to be understood by the public, or even outright denies the right of consultation. This is where the most fundamental change is required—otherwise, winning public confidence will remain a losing battle in Malaysia. Let no one be fooled into thinking that sullen silence means support and acceptance.

PRESENT SHORTFALLS OF PUBLIC PARTICIPATION

There presently exist no official or business attempts to inform, consult, and involve the public—an extension of the poor sense of public accountability that prevails in Malaysia; impediments in communications ranging from lack of interest to technicalities of the medium, language, and approach; general lack of confidence in the reliability of official pronouncements and assurances; fear and confusion about the seriousness and hazards of environmental problems, compounded by the general atmosphere of fear that pervades Malaysian society; absence of a history of people's involvement, except in *gotong-royong* or in narrow religious/ethnic/linguistic issues; sense of inadequacy in handling complex technical problems; ingrained distrust and divisions that inhibit people from working collectively for long-term environmental solutions; and frequent lapses in the implementation of existing environmental and other legislation, as clearly demonstrated in the Sg. Buloh incident.

MAKING PUBLIC PARTICIPATION EFFECTIVE

There is no magical formula for making public participation in environmental management effective, but based on the experiences elsewhere and some common sense, the following approaches should be tried.

1. Fear can partially be overcome by providing access to the experiences from a wide range of sources including those from members of the public who have had to face the same problems. Removal of fear-generating legislation like the Internal Security Act and the Official Secrets Act would certainly help.

2. Confusion can be minimized by putting all relevant information into language easily understood by laypersons and reducing the issue to its basics without distorting the problem or the proposed solutions. Another aid would be to coordinate the inputs from all interested parties, especially allowing the environmentalists the same access as the project proponents.

3. Feelings of exploitation and injustice can be allayed by being truthful about intentions, right from inception to operation. If necessary, hard evidence should be provided to show exactly who benefits and who shares in the costs. This may be the hardest part, but truth and honesty will go a long way in reassuring the public.

4. Distrust can be overcome by being open in all dealings and inviting public inspection of projects from construction to operation stages. The regular sharing of monitoring data will go a long way to generate trust.

5. Government agencies, ranging from district officers to the Department of Environment, should take pains to inform the public on major environmental issues as and when they occur.

6. The Malaysian mass media, especially the electronic media, must initiate a sustained program to fully educate the public on the nature of environmental problems and how they can be managed. Promulgation of a Freedom of Information Act and repeal of the Printing Presses and Publica-

tion Act would make tremendous contributions to information flow and result in a quantum improvement in public involvement.

7. Government, the private sector, and public interest organizations should involve the people in all stages of environmental management by consulting and briefing them. A greater display of public accountability by all relevant sectors will certainly encourage the public to participate more positively as will practicing public consultation rigorously in increasing numbers of comprehensive environmental impact assessments (EIAs).

8. Environmentalists and other public interest groups can help educate and guide the public into contributing positively toward environmental management, as long as the local state apparatus does not obstruct them.

SOME SPECIFIC SUGGESTIONS

In view of the prevailing community doubts about the management of chemicals and toxic wastes in Malaysia, I would like to suggest that the Malaysian government come clean on its present inadequacies and start a process of public consultation to finalize an effective management strategy. In the meantime, it should announce and implement short-term measures to prevent the situation from deteriorating any further.

The private sector, especially the SMIs, must stop flouting existing regulations and show meaningful corporate responsibility by curbing pollution of the environment and not endangering their workers' health and lives. The Department of Environment (DOE) should assume the lead agency role in acting against blatant culprits.

The Malaysian mass media need to devote more critical coverage to this issue, and the Malays themselves must become active and concerned about the dangers posed to their lives and to the lives of future generations (that much-talked-about intergenerational responsibility).

CASE SUMMARY

- Toxic waste presents a nontraditional new kind of problem in Malaysia.
- Both the government and the private sector ignore the possible dangers to locals.
- Local businesses generally operate unregulated for reasons of profit.
- The fireworks factory that blew up made the problem a public issue.
- The public is generally unaware of and uninformed about the problems.
- Dirty industries are moving to Malaysia for profit reasons.
- The public becomes distrustful of government and private sector agencies.
- Cultural differences between Malays and Chinese coincide with sides of the dispute.
- Chinese residents won in court, but industry continues to pollute.
- Chinese protesters are seen as standing in the way of national interests.
- Policymakers' and technocrats' resistance and mistrust prevent solutions.
- There is a lack of public confidence in mediation.
- There is no progress in obtaining effective public participation in environmental management.

16

The Dumping of Industrial Waste in Teshima, Japan

MASAKI YOKOYAMA[1]
Shikoku Gakuin University, Zentsuji, Kagawa, Japan

This case describes a 20-year, ongoing dispute involving residents of the small island of Teshima over the dumping of hazardous industrial waste. Residents first appealed to the governor of the Kagawa Prefecture to halt the dumping. The company, TSKK, then reapplied to the prefectural government, stating that its intention was to produce fertilizer from waste products. In actuality, however, the company continued to dump tons of shredded plastic by-products from automobile manufacturing.

Over time, residents of the island developed asthma and other respiratory diseases. A police raid from a neighboring prefecture stopped the dumping. Then the problem became the removal of the hazardous waste.

After the expected mediation by the local government failed to materialize, the problem was brought to the Pollution Problems Arbitration Commission. However, its powers are only advisory. Masaki Yokoyama discusses how this one case has implications not only for Japan but for the entire Asia-Pacific region.

Teshima is a small island (about 14 sq. km) in the Seto Inland Sea between the islands of Honshu and Shikoku in southwestern Japan. Its population is roughly 1,600. It is located within the Seto Inland Sea National Park and has always been known for its beautiful white sand beaches and green pine trees.

The residents of Teshima have been struggling against the illegal dumping of hazardous industrial waste since 1975.

THREE STAGES OF THE STRUGGLE

Stage 1: Proposal/Opposition (December 1975-February 1978)

Teshima Sogo Kanko Kaihatu (Teshima Integrated Tourism Development) Co., Ltd. (TSKK) is a company almost totally controlled by Mr. Matsuura Shosuke, with his wife as the nominal president. On December 18, 1975, TSKK first applied to the Kagawa prefectural government (*Kagawa-ken*) for permission to process hazardous industrial wastes.

Soon after Teshima residents came to know about it, they started collecting signatures for an antidumping petition. Almost every resident signed, and 1,425 signatures were presented to the governor of the Prefecture on February 25, 1976. On February 27, 1977, Sangyo Haikibutsu Mochikomi Zettai Hantai Teshima Jumin Kaigi (Organization of Teshima Residents Against the Import of Industrial Wastes, hereafter Jumin Kaigi) was formed by almost all the local residents.

Since then, Jumin Kaigi has been actively campaigning in various ways: lobbying the Kagawa prefectural assembly to pass a resolution requesting that the construction of the dumping facility be halted, holding demonstrations at the Kagawa prefectural hall, planting obstacles on the road to prevent the entry of the dumping trucks to the site from the port, bringing this case to the court, and so on. Mr. Matsuura was once arrested for assaulting and injuring local residents in the opposition movement. The conflict, however, did not end at this first stage. At the next stage, the problem became much worse.

Stage 2: Dumping/Suffering (February 1978-November 1990)

On September 16, 1977, TSKK changed its application to the prefectural administration, asking permission to process nonhazardous materials by the cultivation of earthworms, supposedly to produce fertilizer, and Kagawa-ken approved it on February 1, 1978. Based on this approval, TSKK brought in various kinds of industrial wastes, such as paper mill sludge and animal wastes. However, the production and sale of fertilizer were negligible and soon abandoned, and it was considered more a case of waste dumping than commercial processing.

On top of this, illegal operations of an even more dangerous kind started and reached a massive level in 1983. Some 170,000 tons of shredder dust (shredded automobile plastic waste) were collected from all over the western half of the country and shipped to Teshima. TSKK started burning it, and the smoke was unbearable for the residents near the dump site. Many drums and tank-lorries of dubious liquid materials were also brought. TSKK claimed they were processing shredder dust to recover some metal elements, using those liquids as fuel, and therefore the mountains of shredder dust and liquids were not dumped industrial waste but stored resources with commercial value. On paper, TSKK paid for shredder dust at 300 yen/ton and received 2,000 yen/ton for transporting it, thus making 1,700 yen/ton in profit.

The local residents appealed in an open letter to Kagawa-ken in 1984, but it responded only by endorsing the assertion of TSKK. Kagawa-ken acknowledged that the legitimate business of processing by using earthworms was still in operation, that shredder dust and other substances were raw materials stored for metal extraction, and that proper administrative guidance would be given and the law enforced if any offense was discovered. The residents challenged it a number of times afterward, but the prefectural government paid no attention.

The physical suffering of the people intensified in 1987 and thereafter with the occurrence of many cases of asthma and other sicknesses, mostly diseases of the respiratory organs including throat cancer. Soon after, the rate of asthma incidents in schoolchildren started to rise sharply. Until 1987, the rate was far below the national average, probably due to the previously clean environment, but in 1988 it tripled to 1.8 times the average, jumped to 3.6 in 1989, and reached almost 10 times the average in 1993. The national average is 1.04%, but among Teshima schoolchildren (6-15 years of age), 9.6% had asthma in 1993 (see Figure 16.1).

On November 16, 1990, the Hyogo prefectural police made a raid on TSKK's illegal waste dump because the police of Kagawa Prefecture had made no move to intervene, and some of the waste was brought from the nearby Hyogo Prefecture, which gave legitimacy for Hyogo Police to come in, according to the waste treatment law. The raid marks the transition to the third stage in the development of the problem: The dumping stopped, but the waste remained.

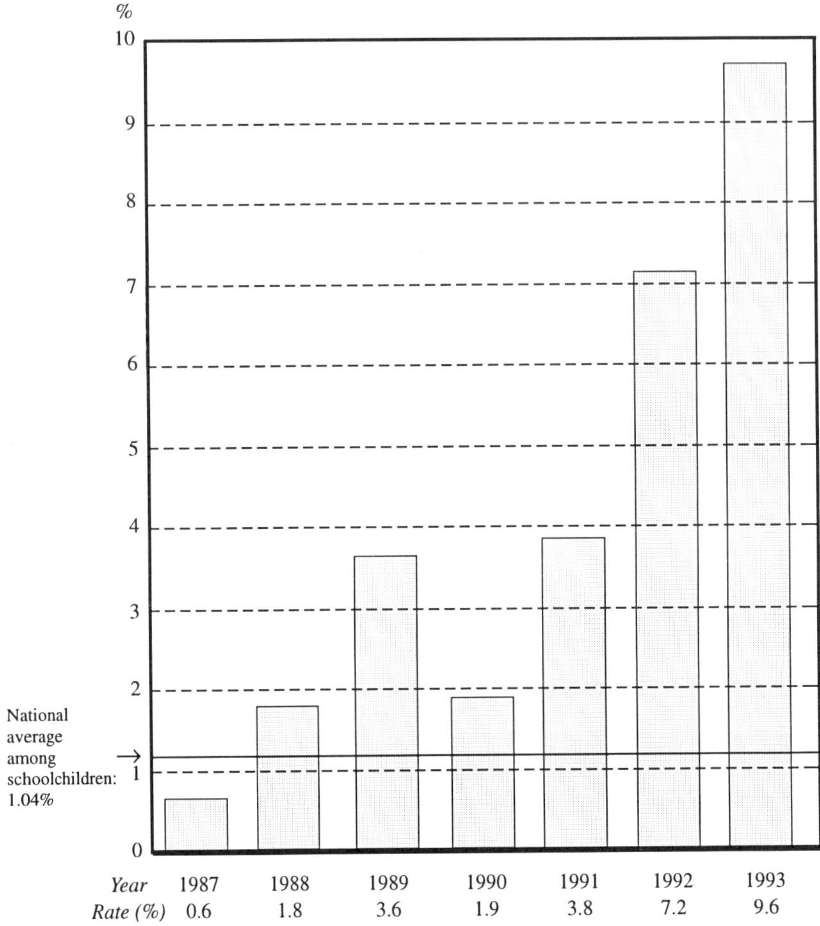

Figure 16.1. Rate of asthma incidents in schoolchildren in Teshima (elementary and junior high schools).

SOURCE: From *Furusato o Mamoru* (p. 12) edited by Haikibutsu Taisaku Teshima Jumin Kaigi, 1993, Kagawa. Copyright 1993 by Haikibutsu Taisaku Teshima Jumin Kaigi. Adapted with permission.

Stage 3: Raid/Arbitration (1990-present)

Even after the face-losing raid by the outsider, for 34 days Kagawa-ken insisted on maintaining its previous position, then changed it 180° to acknowledge that shredder dust was not a material with value but was industrial waste. Scientific inspections were conducted by Kagawa-ken and other institutions, and it was found that the dust contained a massive amount of hazardous materials such as lead, mercury, PCB, arsenic, cadmium, trichloroethylene, and tetrachloroethylene.

The local residents reorganized themselves and formed Haikibutsu Taisaku Teshima Jumin Kaigi (Teshima Residents for Taking Measures Against Industrial Wastes, in short, Jumin Kaigi as before) and demanded that TSKK and Kagawa-ken remove the dumped waste. Kagawa-ken ordered TSKK to remove it by December 28, 1990 but was mostly ignored. Mr. Matsuura and others were arrested on January 23, 1991 and found guilty on July 18, 1991, but this did little toward solving the waste problem.

The problem is one of expenses. The cost of removal has been estimated at up to 4 billion yen, which is beyond the capacity of TSKK, and Kagawa-ken has been refusing up to now to shoulder it because the administration acknowledges no responsibility.

In 1993, Jumin Kaigi obtained the court record of Matsuura's case and made an astonishing discovery. Kagawa-ken not only tolerated the illegal operation, despite having full knowledge of the fact through inspections conducted 118 times on-site in the 13 years after 1977, but actually assisted TSKK in covering up the crime. Two Kagawa-ken official inspectors had advised TSKK to get the scrap metal trader's license to avoid the application of the waste treatment law because shredder dust could be considered a material with value if purchased from producers.

On November 11, 1993, Jumin Kaigi applied to the Pollution Problems Arbitration Commission of the Prime Minister's Office of the national government for settlement of the case, and the first session was held on March 23, 1994 in Takamatsu, the capital city of Kagawa Prefecture. An on-site inspection by Commission members was done the following day. On May 19, 1994, the second session was held in Tokyo, but Kagawa-ken did not admit any responsibility in the case or consent to undertake the costly waste removal operation. After the session, Jumin Kaigi stated that if no satisfactory conclusion could be reached soon, it would seek settlement of the case in court instead of through arbitration.

FINDINGS

Background

There are no apparent cultural differences between the parties involved, for Teshima is a generally monoethnic and also monolinguistic area (all parties speak almost the same Sanuki dialect of the Japanese language). However, there is certainly some difference in the mentality of people, reflecting urban/rural settings and profit-oriented/community-oriented and bureaucratic/nonbureaucratic behaviors.

Conflict Example

There have been a few minor incidents of violent confrontation, resulting in light injury at the time of direct action, such as picketing, inflicted on Jumin Kaigi members. The owner of TSKK is perceived both by Jumin Kaigi and Kagawa-ken officials as a very violent type of person who behaves in an unpredictable and dangerous way. Many of the local residents have been intimidated by fear of his character into allowing waste dumping to continue.

Participants

Jumin Kaigi, the victims. Almost all the local residents of Teshima have organized themselves based on the traditional family, kin, and local community ties for restoration of a healthy environment. The traditional senior leaders of districts are the heads of Jumin Kaigi. However, the younger generation (people in their 30s and 40s) are emerging. They constitute the secretariat of the movement and carry out most of the routine activities. Jumin Kaigi has been very careful not to involve outsiders, such as political parties and nongovernment organizations, so as to maintain their unity and independence.

TSKK, the polluter. This is a small business establishment controlled by one man.

Kagawa-ken, the local government. It was supposed to monitor and control illegal waste dumping, as demanded by the people of Teshima, but it totally failed in performing this function. It has been criticized by Jumin Kaigi for cooperating with the TSKK.

THE MEDIATOR

In the case of a dispute concerning pollution, the prefectural government is expected to mediate the parties from the start, but it did not. Therefore, it has been regarded as a part of the problem rather than the solution. Jumin Kaigi demands that Kagawa-ken remove all the waste to restore the environment because it is heavily responsible for the massive contamination.

The Pollution Problems Arbitration Commission is presently at work. The legal weakness of the Commission is that its function is limited to an advisory role so it lacks the power of legal enforcement. Jumin Kaigi may soon bring the case to the court.

THE MEDIATION PROCESS

It is still in progress. An interesting point is that the major demand of Jumin Kaigi is the restoration of the healthy environment of the island, not monetary compensation for the damage. There is little room for compromise because partial restoration is useless. The demand is qualitative rather than quantitative.

There have been cases of pollution problems being eventually boiled down to deciding the amount of compensation, compromises (x) were made between the two figures ($a > x > b$)—one demanded by the victims (a) and the other proposed by the polluter (b). Ui Jun (1971) once pointed out an empirical law of compromise as observed in those cases. According to Ui's law, the settled figure is not the mathematical average of the two figures $\{(a + b)/2\}$ but the root of a multiplied by $b(\sqrt{a} \cdot b)$. If one party proposed zero, the compromise cannot be made because any number times zero is zero. The compromise between Y1 million (b) and Y4 million (a) becomes Y2 million instead of the average Y2.5 million. Between Y100 million and Y1 million becomes Y10 million, far less than the average Y50.5 million and only 10% of the higher amount proposed. There is a strong tendency of significant reduction of the amount compared to the mathematical midpoint.

As long as the local people maintain their unity in the struggle, there is a good chance of victory, but once they decide to seek monetary compensation as their priority they will probably be forced to settle for only a very small amount, disputes may occur over the distribution of the money, and they will probably be left with a feeling of defeat.

OUTCOMES

The case is not yet settled. However, the public is being made more aware of the problem through the media. Now it would be much more difficult to illegally dump waste for such a long time on such a large scale elsewhere in Japan. It may be an extreme case, but it is not an isolated one. It may possibly result in more exporting of hazardous waste, especially shredder dust, from Japan to other Asian and Pacific countries if the governments and peoples involved overlook or underestimate the danger and the real cost. The same excuse of redefining wastes as "materials with value for metal extraction" may be employed again as the Basel Convention for the international control of waste export has not yet closed this loophole.

CONCLUSION

This kind of environmental dispute is common in various localities in many countries. If a business establishment is allowed to make profit from anything, without effective control, it may sacrifice the environment for an easy profit as seen in this case.

The balance sheet of the case is not yet clear, but one thing can be pointed out. TSKK made a profit of about Y0.2 billion by accepting shredder dust from various auto scrap factories. It is estimated that the waste removal will cost Y4 billion, or 20 times TSKK's profit. This means that TSKK may have gained something by destroying the environment, but this gain is nothing compared with the total damage, of which only a small part can be expressed as a monetary figure. The deaths and sickness suffered by local people and the destruction of nature are irreversible and cannot be compensated for.

Similar cases will occur (or most likely are occurring) in many places in the world when such a free-riding entrepreneurship is tolerated. The unsolved incident of the dumping of radioactive thorium by Asian Rare Earth Co., a Malaysian joint venture with Mitsubishi Kasei (Chemicals) of Japan, is another case just like this. Development for tourism can be very dangerous. A site for golf courses and other facilities can very easily be converted into a waste dump when financial feasibility is grim. One should not forget that the polluter of Teshima, TSKK was supposed to be, or started as, a tourism development company as its name indicated.

CASE SUMMARY

- Conflict is over illegal dumping of hazardous waste.
- All residents signed a petition against dumping, but formal court action and informal protest did not work.
- TSKK radically increased waste, pretending it to be valuable for reprocessing, with local government cooperation.
- Physical illness of locals increased dramatically and locals got outside police to raid, causing the local government to lose face.
- Dumping has stopped, but the waste is too expensive to remove.

- All local residents organized on traditional family ties and outsiders have not been involved.

- Local government (Kagawa-ken, which was supposed to mediate) has taken the side of TSKK.

- The goal is to restore a healthy environment (qualitative) not receive monetary compensation (quantitative), so half-restoration is not acceptable.

- If locals seek money rather than safety, they will end up settling for a small amount and be defeated, making safety and environmental health the common ground.

NOTE

1. Yokoyama is the author's surname. According to East Asian practice, surnames are placed first in all East Asian names given in this case study.

REFERENCES

Haikibutsu Taisaku Teshima Jumin Kaigi. (Ed.). (1993). *Furusato o mamoru* [Protecting the homeland]. Kagawa: Editors.

Ui, J. (1971). *Kogai genron.* Tokyo: Aki Shobo.

PART V

Business Conflicts

17

Child Labor in Nepal's Carpet Industries

GAURI PRADHAN

Child Workers in Nepal Concerned Center, Kathmandu, Nepal

Gauri Pradhan describes the activities of the Child Workers in Nepal Concerned Center (CWIN), a nongovernmental agency working for the rights, dignity, and development of children in Nepal's carpet industry, the country's largest foreign exchange earning industry.

The carpet factories paid commissions to contractors who recruited, supervised, and paid the child laborers in the factories. Most of the children are recruited from ethnic minority communities in distant mountain areas. The children worked 13-hour days, 7 days a week, for little or no wages in unhealthy working conditions.

CWIN confronted the denial of child labor exploitation with a film, publications, exhibits, and a demonstration of a model factory where children's rights could be protected.

On a spring day in 1985, a group of students at Tribhuvan University were sharing ideas on how to start their new lives after graduation. They were activists who were dissatisfied with the then political atmosphere of their country and were linked up with other student movements of the time. By

1987 they had formally established themselves as an organization called Child Workers in Nepal Concerned Center (CWIN). At the time, child rights was an almost unheard-of issue in Nepal. CWIN was the first nongovernmental organization (NGO) in the field of Nepali child rights.

As an activist NGO, CWIN is concerned for the rights, dignity, and development of children living in the most difficult of circumstances and is dedicatedly working for the social emancipation of children in servitude. CWIN believes that every child has an inherent right to justice, peace, and freedom and deserves access to all fundamental human rights, including education, health care, love, respect, security, and protection. CWIN is determined to work for the social, physical, emotional, intellectual, and overall development of children. CWIN believes that children should get first priority in the national development program as they are the future of the country.

From its inception, CWIN has been trying to break down the conservative approaches of the social services. CWIN believes that no child development program would be possible without active participation of children themselves. Its fieldwork, research, surveys, and advocacy have brought the child development program into the mainstream of national development planning.

THE CARPET INDUSTRY

Nepali carpets are world famous. Many people buy these magnificent carpets to decorate their tastefully appointed rooms. However, most of these people do not know the misery behind the looms. Most of them do not even know about the people who make these beautiful carpets. As in India and Pakistan, the carpet industry in Nepal employs a large number of children.

The art of weaving is as old as civilization. It was introduced in India in the 16th century by the Mughal emperors. During the reign of Akbar and Sahajahan, imperial carpet factories were established in Agra, Delhi, and Lahore (Pakistan). In Nepal, carpet weaving has been a traditional occupation of people living in the Himalayan region for years. From the wool of their sheep they make different types of flooring rugs like *raadi, pakhi, lukuni,* and *galaincha* as well as sweaters, jackets, socks, coats, and other items. The Tibetans brought their own weaving technique and unique designs with them when they fled Tibet in 1959 to live as refugees in various areas of the Kathmandu valley. With the help of the International Red Cross and the Swiss government, the first carpet industry in Nepal, the Jawalakhel Handicraft Center, was established in Kathmandu in 1960.

Within less than a decade, carpets became a very profitable export business. Today, the carpet industry has emerged as the largest foreign exchange earning industry in the country. In 1992, the carpet industry earned approximately Rs. 7,300 million, almost double the export earnings of 1991. It provides employment for more than 300,000 people in 2,000 carpet factories throughout the country, 80% of which are located in Kathmandu Valley.

LEGAL PROTECTION OF CHILD LABORERS

Nepal is one of the state parties of the United Nations Convention on the Rights of the Child and the International Labor Organization Convention on Minimum Wage. Similarly, the constitution of Nepal in 1990 prohibits any form of child servitude or bonded labor and child labor in health hazardous areas. The Labor Act of 1992 and the Children's Act of 1992 declared the employment of children illegal. Children below the age of 14 are prohibited from employment in any factory or health-hazardous places. Children over the age of 14 are allowed to work in factories on certain provisions, such as lunch breaks and breaks every three hours of work. Although the laws exist, they have not been put into practice.

A SAMPLE CASE

Laxmi Tamang, 14, came to Kathmandu with her friends six months ago to look around the capital city and learn to weave carpets. At her home in Dhankuta, her parents and four younger siblings live in severe poverty. Her family owns no land, and her parents' earnings as tenant farmers are not sufficient to support the family. The eldest daughter, Laxmi, had the opportunity to attend school for two years. She thought that she might be able to help her family once she started working in Kathmandu. Having always worked hard at home, she thought that she could master the carpet work too in no time. This, however, proved wrong because carpet work was much more than she had bargained for. The congested workplace, dirt, monotonous work on the loom, and long working hours without enough to eat took a toll on her. Within a few months she became sick, grew weaker and weaker, but was not taken to a doctor. Her period of training lagged too; even after six months she had not yet finished the three-month training period. Her sickness grew worse. Then came a point when she could not move her head, which was when the factory supervisor took her to a hospital. The *naike,* or factory broker, informed her parents when the doctors said that Laxmi's condition was really serious. Laxmi's mother came immediately after selling two cows (all that they owned) to obtain money for her fare and Laxmi's treatment. After she arrived in the hospital, the naike fled without giving her any compensation whatsoever.

Laxmi had actually caught typhoid that was complicated by the absence of medical treatment. She had bed sores that developed into an ulcer of the backbone, and she needed to undergo a skin graft. It had been two weeks since Laxmi's mother arrived. The meager amount she had brought with her was gone. She was tense and sick herself when she visited CWIN. She had not been even able to feed her child properly. She broke down when she narrated how Laxmi had one day asked for meat, and when she had said she had no money to buy it, Laxmi had said she would bite her own hand instead.

Laxmi is now under the care of the social welfare department in the hospital that provides her food and medicine. The rest of her expenses are borne by CWIN. She is getting better. That is one relief to her mother who has four other children at home and did not know if they were getting enough to eat or not.

THE CWIN SURVEY STUDIES

In 1989, CWIN brought out for the first time a situation report of the carpet children that was based on a small survey of 10 carpet factories located in different parts of Kathmandu Valley. Since then, much contradictory information has been published on this subject, with the government, industrialists, and business agencies trying to prove that the carpet industry in Nepal is the backbone of the Nepali economy, when in fact it is only the industrialists and businessmen who make money from it.

To get a clear idea of the situation, CWIN decided to conduct a detailed study of the situation and problems of child labor in the carpet industry and undertook the survey research. This in-depth survey study of child labor in carpet factories is the first of its kind. Direct interviews, field observation, and group dynamics were followed in order to reach the depth required of the study.

Different questionnaires were addressed to child laborers, labor contractors, and factory owners and managers of 365 carpet factories scattered throughout Kathmandu Valley; 3,322 working children below 16 years of age were interviewed in detail. Interviews were also taken with 70 labor recruiters, 50 industrialists, and 35 managers. Of the 365 factories visited, the management of 21 of them did not allow the survey team to talk with the children.

MAJOR FINDINGS

Exploitative Labor System

Generally, every carpet factory has an intimate link with the labor contractor, or naike, who will roam around the mountain and *terai* villages and motivate the people to go to Kathmandu to work in the city's carpet factories. They bring the people in flocks, thus receiving a fat commission from the factory owners. Since carpet weaving is done on contract and under the naike's supervision, the carpet factories avoid the responsibility of having to provide workers with benefits and facilities as in other industrial institutions.

In most carpet factories, the naike makes a contract with the factory owner and is responsible for getting a fixed quantity of work finished within a certain period of time. A factory may have one or more naikes, who manage the training of the workers, supervise their work, and fix and pay their wages. In this way, the naike has full control over the laborers, who therefore have little to do directly with the factory owner. They may be driven like flocks of sheep from one factory to another at the whim of the naike if he gets a better deal from another factory owner. They have no job security, no proper registration as workers, and can be fired at any time. They are ill housed and forced to work in very poor conditions and in an unhealthy environment. They have no leave, no medical or education facilities, are made to work long hours, and are ill treated and poorly paid.

Involvement of Child Labor

It is true that the preference for children in the carpet factories is not only due to their nimble fingers that can tie knots on a very tight loom but also because they are easily available, naive, willing, and easy to control and exploit. They constitute an uncomplaining labor force that can be made to do any work, for as much time, for whatever wages. Employing children also means a guarantee of a stable workforce as their labor can be exploited continuously for many years, unlike adults who might not be as easy to control and might have other job options. It is also easy for the naikes to persuade parents to send their children for work in the carpet industry because, in many poor village families, it means not only extra income for the family but one less mouth to feed.

Working Conditions

When the children first arrive to work, they are not paid anything for the first three or four months during what is called the training period. During this time they either stay with their naike or group of acquaintances and learn to weave carpets. Children aged 5 and above work long hours each day in cramped, congested, and stuffy rooms or sheds lacking both air and light and have to breathe in the stale air full of woolen particles. The average workday for the carpet-weaving children is 13 hours, 7 days a week. Their working hours are spent sitting on hard benches. The tight looms scratch their fingers, and the metal combs scrape their knuckles, making them bleed. At night, they huddle together in littered and congested rooms, usually in the back of the factory, after having eaten the watery meal the naike gives them.

Little or No Wages

In some factories, the children work on a piece-rate basis. The naike's commission is usually 40% to 50% of each child's earnings. Most of the remainder is sent to the child's parents, but many complain that it does not get to them.

Urban Migration

Of the child laborers in carpet factories, 97% come from poverty-stricken villages where poor parents have few employment opportunities. The situation of landlessness, indebtedness, and poverty at home is forcefully pushing the poor rural population to the cities. For the rural poor, urban areas offer hope to escape from growing tragedies.

Health and Hygiene of Child Laborers

The unhealthy working environment in the carpet factories adversely affects the health of the children. Working long hours in stuffy dark rooms without proper health care and nutrition causes serious health problems. Continuous work on tight looms causes knuckles to swell up, which leads to arthritis at a young age. The children's eyesight suffers because of the continuous strain of staring constantly at the wool in front of them and because most factories lack proper lighting. They have to sit and work in a crouched position for long hours, and this affects their stomach muscles and back. They get easily tired, but fatigue is ignored, especially if the work is piece rated.

Lack of nutrition makes them anemic and they suffer from perpetual colds due to the damp environment. They also suffer from silicosis, a disease of the lungs, and from many water-borne diseases caused by the lack of clean drinking water in the factories. Common ailments take longer to heal because of general poor health. By the time these children reach the age of 30, they are physically unable to support their families. Thus, they send their own children to work. And so the cycle continues. The profitable carpet business operates not only at the price of the future of children today but also seals the fate of a second generation and a third.

Sexual Abuse and Trafficking in Child Laborers and Young Girls

Young girls and women are regularly subjected to leers, body touching, obscene remarks, and other sexual harassment and abuse, including rape by male coworkers, naikes, and management staff. Such practices are stock-in-trade among the workers in the carpet industry.

It is estimated that there are about 200,000 Nepali prostitutes in India, 20% of them under the age of 16. It is believed that between 5,000 and 7,000 young girls in the 10-20 age group sold in the brothels of India every year are trafficked through carpet factories in Kathmandu.

There is yet another form of child trafficking going on in the carpet industry. More than 25,000 Nepali children work in carpet factories in different parts of India. Most of these children have been trafficked by the naikes from the factories in Kathmandu. The naikes lure the children with the promise of attractive wages and other benefits and better living conditions in the big cities. In fact, the carpet industry children in India are forced to work and live in inhuman conditions. They are cramped together in big labor camps under strict supervision and are forced to work as bonded labor. They are overworked, underpaid, and subjected to poor working conditions, sexual harassment, and severe punishment if they attempt to escape. They live a life no better than that of a slave.

Environmental Hazards

The carpet factories are also partly responsible for contributing to the alarming environmental pollution of beautiful Kathmandu Valley. The chemicals used in different phases of carpet manufacturing, like acetic soda, sulfuric acid, chromium dyes, and bleaching powder, are all harmful to humans. In the 30 years since its inception, the industry has destroyed the quality of the valley's fertile land, consuming enormous resources and polluting land and water.

Children of Indigenous Communities

Most child workers in the carpet factories come from ethnic minority communities in the distant mountain and terai areas. Of these 47% are Tamang,

10% are Sherpa, 11.5% are Magar, 3.3% are Rai/Gurung, and the rest are from other communities, including Dhimal, from eastern Nepal.

ADVOCACY AND CONFLICT MANAGEMENT

For a poor country like Nepal, child labor is a result of its socioeconomic situation, for poverty exists everywhere. However, the fact that the carpet industry earns millions of dollars while exploiting children is disgraceful. The issue has been continuously neglected by the authorities.

In 1992, CWIN conducted a survey study titled "Situation and Problems of Child Labor in the Carpet Factories, 1992." It recently published its research findings in order to make the public aware of the situation and recommended several action-oriented plans to eliminate child labor exploitation in the carpet industry. However, certain vested interest groups are still trying their best to deny the fact that children are, in fact, being exploited:

- The government and business community have denied the existence of child labor exploitation in the carpet factories.
- The carpet producers associations, including the Central Carpet Industries, have denied using child labor in the Nepali carpet factories.
- Members of CWIN and other social workers have been threatened with physical assault and organizational damage.
- Some factories have reacted by removing children from the workforce and sending them out on the streets in order to create direct pressure on CWIN.

As the responsible organization against child labor exploitation and for the rights of children, CWIN has not only exposed the various forms of child labor exploitation in the carpet industries in Nepal but also formulated a number of feasible programs to help protect the children living under the most difficult circumstances. The fact sheet, which was revealed by the 1992 CWIN survey research, was published and distributed both within the country and abroad. The CWIN research report and the fact sheet did not provide any information that spoke against a particular industry. Instead, CWIN tried its best to reflect the general realities of the child labor exploitation commonly practiced inside the carpet factories and provided alternative ideas for improving the situation. In this context, CWIN has organized advocacy, welfare, and rehabilitation programs for the benefit of these child workers. Some are described below:

- Early in 1993, CWIN released a book titled *Misery Behind the Looms.* The book, based on the facts disclosed by the 1992 CWIN survey research, presents case studies, fact sheets, and much important information relating to the situation and problems of children working in the carpet industry of Nepal. This book not only disclosed the facts but also recommended viable suggestions. It caused large ripples of public outrage and shocked the Nepali carpet world. The book received much coverage in the Nepali news media.

- A film, also titled *Misery Behind the Looms,* was shot in early 1992 during the survey research on the situation and problem of carpet children. This film provides an excellent view of the different forms of child labor exploitation existing in the carpet world of Nepal. The film has been shown in Nepal and different parts of the world and effectively exposes the exploitation and condition of child servitude in Nepal. Many copies of the film have already been distributed to concerned people worldwide.
- To make people aware of what exactly is happening to the children working in the carpet factories and to find viable ways of solving these problems, a three-day workshop was held in Kathmandu February 5-9, 1993, soon after the launch of *Misery Behind the Looms.* The discussions and deliberations during the three-day meeting contributed a lot toward developing the idea of a model carpet factory where children's rights will be fully protected. The workshop has also created a better atmosphere of understanding and cooperation among concerned parties.
- During the 1993 Winter Session, CWIN appealed to all members of Parliament to raise their voice in defending the rights of carpet children who are living in risky conditions. CWIN also submitted to them a set of research reports and findings as well as recommendations. CWIN then urged the government and parliamentarians to take the initiative in creating separate legislation for the benefit of carpet workers and to formulate immediate plans for the rescue and rehabilitation of the bonded and sick child laborers. In the session, several parliamentarians spoke up for the rights of the carpet children and urged the government to take immediate action to ensure the security and future of these children.
- Submission of the report to the government was followed by the organization of the National Exhibition on Carpet Children in Nepal in Kathmandu, February 9-12, 1993. Attractions at the exhibition were, among others, a photo and painting display; graphic charts showing statistics from the survey study of child labor in the carpet factories in Nepal; a display of carpets, the carpet production process, materials, looms, and child laborers actually weaving a carpet; distribution and display of publication materials, posters, postcards, leaflets, and a fact sheet on the situation and problems facing carpet children; a slide presentation on the situation of carpet children, showings of the film *Misery Behind the Looms.*

The results of the CWIN survey study of the child laborers in the Nepali carpet factories along with the workshop and the national exhibition were highlighted on Nepal television and radio and by several national and international media.

On the basis of the conclusions reached at the end of the workshop on carpet children, CWIN developed a conception of a model carpet factory free of child labor exploitation. Children at carpet factories would work in acceptable working conditions for no more than 7 hours a day. Children would also have rights to education and health care.

CASE SUMMARY

The students who formed the CWIN chose a course of political activism rather than litigation to confront Nepal's carpet factories. Codified laws were not traditional in Nepal because formal litigation was not consistent with religions that taught peaceful means and methods based on truth and harmony. CWIN's political activism was based on research and education.

- The carpet industry depends on and exploits child labor.
- Laws against child labor have been ignored.
- Laxmi caught typhoid while working, and because her employer would not pay for medical help, her family had to sell all they had to help her.
- Carpet industries are the backbone of Nepal economy, so there is much pressure from the government to cooperate.
- The carpet industries contract with a broker (naike) to avoid responsibility.
- Most children come from poor families who have no choice.
- Other forms of child trafficking also go on under the guise of carpet industry recruitment.
- Public exposure of the injustice had an impact on change by causing the government and industry to "lose face."

18

Arbitration in Thailand

NACHA WORAWATTANAMATEEKUL
Office of the Judicial Affairs
Ministry of Justice, Nonthaburi, Thailand

Nacha Worawattanamateekul describes Thai politics and current economic conflict. With its economic growth, Thailand has been increasingly a party to international commercial arbitration, and business contracts in Thailand have begun to include arbitration clauses. Thailand had a need for its own national arbitration center.

Many parties had competing ideas as to its establishment. However, its lack of immediate success was due more to a lack of acceptance from the public who valued the integrity, acceptability, and enforceability of court awards. This case study presents the actions taken to increase the acceptance of arbitration in Thailand.

In Southeast Asia, Thailand is the most consistently independent country. Nowadays, Thailand, with a population of some 60 million, enjoys a relatively high degree of ethnic, linguistic, religious, and cultural homogeneity. Ethnic minorities account for no more than 15% of the population. Thai, the official language, is almost universally understood, with the possible exception of the hill tribes in the north and the Muslim villages in the southern border provinces. Buddhism is the state religion. About 95.3% of Thais profess Buddhism, 3.8% Islam, and 0.6% Christianity, and the remaining 0.3% Hindu, Sikh, and Confucian.

THAI POLITICAL SYSTEM

Since the 1932 revolution, several aspects have contributed to Thai politics, making it both exciting and confusing. One aspect concerns the nature of the rules of the game and the way the rules are applied. The importance of this matter is that the constitution has always been a subject of continuing political debate and dispute among the politically active and aware segments of the population.

A second aspect of Thai politics is the nature and behavior of Thai bureaucrats and the bureaucracy, particularly the powerful military establishment, the army. Thai politics is essentially bureaucratic politics, although many people, especially the educated middle class, think bureaucrats should serve the public by implementing policies and carrying out orders of the political branches of government, particularly the legislature, which reflects popular will and desires. In fact, bureaucrats serve their own interests rather than public interests.

A third aspect involves the unfolding role and influence of other social groupings, especially the powerful business groups that have emerged as a result of economic and social development. The increased commercialization of agriculture, industrialization, urbanization, the spread of literacy, improved education, development of mass media, and so forth have provided the new urban populations, businesspeople, merchants, professional people, workers, and students with a sense of being able to influence political events and political decisions.

A fourth aspect of Thai politics is the multiparty arrangement. The Thai party system is based on laws, key leaders' personalities, and money instead of ideologies and grassroots support. Therefore, it should not be surprising at all to observe the coming and going of Thai parties. Occasionally, one party splits, with the departing members sometimes forming a new party. All of these actions, including party alignment and coalition building, are based solely on interest and power.

NATURE OF THE CONFLICT

It is a common belief that all organizations are a mixture of opposites of cooperation and conflict, stability and change, and order and disorder.

Thailand now faces many conflicts—political, social, and economic. This case study explores Thailand's economic conflict.

Thailand has witnessed unprecedented economic growth and phenomenal success in international trade and industry. Commerce and international dealings often prefer resolving disputes through arbitration than through court litigation. More and more businesspeople and their lawyers find arbitration clauses a standard part of the contracts they are about to conclude and invariably use arbitration rules and international commercial arbitration centers abroad. Thailand has thus become the receiving end for the enforcement of foreign arbitral awards. It is a matter of economic interest, if not national pride, that Thailand develop an arbitration center of its own to promote and administer domestic arbitration, with the capability of undertaking international commercial arbitration. Thailand, a member country to the June 10, 1958 New York Convention on the Recognition and Enforcement of Foreign Arbitral Awards, enacted Arbitration Act 1987 (B.E. 2530) to implement the Convention. The Act is a great step toward recognizing arbitration as a means of alternative dispute resolution in this country. It is seen by the judiciary as a device for reducing the backlog of cases pending trial and by commerce and industry as a fresh approach to the resolution of commercial disputes that is private, speedy, inexpensive, and conducted with expertise.

In the past, those who had portrayed arbitration as an alternative dispute resolution in Thailand became disillusioned when they put the concept into practice. The Thai Chamber of Commerce had an arbitration program as did the Law Society. Law professors and academics also attempted one. All were unsuccessful. The principal factor responsible for this predicament was the public's unacceptance. The public found it hard to accept the forum as a replacement for the law courts in terms of integrity, acceptability, and enforceability of the award.

Realizing the difficulties faced by the introduction of the concept of arbitration, the Ministry of Justice, entrusted by Arbitration Act 1987 to oversee its administration, decided to establish the Arbitration Office in the Ministry. The role of the Ministry is to lend its credibility to the Office and hence, hopefully, achieve the public's acceptance. The Arbitration Office is under the supervision of an advisory board, which is composed of representatives from various organs within the Ministry of Justice itself and representatives from the attorney general's office, the Ministry of Commerce, the chamber of commerce, the Law Society, and the Federation of Industries. The Arbitration Office represents a combined effort of both public and private sectors in law, commerce, and industry to establish and promote arbitration as a means of alternative dispute resolution in Thailand. The Law Society ceased its arbitration program to join the Ministry of Justice, and the

Thai Chamber of Commerce has pledged its full support. It is hoped that the Arbitration Office will develop into an international commercial arbitration center when the concepts of international and interdependence are deep-rooted into local legal minds.

The Arbitration Office has its own conciliation and arbitration rules. At present, the Office has enlisted 128 eminent lawyers and other professionals as arbitrators. Parties are free to nominate other qualified professionals to serve as arbitrators. The list of arbitrators is classified into 15 categories—for example, international trade, investment, intellectual property, carriage of goods by sea, malpractice, and construction contracts. Although Thai and English are the languages most often used in arbitration at the Arbitration Office, parties are free to choose any language. Chinese is sometimes used in the arbitral process. Foreign lawyers are welcome either as arbitrators or as legal advisers in arbitrations involving foreign parties.

Albeit a body sponsored by the government, the Arbitration Office maintains its independence and integrity intact from the Thai government. The Office has no control over the discretion of the arbitrator in each case. It merely acts as secretariat to the arbitral process. In the meantime, the Arbitration Commission, appointed by the Cabinet, comprising both the public and private sectors, oversees the neutrality and independence of the Office.

In an effort to raise the standard of the legal profession to meet international demands, the Ministry of Justice has recently entrusted the Arbitration Office with the task of running the Centre of Promotion of Commercial Law and Alternative Dispute Resolution. The Office, in that capacity, frequently holds seminars and conferences on commercial law and alternative dispute resolution. The Office has also published *Cases and Materials on Arbitration,* a two-volume treatise on arbitration law. It is now working on cases and materials on international trade law. The Arbitration Office considers its dual role of promoting both arbitration and the legal profession with international practice a significant and fundamental contribution to Thailand in its campaign to become the leader in commerce and industry in this part of the world.

CASE SUMMARY

- The controversy concerning the interpretation of the constitution continues.

- Politics and bureaucracy are driven by a powerful military establishment.

- Businesspeople have emerged as a powerful group.
- Personalities, money, and law are more important than ideology and public support.
- Economic growth has resulted in conflict.
- The Arbitration Office is established as a government agency.
- The Arbitration Office has two roles: promoting arbitration and the legal profession.

19

China and Japan Dispute Copyright of "Ultraman" Toys

LU GUOJIANG
Shanghai High People's Court, Shanghai, China

Perhaps because of Confucian beliefs and experience with reactionary governments and unjust courts in China, people tended to avoid courts and turn to elderly community members to resolve disputes. The Chinese Communist Party has attempted to continue this tradition. In the legal sense, in Chinese translation the terms for mediation and conciliation are not different and refer to a range of methods by which a third party seeks to resolve a dispute without imposing a binding decision.

In China, court mediation is conducted by a judge who first determines the facts through investigation and study to distinguish right from wrong and then works with the disputants to settle the dispute on the spot so as to promote mutual understanding and a compromise agreement. Over 70% of all civil cases handled by the People's Court are settled through mediation.

In this case study described by Judge Lu Guojiang, a Japanese animation company with a studio in China produced a popular television series Ultraman. *A local store began selling "Ultraman" toys in violation of copyright laws. The judge first established the facts to distinguish right from wrong and then explained the liability to the disputants and offered to mediate. Mediation involved arranging for an apology, compensation, and a signing ceremony in the plaintiff's office.*

This case is about a copyright dispute that was successfully mediated by a court in China. In China, court mediation refers to the activities under the charge of a judge or a collegiate bench to bring together the disputed parties to talk over their disputes on the basis of equality, reach agreement, and end litigation through mutual understanding and accommodation. Court mediation covers cases involving civil disputes, economic contract disputes, criminal cases with private prosecution, individual civil actions in criminal cases, cases in which citizens, legal persons, or organizations take legal proceedings against administrative organs or their staff members with a demand for damages when their legal rights are infringed upon by the latter's administrative actions and cases in which citizens start legal proceedings exclusively for damages.

In China, court mediation is one way the People's Court exercises its judicial authority. Court mediation has the following characteristics:

- The state judicial organs preside over court mediation, and court mediation carries the nature of litigation.
- Once signed upon receiving it by the parties concerned, the conciliation agreement has the same legal effect as a court judgment. This embodies the principle of final ruling of the court.
- If one party refuses to implement the conciliation agreement with legal effect, the other party has the right to apply for enforcement of it by the court.

At present, over 70% of all the civil and economic cases handled by the People's Court are resolved through mediation. Court mediation is conducive to settling disputes appropriately, enhancing unity between the disputed parties and strengthening the legal education of the parties concerned and of the citizens at large.

DETAILS OF THE CASE

The two disputed parties in this case were a Japanese animation studio and a Chinese shop. Due to the differences in the economic development and cultures of China and Japan, however, there also exist differences in the legal sense of the citizens of the two countries. Copyright protection has a relatively long history in Japan, where the current copyright law was promulgated in 1970 and revised in 1978. The Chinese government has also attached great importance to the protection of copyright by the law. In 1990, the Copyright Law of the People's Republic of China was officially enacted for the protection of intellectual property.

In July 1992, China officially acceded to the Berne Convention for the Protection of Literary and Artistic Works and the Universal Copyright Convention. In November of that year, China also acceded to the Geneva Convention of the Protection of Producers of Phonograms Against Unauthorized Duplication of Their Phonograms. All this shows that China has begun to integrate with the world in the field of copyright protection. China is a country with a population of over 1.1 billion, and there exist differences in economic and cultural development from region to region, so it will take some time for Chinese citizens to improve their understanding and knowledge of copyright law. It was against this background that the dispute described in the case study took place.

Parties Involved

Plaintiff: A Japanese animation studio (referred to hereafter as the plaintiff). Founded in 1963, this Tokyo-based company mainly produces animation pictures and cartoons. It also has subsidiaries in seven regions including the United States and Hong Kong, with a total of 120 business offices. In 1966, the company produced a 500-episode TV series called *Ultraman.* The image of "Ultraman," the hero in the series, was used on over 100 commodities, and the company reaped an annual income of 1.2 billion yen from its copyright of the character.

Agent: An animation studio in China. The company, a Sino-Japanese joint venture with the status of a legal person in China, is engaged in processing operations for telefilms and videos, such as coloring, animated pictures, original pictures, artistic background, film shooting, and dubbing for foreign cartoons. All its products are for export.

Defendant: A department store in "S," a city in China (referred to hereafter as the defendant). The store sells mainly women's and children's articles.

The Japanese animation studio company signed a cooperation agreement with a TV station in "S" in October 1992, which provided that the Japanese side supply 39 episodes of *Ultraman* (16 hours' worth), with the Japanese retaining copyright. When it was shown on TV, the series aroused wide repercussions, particularly among the young. There was an "Ultraman" craze among the children, who took the heroic character as their idol.

The defendant began selling "Ultraman" toys in July 1993. The Japanese side noticed the sale a few days later and entrusted the animation studio in China with full authorization to handle the dispute. The authorization included the management of the copyright, permission to use the "Ultraman" image on commodities, and the investigation of responsibilities for torts.

After it found the defendant's tort, the plaintiff twice sent letters to the defendant, requesting that the latter stop its tort and provide the name of the producer of the toys. The defendant, however, firmly held that it had not infringed on the rights of the plaintiff because the toys sold at the store had been purchased from a small commodities market in "S," and it therefore paid no attention to the plaintiff's letters. Under such circumstances, the agent of the plaintiff sought prosecution against the defendant in the Intermediate People's Court located in "S."

In the plaintiff's view, the image, shape, name, and plot of the story of *Ultraman* all fell within the scope of copyright, and the defendant's use of the image of "Ultraman" without permission and its act of selling such toys constituted a tort of the plaintiff's copyright. The plaintiff therefore demanded that the defendant publish apologies and admit its fault in the newspaper and that it make a compensation of 2,000 yuan to the plaintiff for its tort and pay all litigation fees of the case.

MEDIATION AND OUTCOME

The Intermediate People's Court accepted the case in accordance with the law of China and appointed Judge L to handle the case. Judge L held a master's degree in law and had been with the court over 10 years, during which he had gained much work experience in the mediation of civil cases. Judge L observed that civil disputes involving, say, marriage, property, or neighbors, sometimes turned into criminal cases, such as murder and assault. Had those civil disputes been mediated in a timely manner and handled appropriately, many serious consequences could have been avoided. Mediation is an effective means of resolving civil disputes through persuasion and education. In the view of Judge L, the court should first try to mediate disputes when handling civil cases.

After taking the case, Judge L adopted the following mediation methods and steps:

1. *Finding out the facts and distinguishing right from wrong.* According to Chinese law, the court must base its mediation efforts on facts and distinguish right from wrong in mediation when the facts are clear. This is so because only by identifying the liability of the parties concerned can the court urge the disputed parties to make mutual accommodation and reach a conciliation agreement. At the same time, court mediation must abide by the law, that is, the conciliation agreement cannot contain any content that goes against the law, nor can it harm the interests of the society and other people.

Judge L discovered from his full investigation that the defendant had sold 217 "Ultraman" toys from July 6 to 10, 1993, with total sales of 614 yuan. The toys had been bought from a trader at a small commodities market in "S," but it was not possible to find this trader. As soon as the defendant received the plaintiff's letter about its tort, it stopped selling the toys. Judge L expressed the view that the plaintiff's copyright of "Ultraman" is protected under Chinese law. Because China is a member country of the Berne Convention and the Universal Copyright Convention, it conscientiously observes the provisions of the two conventions. China's copyright law also contains clear provisions for the protection of copyright of the citizens and legal persons. The defendant's act of selling "Ultraman" toys violated these provisions. In view of the fact that its act constituted an infringement of the plaintiff's copyright, the defendant must bear civil liability accordingly. With regard to the defendant's pleading that its act was unintentional, Judge L pointed out that this would have no effect on the fact that it was a tort. The fault lay with the defendant, and it would be obliged to bear all the liability.

2. *Conducting mediation and reaching an agreement.* When the facts of the case had been established, Judge L called in the two parties separately and made clear to them where the liability lay in the case, and he also asked them if they would accept the mediation of the judge. The Chinese law stipulates that court mediation must follow the principle of free will of the disputed parties; that is, the two parties must agree that they want the mediation, that any conciliation agreement must reflect the genuine mind of the two parties, and that no party should be forced or coerced in disguised form to accept mediation. If one or both parties refuse mediation, the case is decided in court. When conducting mediation, the People's Court may invite the assistance of the units and individuals concerned and notify in summary procedure the parties and witnesses to appear. In this case, both parties agreed to have Judge L mediate the case.

At a mediation meeting presided over by Judge L, the defendant first admitted to the plaintiff that it was wrong. The defendant said that its tort was due to its lack of knowledge of the copyright law and its poor legal sense of copyright infringement. It expressed its willingness to draw lessons from the case and pay greater attention to the protection of copyright. To show its sincerity, the defendant proposed that it go to the plaintiff's office to extend its apologies and expressed the hope that the plaintiff would extend forgiveness. The plaintiff also spoke at the mediation meeting, saying that in consideration of the fact that the defendant's tort was unintentional it would forgive the defendant. Thinking that it would work in favor of a successful settlement of the case, Judge L decided to arrange the signing ceremony of the conciliation agreement at the plaintiff's office.

With Judge L presiding over the ceremony, the two parties reached the following agreement of their own free will on December 18, 1993: The defendant makes apologies to the plaintiff in written form within one week after the conciliation agreement takes effect; the defendant pays a compensation of 614 yuan to the plaintiff for losses incurred to the latter; and the defendant pays the litigation fees of 190 yuan for the case.

3. *Implementing the conciliation agreement and fulfilling obligations.* According to Chinese law, the People's Court should prepare a conciliation agreement in written form once such an agreement is reached. It is signed by the judge and the clerk, stamped with the seal of the court, and then sent to the parties involved. The conciliation agreement goes into effect when the parties concerned sign it. The parties concerned must implement the legally effective conciliation agreement; if one party refuses to implement it, the other party can apply to the People's Court for its enforcement. Judge L prepared the conciliation agreement according to this provision and hoped that the two parties would carry out the agreement in its full content. In fact, they fulfilled their obligations specified in the agreement three days after it went into effect.

Both parties expressed hope that they would become cooperating partners after the case was closed. At present, they are discussing the ways and form of their cooperation. Meanwhile, Judge L sent a judicial proposal to the Administration Bureau of Industry and Commerce of "X" district in the name of the court, suggesting that the Bureau strengthen its administration of "X" 's small commodities market; punish, in accordance with the law, those acts that violate the law; and protect the rights of the citizens and legal persons through administrative actions. The plaintiff was satisfied with the successful mediation of the case by the Chinese court in accordance with the provisions for the protection of copyrights carried in the relevant international copyright conventions and the copyright law of China.

CONCLUSION

It is natural that the differences in the legal foundation of different countries can give rise to differences in their laws and cultures. Take any ordinary legal issue, for example. Countries may differ in their understanding of it, which reflects legal and cultural conflicts. To solve this contradiction, one should recognize cultural differences, which are bound to cause cultural conflicts, and seek to narrow existing cultural differences.

CASE SUMMARY

- Court mediation is an extension of the People's Court.
- This dispute is between a Chinese and a Japanese system over a copyright issue.
- A department store began to sell "Ultraman" articles.
- The defendant was charged to publish apologies and admit fault plus pay compensation.
- The first step was to find the facts and distinguish right from wrong to establish liability before beginning mediation.
- In the judgment of the mediator, the store broke the copyright law by selling the "Ultraman" toys.
- Whether the selling was intentional or not did not matter.
- The store agreed to apologize and ask forgiveness for this unintentional error.
- The defendant paid a penalty and mediation fees.
- Both parties expressed a wish to work together in the future.
- Mediation was made in a special signing ceremony.

PART VI

Neighborhood Disputes

20

Han and Hui and a Shared Cooking Stove

LU GUOJIANG
Shanghai High People's Court, Shanghai, China

History suggests that mediation has existed in China since the Zhou Dynasty as early as 1100 years before the Christian Era. The 1982 constitution established mediation committees in urban and rural areas to handle primarily marriage, family, and neighborhood disputes. China has over 1 million of what is called the People's Mediation Committees (PMC) staffed by over 6 million people. More than 7 million civil disputes are handled annually.

People's mediation is not the same as court mediation, does not involve the courts, and is voluntary. A PMC usually consists of from 3 to 11 nominated or elected members who serve without pay. In rural areas, the process is village based.

The case study presented by Lu Guojiang describes a dispute between families of two "nationalities" in China—the majority Han and the minority Hui. The Hui do not eat pork and objected to the Han family's preparing pork at a communal cooking stove. A fight developed. The PMC in this case was invited to mediate by the disputing parties. After an investigation of the facts, the mediator determined liability.

This case involves a dispute between neighbors that was successfully mediated by the People's Mediation Committee (PMC) in China. In China, the PMC is known simply as people's mediation and refers to activities under the PMC to—in accordance with the law, regulations, rules, policies, and social ethics—persuade the parties in civil disputes to talk to each other on an equal footing, achieve mutual understanding and make mutual accommodation, end their estrangement, and finally resolve disputes.

The PMC is a mass organization under the neighborhood committees in the urban areas and the villagers' committees in the rural areas, which mediates civil disputes under the guidance of the government and the People's Court at grassroots levels. It is not a judicial organ, nor is it a state administrative organ. Therefore, it does not have the judicial authority and the authority to take administrative disciplinary actions. Its main tasks are to mediate civil disputes, such as those among the citizens over personal and property rights; to publicize the law, regulations, rules, and policies through mediation work; and to educate the citizens to abide by the law and observe social ethics.

At present, there are over 1 million PMCs in China, with a staff of more than 6 million. On average, they mediate over 7 million civil dispute cases each year, which cover mainly marital, inheritance, maintenance of the old and the young, house land, debt, production and business operations, compensation for damage, and neighbor conflicts. In China, people's mediation is a good means of resolving civil disputes and plays an important role in ensuring the peaceful life of the people and social stability. It is also an effective way of preventing civil disputes from getting worse, an essential link in public security work, and an important step in preventing crimes.

The people's mediation system has existed for over 50 years. In 1954, the State Council of China issued *Provisional Regulations on the Organization of the People's Mediation Committee,* which stipulates the nature, tasks, organization, function and powers, work principles, methods, and disciplines of the PMC. This document marked the establishment of a legal system in China. The current constitution, which was promulgated in 1982, makes clear for the first time the status of people's mediation in the legal system, which has promoted the work of people's mediation. In 1989, *Provisions on the Organization of the People's Mediation Committee* was issued, which has further improved the people's mediation system.

DETAILS OF THE CASE

The two parties in dispute in this case were from the Han nationality and a minority nationality, respectively. China is a country with as many as 56 nationalities, including the Han, the Mongol, the Ugyur, and the Hui. Of all the nationalities, the Han has the largest population, accounting for 94% of China's 1.1 billion population, with the other 55 nationalities constituting only 6%. Although the minority nationalities are a small percentage of China's population, they are spread across between 50% and 60% of the country's land mass (9.6 million sq. k). A striking feature is that the nationalities intermingle with one another. On the one hand, the overwhelming majority of the minority nationalities have their own areas of different sizes where their respective populations concentrate, and on the other, they spread out and mix among the minority nationalities and between the minorities and the Han nationality. Take the minority Hui nationality, for example. It has a population of over 7 million, of which more than 1 million live in Gansu Province and Ningxia Hui Autonomous Region and the remaining millions are spread over different parts of the country, including almost all the cities.

Due to the fact that each nationality has a different cultural background, each has its own language, religion, customs, and habits. The case discussed here, which involves a dispute between two families, occurred against such a background.

Party A, a Hui by nationality, was a retired worker, who used to work in a cotton mill in "T" city before. Party B, a Han, was a retired bookstore clerk in "T."

In December 1991, Party A moved from "W" city to "T" and became Party B's new neighbor. Due to historical reasons, the residents in some cities in China still live in crowded spaces. In these places, it is common for several families to share a water tap and a cooking gas stove, and this was the case with Party A and Party B. Because the two families had different habits due to their different backgrounds, there gradually developed some problems between them.

As a Hui, Party A customarily did not eat pork and naturally did not like the sight of his neighbor washing and eating pork, so each time Party B used the public water tap to wash pork and cooked it on their shared gas stove, Party A would strongly protest against his neighbor. Party B did not buy that, saying that it was the way they had lived for dozens of years and no one had the right to interfere with their habits. As a result, the two families often had quarrels. One day, when Party B was away, Party A dumped the pork soup being cooked on the stove into a garbage container nearby. As soon as Party B discovered this, the two families started a fierce quarrel, in which Party B beat Party A, causing injury.

Following the fight, the disputed parties went to the PMC of the local neighborhood committee to report the incident and ask it to help resolve their dispute. Party A demanded that Party B pay compensation for medical expenses, and Party B asked Party A to pay for the pot and soup he'd dumped. Mediator D of the neighborhood committee received them warmly.

MEDIATION AND OUTCOME

In China, the PMCs must observe the following fundamental principles in their mediation work:

1. Free will, which means that the PMCs must carry out their mediation activities on the basis of free will of the parties in dispute
2. Abiding by the law, which means that the PMCs must conduct mediation in accordance with the laws, regulations, rules, and policies or, where there are no clear provisions in these structures that they can apply, with social ethics
3. Equality, which refers to applying the law and policies equally to all the parties involved in a dispute, regardless of their respective social and economic status
4. Respect for the litigation right of the disputed parties, which means that the PMCs must not prevent the parties in a case from going to the People's Court for litigation in lieu of mediation

PMC members must also observe the disciplines that prohibit them from engaging in favoritism and malpractice, accepting entertainment and gifts from the parties under their mediation, repressing the parties and retaliating against them, humiliating and punishing the parties in dispute, and disclosing their secrets. The PMCs charge no fees for mediating civil disputes. The PMC members may be subsidized in light of their respective conditions. The villages' committees and the neighborhood committees decide the budget of the PMCs and the amount of subsidies to their members.

In China, the PMCs comprise three to nine members, with one chairman. Besides those who are concurrently members of the neighborhood committees or villagers' committees, other members of the PMCs are elected by the masses. They have a term of three years and can be reelected. In view of the fact that the members of the neighborhood committees and villagers' committees are also elected by the masses, they may become concurrent members of the PMCs without election. In areas where many nationalities live together, the PMCs should include members from minority nationalities. If members can no longer serve on the committee, their original units can elect new members to replace them. If members are dismissed by their original units for serious neglect of duties and violation of the law, they are replaced by new members elected by the same units. The PMC members should have the following qualifications: fair-minded adult citizens who stay in close contact with the masses, have a positive attitude toward mediation work, and possess adequate knowledge and understanding of the law and policies.

Mediator D, who was responsible for the mediation of the dispute between Party A and Party B in this case, was a retired worker from a textile mill. She had been a mediator in the trade union of her factory for more than five years before retiring. She often helped local residents solve their difficulties and thus had the trust of the residents in the community. After retirement, she was elected to the PMC in the neighborhood where she lived. For this particular case, she adopted the following mediation methods and steps:

1. *Accepting the case.* This is the first step in all mediation activities. There are two ways for the PMC to accept a request for mediation: Disputed parties ask orally or in writing for mediation or the PMC takes the initiative to mediate a dispute. In this case, the disputed parties directly asked the PMC to mediate, so the PMC directly placed the case on the file and the mediator filled out a case acceptance registration form. In the process of accepting a case, if one or both parties change their mind and insist that they no longer want mediation, then the PMC should not force its mediation on the parties involved, nor should it prevent the parties from bringing their case to the court if the case is not mediated.

2. *Investigating the case.* This is to find the nature, time, place, cause, course, and liability of the dispute. After accepting the case, Mediator D first patiently listened to the parties in dispute and then went to the location where the dispute took place to conduct firsthand investigations. She found that the dispute between Party A and Party B was caused by none other than the fact that two families with different cultural backgrounds and habits shared a kitchen. In the process of the dispute, Party A threw away Party B's pot and soup and thus should bear the main liability, but Party B was also at fault for physically hitting and injuring Party A. Realizing that an appropriate arrangement must be made for this shared kitchen before the conflict between the two parties could be resolved, Mediator D went to the housing administration department in the community to enlist its help. The housing department, upon hearing the case, responded positively, saying that it would fully support the mediation effort of the PMC.

3. *Holding a mediation meeting and urging the two disputing parties to reach agreement.* The PMC may appoint one or more of its members to mediate a dispute. It may also invite the units and individuals concerned to contribute to the mediation effort, and those invited should support the work of the PMC. When facts became clear, Mediator D called in the two parties and also invited

the representative from the local housing department to the mediation. At the meeting, the mediator made the parties aware of the state law and policies, pointing out that although the two parties were of different nationalities they were both members of the big family of the Chinese nation. The constitution, laws, and regulations stipulate that all nationalities are equal, and therefore their languages, habits, and religions should be respected. They should unite and respect each other and should not discriminate against each other.

Then she announced the respective liability of the two parties. Both parties spoke at the meeting, admitting their fault and extended apologies to each other. As a result, they ended their estrangement. Party B said that he did not know that Party A was a Hui and had his own habits, so he just thought Party A was being obstinate. It was clear that he did not know Party A enough and had been disrespectful, so he said that he was the main faulty party and therefore would like to apologize. Party A responded by saying that although he was from a minority nationality and had his own habits he should not try to force his habits on the Han brothers. He also realized his fault in the dispute, so he expressed his willingness to apologize to Party B. Under the mediation of Mediator D, the two families reached the following written agreement:

- The two families will respect each other's habits and live in harmony.
- Both parties give up compensation requests.
- The tap basin and gas stove originally shared by the two parties will be left for the exclusive use of Party A. At the same time, a wall will be built about two meters to the left of the originally shared utilities to separate the shared space, and a new water tap and cooking stove will be installed for Party B's use only.
- The cost for building the partition wall and installing the water tap and cooking stove will be borne by both parties, and the construction will be done by the local housing department.
- This agreement will take effect within one month of the date of signature by the two parties.

4. *Implementing the agreement.* This refers to the conscientious implementation of the conciliation agreement reached by the parties concerned in a case. In China, implementation of the conciliation agreement of the PMC usually takes one of two forms: conscientious or supervised. The latter form is not implementation by force; rather, it is the means by which the PMC urges the parties to fulfill their obligations on a voluntary basis. If one or both parties go back on their word after mediation, either party can ask the local people's government to handle their conflict or bring their case to the People's Court.

Both parties conscientiously implemented the conciliation agreement in its full content within one month of signing it, and they have lived in harmony since then.

CONCLUSION

As shown by this case, cultural conflicts between nationalities are bound to occur in a country or a region having different nationalities. This is a reality. The resolution of such conflicts depends on that country's or region's formulation of correct policies on nationalities and enacting appropriate laws, which are based on respecting the religions, languages, customs, habits, and cultures of the different nationalities and promoting their unity, harmony, development, and prosperity. It also depends on the concerted effort of the government and judicial organs of that country or region to attach importance to the work on national cultures and resolve any problems and conflicts at their earliest stage so as not to harm national unity and progress and impede national cultural development.

CASE SUMMARY

- Mediation's primary purpose is to keep civil disputes from getting worse.
- A dispute arose between two families about cooking pork on their jointly owned stove.
- Cooking pork was a tradition for one family that had gone on for years.
- The other family dumped pork soup in the garbage, starting a quarrel and violence.
- One party wanted compensation for the soup and the other for medical bills.
- A mediator accepted the case with the agreement of both families.
- The mediator was able to get separate facilities for the two families to prevent future conflict.

- Both families claimed not to have known the culture of the other, leading to the conflict.
- Although the two families were from different cultures, they were members of the same nation.
- Both parties admitted fault and apologized.

21

Citizens' Right to Their Reputation

LU GUOJIANG
Shanghai High People's Court, Shanghai, China

In this case, two university teachers brought suit against a store for impugning their reputations when they were stopped and searched at the store by a clerk with only a middle school education. The store contended that it had signs posted indicating that bags and handbags could be inspected by the cashiers.

After investigation, the court determined that the sign and the search were not legal. The court asked if the parties would accept mediation. The store apologized and paid compensation for economic loss and mental insult.

NATURE OF THE DISPUTE

The plaintiffs, two local university teachers, alleged that when shopping in the defendant's Huikang Supermarket they were suspected of pilferage and forced by the defendant's staff to unbutton their clothes and open their handbags for inspection. Because this act insulted their personal dignity and impugned their reputation, the plaintiffs took the case to the court, asking that the defendant apologize and compensate them for mental insult.

The defendant alleged that according to their policies at their Huikang Supermarket, the attendants have the right to inspect handbags and bags brought into the market by customers at the cashier's counter. A notice to this effect is posted at the market's entrance. They alleged that customers accept this policy willingly when they enter the market. They also alleged that the defendant's staff inquiring if the plaintiffs had taken things without payment and inspecting their handbags inside the market did not affect the plaintiffs' social standing. Therefore, this act did not infringe on the plaintiffs' reputation right, so the plaintiffs' pleading should be rejected.

HEARING AND MEDIATION

People's Court in "X" district accepted the case, and a collegiate bench of Judge Zhang and two others was formed in accordance with China's civil procedure law. The collegiate bench heard and mediated the case.

Facts Found

People's Court determined that the defendant's Huikang Supermarket displays goods in the open and allows customers to enter the market with their handbags and bags. The notice posted on the entrance reads "Instructed by the Company, cashier shall inspect the handbags (including plastic bags) brought into the market by customers. Please open your handbags so that the cashier can have a look."

About 5 p.m. on December 23, 1991, the plaintiffs went into the market to shop. They stopped at and glanced over the sweets counter, then chose a picture frame at another counter, paid for it at the cashier's counter, and went out. No sooner were they five to six meters' distance from the entrance when Fu, a store attendant, ran after and stopped them. Fu inquired, "Miss, have you taken things out of the market without payment?" The plaintiffs replied, "No." Not believing them, Fu inquired again, "Have or have not?" The plaintiffs still replied, "No! Not at all." Taking them to the entrance, Fu pointed to the notice on the wall and said, "We have the right to inspect your handbags." Then Fu took them to the market's office and questioned them again and again. With tears in their eyes, the plaintiffs had to open their handbags, unbutton their clothes, and take off their hats to let the store's attendant inspect them. But nothing was found. At last Fu said, "We are sorry, but someone said you had taken away things without payment. Now you may go." The plaintiffs asked to see the market's manager, but they were told he was not in.

Responsibility Divided

The court held the following opinions:

1. Right means an act and interest which the law grants a citizen or a juristic person to execute and enjoy. Because the market's staff have never been granted the right to question customers and inspect their belongings by law, the store has no right to post a notice demanding that customers open their handbags for inspection. This notice has no legal ground and is null and void. Customers have the right to refuse to comply.

2. Article 101 of General Provisions of Civil Law of P.R.C. (People's Republic of China) states, "The reputation of citizens and juristic persons, and the personal dignity of citizens, are strictly protected by law. It is forbidden to injure the reputation of citizens or juristic persons by such means as insults of defamation, etc." Though having no conclusive evidence, the defendant's staff suspected the plaintiffs of pilferage and stopped them to inquire whether they had taken things without payment. The defendant forced the plaintiffs to open handbags, unbutton clothes, and take off their hats for inspection. This act is in the nature of a search of the customers by a market staff member. However, this kind of search can only be enforced by a judicial organ. Therefore, the act of the market staff member has infringed on the reputation rights enjoyed by the plaintiffs in accordance with the law.

3. When there is an infringement against citizens' right to their reputation, they have the right to demand cessation of the infringement, restoration of their reputation, elimination of its effects, and an apology. Moreover, they may demand damages. Therefore, the plaintiffs' lawful pleading should be supported.

4. Article 43 of the General Provisions of Civil Law of P.R.C. says, "Enterprise juristic persons must bear civil law liability for management activities of their statutory representatives or other employees." The defendant's staff executed this infringement while performing their duties as established by the defendant. Therefore, the defendant should bear civil responsibility of infringements.

Mediation in Accordance With the Law

On the basis of the facts found and on the determination of responsibility, the court asked the two parties' opinion whether they would accept mediation willingly. The defendant apologized face-to-face to the plaintiffs and compensated each one RMB ¥ 1,000 for economic loss and mental insult. The plaintiffs accepted the compensation fee and requested withdrawal of the case, which was approved by the court.

CONCLUSION

The plaintiffs and defendant had the same cultural background. In this case, the difference in their education level may have led to the conflict. The plaintiffs were university teachers, and the store attendant was a middle school graduate. This difference in educational background can lead to different views of the same issue. How should such conflict be solved? Once the facts of the case are determined and right and wrong are clearly distinguished, the parties' knowledge of this helps minimize the difference of views during the mediation.

CASE SUMMARY

- Citizens were embarrassed by having to unbutton clothes and open their handbags at a supermarket, which suspected them of pilferage, causing insult.
- The store claimed that signs protected them but were not intended as an infringment on reputation rights.
- The court-appointed mediator decided the store had no right to post signs or inspect belongings and that customers can refuse to comply.
- Citizens' reputations and dignity are protected by law.
- Citizens have the right to demand restoration of their reputation and an apology plus payment of damages.
- The defendant apologized and paid compensation.
- The plaintiffs were university teachers and the store person a middle school graduate, leading to the misunderstanding.
- By first finding out the facts, both parties could reach the same optimal solution without different views.

22

Manakamana Village's Demand for Drinking Water

JAGADISH C. POKHAREL
Center for Alternative Dispute Resolution, Kathmandu, Nepal

In Nepal, Panchayat, the traditional process of mediating conflicts, was conducted by respected, public-service-oriented elders to achieve truth, justice, peace, and harmony. Their suggestions were readily accepted by the disputing parties. More recently, the Panchas are composed of elected public officials who may not be viewed as embodying the same values.

Jagadish Pokharel describes a case in which one village had its only water supply from another village cut off at the source. Traditional dispute resolution was not possible as the village with the water refused to even talk with the other village. A team of elected officials, police, and administrative staff issued a decision to restore the water supply, but nothing happened. A unilaterial action taken by the villages' young people restored the water supply by demonstrating the villages' interdependence.

Manakamana village in the Nuwakot district in central Nepal is inhabited by the Tamangs. It is a mountainous village about an hour's walk from the road. There is only one high school, one post office, two small stores, and a village community office.

Drinking water is very scarce in Manakamana. For the past eight years Manakamana has been getting its water from a spring located in another village about three kilometers northwest. All together there are 18 taps. This is the most reliable drinking water source that Manakamana has access to. Manakamana residents have relatives (married daughters and sons) in the source village. A young Tamang national leader who commands respect in this area also lives in Manakamana.

Manakamana had no problem in the past. It was getting water without any interruption. Then in 1993 something happened. The other village's people destroyed the water tank and cut their polyethylene pipes. Manakamana people went to the source village, but they found a hostile crowd, mostly women, waiting for them. They were not allowed to repair the tank and pipes. They retreated and tried again. The source village was not ready to share water with Manakamana. They allegedly needed it for themselves, mainly for irrigation.

Usually, the Tamangs resolve such disputes through traditional methods. They sit over drinks and food and talk. In this case, though, the other village's leaders would not even talk to them. As the situation worsened, the Manakamana village leaders went to the chief district officer (CDO), who maintains law and order in the district. The CDO dispatched a team to study and resolve the dispute. The team included elected officials, police, and administrative staff.

The team's on-site assessment of the situation concluded that the source village was overdoing things and that they should let the water flow to the Manakamana village. It was also decided that the damage the source village inflicted on the water supply facilities had to be repaired at their own cost. The district team left.

But nothing happened. Water did not flow to Manakamana. The Manakamana people did not dare go to the source village, but they did not want to suffer either.

Then some young people in Manakamana came up with an idea. They said, "If the source village does not let us have water, then they are not going to pass through our village to Trishuli, the center of the district, either." They dispatched a team to guard the passage. They decided to beat up anyone from the source village who tried to break their decree. The news was widely circulated.

Obviously, the source village got the message. As the passage through Manakamana was the shortest and the most reliable one to connect with Trishuli, the source village people could not ignore the message. In the rainy season when streams overflowed in the region, the passage was the only possible path to walk.

The water began to flow from the taps in Manakamana. No one said anything. However, the source villagers still maintain that "we do not want to share water with them. If they demand water we are not going to talk to them even if they are our relatives. We do not even care for our daughters!"

Clearly, the source village did not mind sharing water but would do so only under a temporary arrangement; the Manakamana people could not establish permanent right to the water. A permanent structure at the source, maintained and operated by Manakamana villagers, would establish their right over the resource. Also, the source villagers did not want to show they had succumbed to Manakamana's pressure (blackmail): nonpassage to the road. The ad hoc solution has worked so far.

CASE SUMMARY

- The source village was unwilling to allow the user village access to its water.
- Traditional mediation methods of talking did not work.
- An outside government team was brought in to mediate.
- The team charged the source village to repair the pipes they had damaged at their own expense so that the other village could get water again.
- The user village blocked their road to the district center and did not allow the source village people to pass.
- The source village people needed to pass through the user village streets to get to the district center.
- The water began to flow in the user village without further discussion.
- The source village continued to claim the right to cut off water at any time and refused to "lose" the argument.
- Order was restored—so far.

PART VII

Conflicts Involving Indigenous Peoples

23

An Indigenous Perspective on One Aspect of Reconciliation

PAULINE TANGIORA
Mahia, Aotearoa, New Zealand

With the reestablishment of the Treaty of Waitangi between the representatives of Queen Victoria and a number of Maori chiefs, conflict resolution in New Zealand has increasingly incorporated Maori interests and traditions and the Maori way of community. Among the influences on conflict resolution have been the importance of the marae, *or meeting ground, as a location for talking and resolution; of the value of the* hui, *or meeting, as a framework for talking through issues; of tradition, status, and* mana *(the complex of norms that surround and support the sense of self and shared identity and esteem); and of cultural location, of* turangawaewae, *or having a place to stand, and of community.*

New Zealand is often described as a bicultural society rather than a multicultural one. The intent is to create a society that acknowledges the unique and irreplaceable attributes of maoritanga together with all other non-Maori races.

In this case study, Pauline Tangiora reports on a conflict between local tribal people in Aotearoa, New Zealand, and outside developers over the construction of a hotel. The tribe called upon the Minister of Conservation and Environment for assistance. In meetings held between the tribe and the developer, the mediator/spokesperson allowed members of the tribe to say what the waters and land meant to them. The tribe's consensus decision making, while not taken into account by the developers, was critical for dealing with the conflict.

Aotearoa, New Zealand is a country populated by two principle peoples: Maori—the indigenous peoples of the land and Pakeha—and all others who came after the Treaty of Waitangi was signed in 1840.

When the Maori offered to share this country with strangers they did not give up their sovereign rights. Ownership was and still is retained by the tribes of this country. The ideal was to live together in peace and harmony in some semblance of order. The Maori peoples had their own laws of living and governance, each tribe having jurisdiction within its tribal area. The *mana* of the tribe was ever paramount, and intertribal disputes were addressed by the country under the tribe's collective decision making.

The forests, waters, mountains, and lands were sacred, and each tribe gave respect to its own *Kaitiaki* (caretaker). In the context of this case study, the Kaitiaki is Taniwha, who resides at the bottom of Whangawehi harbor at Mahia Peninsula in Aotearoa, New Zealand.

NATURE OF THE CONFLICT

The conflict arose because outsiders viewed the beauty of this peninsula, with its peaceful and harmonious disposition, as an ideal place to build a hotel for tourists. This decision was made without first consulting the inhabitants, although a few persons approached thought it was a good idea, with no prior research into how this would affect the historical background of the tribe, with no recognition of the significance of the "living" heritage this area has in the everyday movement of the people, and not accepting that, first and foremost, this area is a food resource for the tribe, namely, cockles and whitebait, and a major disturbance would adversely affect this important food source. The hotel developers' approach amounted to cultural insensitivity.

On hearing through the "grapevine" what was proposed, several of the local tribal peoples moved in to physically stand in the water to declare the tribe's displeasure at what was being proposed.

Then the hard work began. Letters were sent and visits made to the Minister of Conservation and Environment—both of these departments the tribe felt were players. Environment was the living ethos of the people, and conservation was concerned with the possible eradication of the cockles and whitebait.

Meetings of the tribe were called. Elders and the young, male and female, stood to voice their opposition to the move to invade their territory.

Costs were borne for a legal opinion that tribal peoples can ill afford and is really not a part of their culture. The developers brought their plans and ideas and painted a really glossy picture:

1. That one of the partners was a tribal person from the area was accepted, but decisions made by the tribe in community.
2. That the project would create jobs for the people in an area with a high unemployment rate—it worked out to be only a minuscule number of jobs and all would be in the cleaning area.
3. That the hotel/marina would open up the area for tourism—the tribal people found they were not ready for this as they did not have the infrastructure in place.

The developers heard that there was a barrier to any common ground that could be discussed. They had shown a lack of respect for the tribal way of life by attempting to "bulldoze" a development for purely financial gain. Directions were then given by the appropriate ministries that the developers must gain the consent of the tribal people as well as adhere to the policies as laid out by the Ministry of Environment and Conservation.

THE MEDIATION PROCESS

More gatherings were called of the tribe and the developer. A spokesperson knowledgeable of the consensus decision making of the people was given permission to speak on their behalf. In this case, the mediator and tribe spokesperson were the same person.

It was seen as paramount that the parties understand, personalities aside, why, in this modern-day world of business, respect for traditional teachings and cultural values is so important. The spokesperson asked members of the tribe to tell in their own words what their waters and land meant to them. All members present took up different areas of mediation—spiritual, economic, environmental, conservation, and fishing. The presentation was like a circle, with no one being told their role and each working with each other to give an oral picture of where they fit in. The tribal mediation allowed members to take their place in the holistic mediation process. Their oratory of the land, water, wind, mountains, sea, and the life forms that grow in these areas was interwoven with reasons why there could not be a marina at that particular spot, as was demonstrated in the following comments:

> The water covers our Kaitiaki. If you put your bulldozers in and move the seabed, things will happen. On special days and low tide you can see it laying there. Our Kaitiaki is us. Leave it alone.

> We know our peninsula is a haven. That's why we are so protective of it. We don't want people crawling over us. We have so many special places here on the peninsula, we want to take care that our children of the future are able to feel, and know, who they are. Once one developer comes, the rest will follow. Then we become like the rest of the world—lost and abused, all for the dollar.

The nontribal recognition of the European missionaries who came and baptized some of the tribal peoples was a part of the reservations expressed about the proposed marina: "How can you push over the font where the first baptism occurred and set it up somewhere else? We respect those stones—that is a Tapu place for us."

The developer countered with these comments:

> The marina will benefit you. Money will be spent in the area. Jobs would be yours. You can start a tourist industry.

> You have to move into tourism sometime. One can't stop progress.

> The local boaties who come in the holidays need a marina to tie their boats up.

After all the talk, the mediator/spokesperson tied it together:

> We live here, the land is us, the sea is us, but we are working toward a sustainable future but our people will do it our way, in our time, keeping in mind that we are a living embodiment of our living history, we are a part of the past and live in the present with those things that came from our past. We cannot accept doing what you want. We're not ready, and when we look to moving into such ventures it will be done with the consensus of the people. Here we are a community. We would like to retain this traditional and cultural mode of living. Maybe at some future time we can look to continuing a dialogue but for the present we cannot agree to this proposal.

OUTCOME

The conflict motivated the local district council and conservation department to meet with the tribal people to develop a plan for the peninsula that would cover more than just a marina but also waste disposal, water, housing, recreation, and any business proposals that might be envisioned.

The mediation process in this case, although its decision was not to the benefit of the developers and their overseas syndicate, benefited from the tribal conflict-resolving process. The approach taken is not multicultural but bicultural, as what is done at the bicultural level, needless to say, would be good for any other groupings within society.

CASE SUMMARY

The case suggests that a small number of the tribe thought that development was a good idea and that one of the developers' partners was a tribe member. What was important, though, was that the tribe arrive at a consensus. The developers did not recognize the importance of the tribal group's interrelationship, harmony, and consensus.

The following points were illustrated in the case study:

- The conflict was largely due to outsiders disrupting the peaceful and harmonious people.
- Tribal authority opposed development and control by national authorities.
- Developers' disregard for tribal authority prevented finding common ground.
- National authorities required developers to get permission from tribal authorities.
- Personalities were less important than traditional teachings and values.
- The mediators tried to make "future" the common ground.
- The developers were not able to reach an agreement with the tribe but benefited from the educational experience.

24

Philippine Rural Development and Indigenous Communities

AYTAS AND THE SACOBIA PROJECT

EDUARDO C. TADEM
Asian Regional Exchange for New Alternatives, Hong Kong

Historically in the Philippines, disputes were customarily brought to the village headman for resolution in a desire to maintain peace and harmony in the community. That tradition was institutionalized in the Katarungang Pambarangay Law of 1978 that established a system of settling disputes at the barangay (village) level. In each of the approximately 42,000 barangays throughout the Philippines, conciliation bodies were established. Except for certain types of disputes, disputants cannot resort to the courts or government offices without first attempting amicable settlement at the barangay level.

Yet Muslims in the southern Philippines and highland tribesmen in the Cordillera region of the north strongly resist the conciliation law and follow their own customary way of settling disputes that involves Punong barangays (community headmen). The courts, however, recognize only those settlements reached by barangay officials.

Eduardo C. Tadem reports on the situation of the Aytas, a Filipino ethnic group whose cultural and spiritual bases of identity have been disrupted by not only the dominant Filipino culture but also by Clark Air Base, a U.S. facility, which took over the ancestral Ayta lands and later, after the base reverted, two Ayta villages were relocated to Sacobia. The destruction resulting from nearby Mount Pinatubo's 1991 eruptions brought about more ethnic conflict. Three personal case studies show how Aytas' lives were affected.

Tadem's report is based on a larger study of a Philippine integrated rural development (IRD) project of the Marcos regime implemented in three rural villages located near Mount Pinatubo. His field research was abruptly terminated in June 1991 when volcanic eruptions devastated the entire project site. The final research report was completed in September 1992.

THE PINATUBO AYTAS: AN HISTORICAL BACKGROUND

The Aytas belong to a Filipino ethnic group known as "Negritos." Numbering just over 100,000 of the Philippines' 60 million inhabitants (as of 1993), they are also considered the country's aborigines. Their economy is based on hunting and gathering and some shifting cultivation. In their culture, all natural resources are held in common. The concept of private property is generally nonexistent.

Long before the first Western colonizers arrived in the 16th century, the Aytas inhabited the coastal and forested lowland areas until waves of Indo-Malay settlers pushed them to the hills. Reduced to being a minority ethnic group, they suffered various forms of discrimination at the hands of the majority Indo-Malays. As late as the 1970s, the process of dislocation continued as lowlanders unrelentingly encroached further on traditional Ayta upland areas.

In Central Luzon, the urban towns now known as Angeles City and Mabalacat in Pampanga province were predominantly peopled by Ayta communities as of the late 17th century. By the early 18th century, however, most of them had been pushed back to hilly as well as lowland areas around Mount Pinatubo. This now famous volcano became an object of veneration by the Aytas as the source of life and death and home of the God-entity they called Apo Namalyari. Socially organized into nomadic family groups of 20 or 30 members, they roamed the mountain ranges around Pinatubo in search of wild game such as deer and boar.

AYTAS AND THE U.S. MILITARY BASE

After U.S. forces took over the country from the Spanish colonizers in 1898, they designated a large area west and southwest of Mount Pinatubo as a military reservation, which later came under the jurisdiction of Clark Air Base. Over the years, it grew from an initial 3,000 hectares to 63,200 hectares and included, among others, the air base proper (home of the 13th U.S. Air Force) and the Crow Valley bombing/target range.

Much of the land occupied by the U.S. military was ancestral Ayta land. The aborigines were once again forced to move further up in the hills or to marginal lands outside the perimeter of the U.S. base such as Porac, Pampanga, and Bamban, Tarlac. At the same time, local landgrabbers continued encroaching on the Aytas' ancestral lands to establish sugar plantations and grazing lands.

A few Ayta families were allowed to stay on within the base, and some were hired as security guards, jungle survival trainers, domestic helpers, or cleaning and maintenance personnel. In addition, those relocated to the Negrito Reservation at New Cabalan were granted the "privilege" of scavenging at the huge garbage and dump site within the base for any scrap or recyclable materials which they could sell in Angeles City or Mabalacat.

It has been chronicled that since the U.S. base was established, the Aytas who continued to live in lowland areas or worked for the Americans have been relocated no less than five times. Outside the southwestern perimeter of Clark Air Base, two slum communities sprang up, oddly named "Macapagal" (for President Marcos's immediate predecessor) and "Marcos." Macapagal was originally a government relocation site for Aytas from one part of Angeles City. Later, U.S. military officials asked the Ayta families to move once more and settle in San Joaquin village, which was situated within the base compound. The Aytas acceded and sold their rights in Macapagal to non-Aytas only to be later forced to move one more time by the Americans to a site right beside their old village. This new site was named Marcos village.

In exchange for their communal lands, the Aytas were offered "presents" by the U.S. military, such as American canned goods, medicines, and various base privileges such as priority for employment.

In the late 1970s, Marcos village had a population of 1,491, of which 25% were Aytas, 32% were of mixed ethnicity, and 43% were non-Atyas. Although 58 Ayta residents were employed by Clark Air Base, the Ayta unemployment rate stood at 80% compared to 40% for non-Aytas living in Macapagal. Both villages registered low levels of educational attendance and limited access to health and other social services.

Clark officials began feeling uncomfortable about the presence of two economically depressed communities just outside its fence. Cases of pilferage of base properties were frequently reported. On several occasions, Clark security guards shot and killed intruders or set killer dogs on both Aytas and non-Aytas on the excuse that they were mistaken for "wild pigs." Such incidents often threatened to disrupt the otherwise harmonious state-to-state Philippine-American relations and became the rallying cause of anti-American mass demonstrations in Manila during the 1960s.

As a solution to the security issue, plans were made for still another relocation of the residents of both Marcos and Macapagal villages. To rationalize such a move, two other reasons were cited on top of the security problem, namely, that the residents were squatting on lands belonging to the U.S. military and that the sites were considered unfit for human settlement due to health and peace-and-order problems. Executing these plans was made possible when the U.S. military in 1979 formally turned over to the Philippine government 40,000 hectares of unused base lands north of the air base, following a series of negotiations between the Philippine and U.S. governments that began as early as 1973.

DEVELOPMENT PROJECTS IN THE REVERTED LAND

As part of the reverted U.S. base lands, Sacobia was identified as the site of a government-sponsored integrated rural development (IRD) project managed by the Sacobia Development Authority (SDA). It had earlier been identified as an agrarian reform resettlement area but was incorporated into the plans of Imelda Marcos and her made-to-order Ministry of Human Settlements to undertake rural development experiments based on her much publicized vision for human development. Sacobia seemed an appropriate site and the fact that Ayta families were living in both the squatter community to be relocated and the target area itself was an added incentive for the high-profile First Lady to identify herself with efforts to alleviate conditions of the most marginalized ethnic groups in the country.

Sacobia History

Prior to the entry of the IRD project, Sacobia's three *barangays* (villages), San Vicente, Calumpang, and Sto. Nino, had a small population (less than 1,000) of lowlander Pampango settlers and seminomadic Ayta families. Socioeconomic conditions in the barangays paralleled those in Macapagal and Marcos. Unemployment rates ranged from 40% to 42%. Educational attainment was low: 20% had no formal education, less than 15% had some form of secondary education, and only 1% had a college education. There was no electricity or water system, and regular health care was absent. The lack of basic social services was made more pronounced by the area's relative inaccessibility to the town centers, with the main access being a dirt road that was difficult to negotiate and would often be washed away during the rainy months.

The land was nominally under the Clark Air Base military reservation, but as far as can be gathered, neither the American military officials nor the Philippine government interfered much with the settlers' lives, except when pursuing leftist insurgents.

Insurgencies

Left-wing guerrillas took advantage of the relative isolation of the Sacobia villages to conduct organizing and mobilizing work beginning in the 1950s under the pre-war Hukbong Mapagpalaya ng Bayan (HMB, People's Liberation Army) and later in the 1970s under the New People's Army (NPA) led by legendary Bernabe "Kumander Dante" Buscayno. The villages were seen as a natural sanctuary from pursuing government troops and actually functioned as a de facto "rest and recreation area" for the guerrillas.

A significant number of barangay residents, including the Aytas, either joined the NPA or were active supporters. Some of the more colorful Ayta rebels went by such "noms de guerre" as "Kumander Tricycle" and "Che Guevara." On the whole, the NPA took on the functions of the local government and their management of village affairs was apparently appreciated by the residents. Government troops would occasionally penetrate the area but would often withdraw into the safety of the town centers.

Planning Rural Development

The Sacobia Human Settlements Plan for 1979-1983 became the blueprint for IRD implementation in the targeted area. It was put together by a 21-member, interagency, technical coordinating committee representing 7 cabinet ministries, 9 ministry bureaus, 4 government corporate-type agencies, and the Philippine armed forces. Its general objectives were to develop "a new self-contained settlement, promote balanced integrated development, alleviate living conditions of the poor, enhance and preserve Ayta culture, and facilitate delivery of basic services."

As events would subsequently show, the objective of "enhancing and preserving Ayta culture" was merely a token gesture. In the Sacobia plan, however, an insensitivity to Ayta culture was already evident, as revealed in the use of the derogatory term "Balugas" in reference to them. This term is commonly used in a derisive sense by lowlanders when conversing among themselves. During my fieldwork, however, I noticed that the lowlanders never used it in the Aytas' presence and instead preferred the less pejorative *kulot,* meaning "curly-haired," a term more acceptable to the Aytas, who in turn referred to the lowlanders as *mat,* or "straight-haired."

A presidential proclamation created and defined the task of the Sacobia Development Agency (SDA) in terms of the BLISS[1] program: "an integrated human settlements approach in delivering basic services and facilities for the development of a new self-contained community, incorporating not only the housing component, but livelihood and ecosystem development as well." In Sacobia, the SDA engaged in livelihood projects, community development projects, and infrastructure development.

Rural Development Imelda-Style

Upon Sacobia's selection as the site of the IRD projects, the first task was to purge it of the insurgents. This was accomplished by stationing two battalions of heavily armed military troops who went after known rebels and sympathizers and through various forms of persuasion (including physical torture) convinced them to return to the fold of the law. To establish a strong administrative structure and ward off further guerrilla threats, the SDA was placed under the command of a retired Army major general.

As the slum dwellers from Marcos and Macapagal villages were being relocated to Sacobia, the original settlers were forcibly deprived of the landholdings they had been tilling for almost 30 years. Instead, they were promised a rapid development of their area that was intended to turn them into self-sufficient and prosperous farmers. In the meantime, the soldiers took over the operation of their farms and hired some of the erstwhile small holders as farm wage workers. Other settlers who could not accept the new dispensation simply left the area in disgust.

One project was the shelter program that built 100 cottages for lowlander settlers in the main pilot village of San Vicente and 50 semibrick cottages for Ayta families in San Martin. The overall plan for 1,800 units to be constructed was later scaled down to 763 units for San Vicente and 100 units for the Aytas in San Martin. Later, a dispute arose between the occupants and the SDA over their ownership status.

As a pet program of Imelda Marcos, Sacobia generated enough showcase projects and was provided with amost unlimited funds. One such project was a goat breeding, dispersal, and dairy farm which imported 1,200 Anglo-Nubian goats and planeloads of Napier grass from Australia. The SDA field command center was perched on top of a hill overlooking San Vicente village and consisted of modern brick buildings that set them apart from Sacobia's pristine environment.

Social and political problems arose involving issues related to insecurity of land tenure, the high-handed SDA administration, and lack of social services and job opportunities. A few residents were hired as "emergency laborers" but received less than the mandated minimum wage, a situation that would remain unchanged over the years. Poverty and unemployment were widespread: More than half of the residents were unemployed, and 54 families had incomes below US$75 a month. One fourth of the residents were illiterate, and nearly half of the youth population was out of school.

AYTAS AND IRD IMPLEMENTATION

From interviews with Ayta families, it was obvious that the memories of the first years of the rural development project were particularly bitter. Aytas who used to live in the San Vicente area and refused to give up their farms were threatened with force. They attempted to hold meetings to deal with the problem but an Army colonel would always appear during these gatherings and forestall any planned protest action. One Ayta tribal chief[2] recalled soldiers showing them a copy of an alleged presidential decree authorizing the land seizures. The document was probably nothing more than the presidential proclamation creating the SDA, but because the Aytas could neither read nor understand the paper, they were sufficiently intimidated.

Amado Gomez, another Ayta from Calumpang village, remembered the soldiers explaining to them that since they had not been paying any taxes on the land and on their income, they were to hand over to the military 30% of their harvest. Those who refused to give this share were forced out, and the military assigned the land to other residents.

The Ayta settlement area in San Martin with its brick houses was an incongruous project. Many of the occupants simply used the houses as temporary dwellings, for they often spent weeks or months roaming the forest near Mount Pinatubo in search of game and fruits. One informant thought that the idea of setting up Aytas villages went against their culture. According to him, "If you force them to stay in a house with cemented four walls, they would escape because that is not their culture. They would feel imprisoned." In the end, many Aytas who became Christianized did adopt lowlanders' ways of settled agriculture and permanent dwellings.

At the same time, the indigenous tribes fulfilled the purpose of showcasing the Sacobia project. They were used (as one official put it) for "mobilization" purposes and paraded before visiting dignitaries as "satisfied" project beneficiaries. On the occasions when Marcos himself or Imelda visited Sacobia, the Aytas would be gathered together in the presence of newspaper and television reporters.

AFTER IMELDA'S FALL

When the February 1986 uprising forced the Marcoses to flee the country, the SDA experiment had not yet fulfilled its mandate to provide its beneficiaries with the promised 11 basic needs. The new administration of Corazon C. Aquino reorganized the cabinet and abolished the Ministry of Human Settlements. The SDA was temporarily placed under the presidential management staff pending its final disposition. In any case, its close identification with Mrs. Marcos made the Sacobia project a low priority in Mrs. Aquino's government.

Sacobia became a grab bag, with its projects and offices stripped of resources like equipment and farm animals. Officials and employees hurriedly left, taking with them the agency's records. In January 1991, Aquino certified a bill dissolving the current SDA and transferring jurisdiction over the Sacobia area to the appropriate local governments.

The new SDA administration tried to introduce livelihood projects, but the response of the increasingly cynical residents was lukewarm. A basket-weaving training project using Sacobia-grown rattan was initiated among the Aytas but abandoned when it was discovered that the tribal families were using the rattan for cooking fuel. A tilapia fish farm and a duck raising project were also attempted, but (to the SDA's frustration) the Aytas simply ate the products instead of marketing them. There was a plan to distribute mango trees for free among the Aytas, but nothing came of it.

CONFLICT OVER LABOR ISSUES

Although the Sacobia Aytas generally accepted the project's impositions on their daily lives, there were at least two occasions when major conflict situations arose. The first had to do with a complaint filed against the SDA by several Ayta residents of Sitio Burog in Sto. Nino barangay who were employed as contractual workers in SDA's agro-forestry projects. Three issues were raised: First, that the SDA had not been paying them the minimum wage as required by law and therefore was engaging in "unfair labor practice"; second, that in paying the wages, illegal disbursements had been made; and third, that the SDA had violated the Aytas' ancestral land rights by taking over their lands.

It was the first two complaints that received the most attention. The Sacobia Aytas were assisted by representatives from the Office of Northern Cultural Communities (ONCC), a government body responsible for minority ethnic affairs in the Luzon area. The ONCC facilitated in having the complaints brought to the attention of the Philippine Senate.

For Sacobia as a whole, the degree of dependence on SDA employment was high for such a small population. Through this long-running emergency employment program, SDA managed to maintain a semblance of goodwill among a significant number of settler families and avoided the resentment for the failed livelihood projects of the early 1980s to be fully directed at it. The employment program thus functioned as a patronage system the SDA skillfully managed, temporarily winning over a number of residents (both Aytas and non-Aytas) to its side.

Despite being favored with the choice job positions, SDA workers often expressed their dissatisfaction with aspects of the employment program. For one, its "emergency" nature precluded any security of tenure. Under Philippine laws, government workers are classified either as emergency, contractual, temporary, or permanent employees reflecting the levels of job security. The second more obvious grievance was the low wages. The daily wage was US$2.10 (P58.50), and monthly earnings ranged from US$36 (P1,000) to US$54 (P1,500). But it wasn't until the Aytas filed a formal complaint that these issues were brought out in the open.

Three public hearings were conducted in the Philippine Senate on October 5, 1990 and on February 7 and 21, 1991. They were called jointly by the Committees on Cultural Communities and Rural Development, which were both chaired by then Senator Joseph Estrada (later elected vice president of the Philippines in the May 1992 national election). SDA Executive Director Arsenio Dizon and other agency officials were summoned to appear before the hearings and respond to the charges.

In his testimony before the Senate committees, former Burog Tribal Mayor Lucio Navarro alleged that Ayta workers had been signing weekly payrolls for seven days of work when in fact they would receive wages for only five days' work. Moreover, the forms they signed were blank. A document that was presented, titled "SDA Field Payroll" for August 20-26, 1990 for a mango orchard project in Sitio Sta. Rosa, listed the names of nine laborers with eight corresponding thumbprints and one signature. Except for one laborer who was a "leadman" and received P69.00 a day, all the others had a daily wage rate of P58.50.

In response to the accusations, Director Dizon asserted at the October 5th hearing that the P58.50 a day is in fact the minimum wage as provided for in the implementing guidelines of Republic Act 6727. The reference was to cases where the legally mandated minimum wage may not apply, as in experimental or pilot farms which the Sacobia apparently fell under. He denied that the document presented by the Aytas was a payroll document and instead called it an "appointment paper." Finally, he claimed that his agency respected the Aytas' ancestral land rights and had even taken measures to "protect them against intruders." In response to a request from Estrada, Dizon promised to provide the Senate committees with original copies of the payroll and other relevant documents.

The documents turned over to the Senate consisted of payroll slips, appointment papers, and attendance worksheets. They were subsequently reviewed by Estrada's technical committee and representatives from the Commission on Audit (COA) and the National Bureau of Investigation (NBI). The COA representative confirmed Dizon's statements, but a new twist in the case developed when the NBI expert discovered that the field payroll documents had been tampered with. During the February 7, 1991 committee hearing, NBI fingerprint expert José Palma testified that only one person made the thumbmarks for several workers that were affixed on payroll documents.

At the same hearing, the Aytas also testified that the SDA had been harassing them since the complaint was filed. One reported that he was removed from work immediately following the October 5, 1990 hearing. Another claimed that he was being tagged a "rebel" and placed on an SDA "wanted list." Dizon dismissed these charges as "baseless," saying that "it was not his style to threaten people." He instead accused Ayta leader Lucio Navarro of "blackmailing the SDA" into giving him a job.

At this point, Estrada, impatient with the slow pace of the Senate's investigation and what he felt were delaying tactics by the SDA, cited the NBI's findings as reason enough to file charges against the SDA persons responsible for the anomalies. Dizon countered that the anomalies referred to by the NBI took place during his predecessor's tenure and therefore he needed more time to respond to them in accordance with what he called "due process." Estrada, who was in no mood for legal niceties or further delays, told Dizon that "this has been going on since 1980. There is no longer due process but overdue process. I pity our poor Ayta brothers because no one seems to care for them."

In an interview I had with Dizon, he explained that the SDA's unusual salary payment procedures were instituted to spare the Aytas the 24-kilometer walk from Burog to the SDA office. Arrangements were therefore made for one person to collect the salaries of all the laborers. Furthermore, since few of the Ayta workers could read or write, thumbprints were allowed.

During the last inquiry on February 21, 1991, Estrada was eager to refer the case to the full Senate for a more thorough investigation of the alleged anomalies. Ayta leaders from Burog whom I interviewed at the San Clemente, Tarlac evacuation site in August 1991 said that as far as they knew the issue remained unsettled.

One aspect of this case that bears mention is that not all Sacobia Aytas supported the cause of the activist group. Those from other sites were either indifferent or hostile. The SDA played on these intertribal differences by offering privileges and incentives to those who would cooperate with the Sacobia project.

THE MOUNT PINATUBO DISASTER

The summer 1991 eruptions of Mount Pinatubo and the even deadlier volcanic flows (*lahar*) over the succeeding years caused hundreds of deaths and widespread damage in surrounding areas and displaced thousands of people. A major casualty was Clark Air Base, which was so heavily damaged it was permanently abandoned.

The destruction wrought by Mount Pinatubo put on hold the interagency dispute over who would take over the SDA. Indeed, the extensive damage to the once charming rolling hills of Sacobia had made it a less attractive prize. Many residents left Sacobia further diminishing its population base. Since the Ayta villages were nearest the volcano, their communities became virtual ghost towns.

One could say that nature had passed final sentence on the IRD project and common sense dictated that the SDA be mercifully abolished, but for some unfathomable reason it continued on. Sometime in 1992, it was reportedly transferred to the Department of Agriculture for direct supervision.

CONFLICTS OVER RELIEF AND RESETTLEMENT OPERATIONS

A culturally divisive consequence of the Mount Pinatubo eruptions on the Sacobia Aytas was the disruption of their politico-administrative structures and the emergence of rival tribal factions. A primary source of conflict was the perception of the SDA in particular and the IRD project in general.

Although the Aytas had long been divided in their attitude toward the SDA, the volcanic eruptions and the dispersal of their communities in three and later four areas, sharpened the differences. This brought about the second major ethnic conflict situation in Sacobia. Previously, José Vergara, a San Martin resident, was the acknowledged tribal mayor of all Ayta communities in Bamban, Tarlac, including the Sacobia Aytas. After the eruptions, different

Ayta factions went their separate ways and formed their own distinct leadership structures.

One group led by Vergara opted to stay in an evacuation center within the Sacobia area. This was regarded as the pro-SDA faction. Another group led by Juanito Alfonso moved to Bamban town proper after a few days and then was taken to an evacuation center in Maasin, San Clemente, Tarlac. This group then chose Alfonso as its new tribal mayor. Still another group from Sitio Burog consisting of 50 families was reported to have been brought to Palawan province by an American missionary who had been working in San Martin for several years. Their fate remains to be ascertained.

Aytas in San Clemente were critical of the SDA's handling of the evacuation from their villages. In an interview on July 17 with Nicolas Castro, San Martin barangay captain, I was told that the SDA failed to provide vehicles for their evacuation to a safer place after the major eruption on June 15. Castro charged that as they were making their way on foot down to Bamban town proper, SDA Director Dizon himself blocked their way and forced them to go instead to the SDA evacuation site. He added that the SDA was still trying to get them to go back to Sacobia, despite the continued eruptions and the lahar threats. Castro also echoed the lament of lowlander residents that the SDA did not provide them with relief goods.

In a letter to a newspaper editor, SDA Director Dizon denied that he was holding the Aytas hostage in Sacobia. He claimed that the Aytas went back to Sacobia voluntarily and that he had an agreement with village and tribal leaders for their constituents to do voluntary rehabilitation work.

Not surprisingly, Aytas in the SDA evacuation site expressed confidence in the SDA administration. Honrado Sanchez, tribal chieftain of Sitio Mataba, said that they continue to recognize José Vergara as tribal mayor of Bamban and not Juanito Alfonso or Carlito Lapuz. He further declared they had no intention of moving to the San Clemente resettlement site.

In an interview aired over Radio Tarlac in August 1991, José Vergara denied that they were being held hostage by the SDA and denounced Juanito Alfonso as having usurped authority as Bamban tribal mayor.

In early 1992, however, the Aytas in the SDA evacuation site split up further, with half of them moving northwest to a resettlement site in Calangitan, Capas, Tarlac set up with the help of Dante Buscayno. By this time, the SDA reported that the remaining Aytas had returned to their former homes, with only a few families staying on at the agency's evacuation site. A report in March 1992 from a barangay resident, however, says that the SDA simply wanted to move people out of the buildings in the evacuation site to make way for a poultry project.

RESETTLING THE AYTAS

Although all those displaced by Mount Pinatubo's eruption suffered, the most severely affected were the Aytas, including those under the Sacobia project. Being nearest the volcano, the Aytas lost not only their houses and farms but, with the disappearance of their hunting grounds and surrounding forests, their spiritual ties with Mount Pinatubo as well.

The Aytas found conditions in the evacuation sites nearly intolerable. Shelter from the elements was inadequate, basic sanitation was absent, and there was a lack of health care. Respiratory and gastro-intestinal ailments were common, sometimes fatal.

The Aytas were also culturally disoriented by the lowland and near-lowland surroundings. They were unused to the sight of flatlands and plains stretching far and wide in every direction. They obviously longed to once again roam the mountains and hills and commune with nature.

The evacuation center in San Clemente was nothing more than a collection of hundreds of makeshift tents donated by foreign governments. It became the transit point for Tarlac Aytas prior to being resettled in barangay Dueg in the same town, 1,000 meters up in the mountains, which approximates the Aytas' natural habitat around Mount Pinatubo.

A possible source of ethnic conflict looms however, for non-Ayta settlers engaged in ginger cultivation already inhabit the government-identified resettlement site and occupy almost all cultivable areas. Given this, the only uncontested and available lands are along steep inclines on mountainsides, which would make cultivation extremely difficult. When asked about the incoming Aytas, the old-time Dueg settlers, some of them rebel returnees, expressed apprehension at the planned incursion and hoped that their lives would not be unduly disrupted.

THREE LIFE HISTORIES

A more detailed picture of the lives of the Sacobia Aytas is provided by the following three brief life histories, which are based on three separate interviews—the first two (Castro and Lapuz) at the San Clemente evacuation site two months after the first volcanic eruption and the third (Gomez) in Sacobia before the eruptions. As the accounts show, the Sacobia Aytas are in a transition stage from the traditional nomadic lifestyle to a more settled way of life. This reflects the type of "development" to which they have been subjected by the inroads of lowlander-type civilization, which reached its height during the IRD project.

Nicolas Castro

Nicolas Castro, 33, was named barangay captain of San Martin after the Mount Pinatubo eruption. He feels closely attached to Sacobia as many generations of his family have lived and died in the area. San Martin used to be known by the Aytas as Balete, but the SDA changed it to San Martin, after the Black Saint Martin de Porres whom the Aytas identify with.[3]

Before the IRD project began, Nicolas' family cultivated 15 hectares of flatland in Balete. They also engaged in forest paddy agriculture, planting mountain-type reddish-brown rice, and grew fruit trees. But as there was no irrigation, harvests were low. Three cavans (150 kilograms) of seedlings would yield a maximum of only 50 cavans (2.5 tons) of palay.

To supplement their income, they gathered banana blossoms, cut down *buho* saplings, and planted *ube,* sweet potatoes, and bananas. The main problem then was the absence of a farm-to-market road. The villagers used a narrow footpath that tall cogon grasses would often cover. Other modes of transportation had to be used. For example, the buho saplings were floated and guided down the river on their way to town.

Their lands were taken by the military when the IRD project was established. Nicolas and his brothers were later able to recover their livelihood mainly through their own efforts when most of the lands were returned after three years. But in cultivating various crops and raising livestock, the Castros did not rely on help from the SDA.

The brothers had two hectares of sweet potatoes, one hectare of *gabi* (a yamlike root crop), four hectares of riceland, with two hectares irrigated and the rest rain fed, and one hectare of bananas. The sweet potatoes yielded a harvest of 200 sacks weighing 80 kilograms each, which would sell for from P3.80 to P4.80 a kilo. The best price was secured by canvassing among several buyers from Angeles City.

Castro's livestock consisted of 25 goats. These economic activities had produced for him a small savings surplus, which was being deposited in a Bamban bank. Despite his dismissal of the SDA, he has been a recipient of the agency's *carabao* dispersal program. However, he considered the debt already repaid because, after all, he had invested a lot of time, money, and effort in caring for the animals. Nicolas, his wife Rosita, 30, and one daughter Bella, 7, lived in one of the SDA-supplied semibrick houses.

All these were lost in the aftermath of Mount Pinatubo's eruption. Nicolas estimates that 200 hectares of productive lands were lost by San Martin residents alone. He sadly notes that if the disaster had not taken place he would have been able to rise above poverty within two or three years. Along with other Ayta families from Sacobia, Nicolas and his family found themselves in the San Clemente evacuation center living under foreign-donated canvas tents.

When asked about the traditional cultural practices of the Aytas, Nicolas objects to some of the old ways, such as parents choosing marriage partners for sons and daughters. The children, not the elders, should have the right to choose whom they marry, he asserted. These changes in beliefs have been brought about by Christian missionary work among the indigenous tribes. All Ayta residents of San Martin have been Christianized and are affiliated with the Methodist church.

Finally, Nicolas said that no tears would be shed for the SDA if it were to be abolished. "The people would lose nothing," he confidently affirmed.

Carlito "Carling" Lapuz

Carling Lapuz was named Sta. Rosa tribal chief after the Mount Pinatubo eruption. I interviewed him at the San Clemente evacuation center where he was temporarily staying along with 144 other Ayta families from Sacobia. Eighteen of the 26 families residing in Sta. Rosa had moved to San Clemente, and the rest were either at the Sacobia evacuation site or at Camp Aquino in San Miguel, Tarlac.

Generally sympathetic to the SDA, Carling regards as a major benefit the advances that workers could make at the SDA-operated store (called the "Superette"). He also cites the SDA's plan for livelihood support among the people such as the transfer of titles for rice lands and a new community fishpond.

When asked about negative aspects, Carling pointed to the case of his son-in-law Fernando Mejia, who was a recipient of the cattle dispersal program. The cow was lost in the chaos arising from the eruption, but an SDA project officer still demanded that it be produced or he would have Mejia arrested.

Carling is a Christian convert, but when asked what denomination, he had to call the village pastor to ask. Reminded that he belongs to the Methodist church, he noted that in San Martin, it is the Baptists who are dominant. The Christianized Aytas do not make fine distinctions between the sects, however. When "born again" proselytizers came, the people also attended their services because, as Carling put it, "there is only one God."

Ayta Christians have generally turned their backs on their old beliefs about *anitos* causing illness, the giving of dowry by a bride (money or *carabao*), and of Mount Pinatubo being the source of all fortune and luck of the Aytas. However, Carling still believes in a "forbidden place" *(pulong maselan)* in the volcano, which brings misfortune.

Carling has had an interesting life. For 10 years, he worked as one of 52 jungle survival training instructors at Clark Air Base. He remembers being questioned about the many uses of the banana plant. He responded that the trunk can be used as an air mattress, the bark fiber as suture for stitching wounds, the bark sap as a blood coagulant, the root bed and the trunk as sources of drinking water, the water itself as a remedy for stomachache, and the leaves as a poncho raincoat, eating plate, or head cover.

After Carling's jungle survival training experience, he became a privately hired security guard for an American Air Force major. Finding the P500 fortnightly pay too low to support his family of eight children, he asked for a raise. But his employer refused and instead recommended him for a janitor's position at the Base. He had to take a simple qualifying exam that included a written test and thought that he did well. But to his surprise the recruiting office informed him that he had failed it. He says the reason he didn't get the job was because he did not have a "patron" to back him up. Now jobless, Carling moved his family to Sta. Rosa in Sacobia where relatives had been farming for many years. This was in 1987.

Carling said that he has found it easier to earn a living in Sta. Rosa unlike at Clark where, if one did not have the backing of someone powerful, there was no steady work. He criticized the treatment of his fellow Aytas by Clark American and Filipino officials. Life was good in Sta. Rosa, and he wanted to live in the area permanently. He had no enemies and the people got along well with each other.

Carling was never employed by the SDA. He was, however, looking forward to the fulfillment of SDA Director Dizon's promise to give employment to barrio residents. He blames Lucio Navarro and his group who he feels spoiled his chance of getting hired by the SDA because of their complaint against low wages.

Amado Gomez

An Ayta native, Amado is 35 years old and a resident of Barangay Calumpang. His parents moved into the area in 1950. He is one of seven children (two brothers and five sisters), all of whom lived and farmed in Calumpang. Amado has been a barangay councilor since 1979.

He worked for Clark Air Base as a night-shift security guard in the housing area and received P1,200 every 15 days. Additional income was obtained from collecting aluminum cans from the servicemen's garbage. He sold these to a buyer in Marcos village for 25 centavos per can. Amado sometimes made P30 a day from this sideline occupation

Long before the SDA came, Calumpang was a sugar-producing area, and the Gomez family were cane farmers. Life was good then. "For every effort exerted, the farmer was paid," Amado said. The share from the cane harvest would sometimes reach P10,000 per harvest and was more than sufficient to live on. The people enjoyed their traditional celebrations such as the barrio "fiesta," birthdays, and community dances.

When the NPA started entering the area, the Army followed and harassed the villagers. In response, many Aytas joined the NPA and tension ruled the lives of the people. When the CABCOM (Clark Air Base Command) soldiers came in 1979 followed by the SDA a year later, the settlers' lives turned from bad to worse. The Gomez sugar farm was taken over by the SDA cattle ranch. On top of this, the soldiers demanded a 30% share of the harvest of their other crops.

Amado feels deeply about the condition of his fellow Aytas. Before the IRD project, Aytas would get priority employment at Clark, could go in and out of the base, and received free education and medical benefits. Ayta base employees would be fetched for work by a Clark bus. Amado said the Ayta tribal head, whom he called King Alfonso, was given the honorary rank of "general" by the Americans. He is resentful of Capampangans (lowlanders) who married Ayta women for opportunistic reasons (e.g., to secure land rights). He calls them *magnanakaw* (thieves).

Amado recounted an incident involving conflict between Aytas and lowlanders in Sapang Bato, Angeles. In 1985, a group of Batangueno coffee planters entered Ayta lands and requested to cultivate an area for three years after which the land would be returned. When the Aytas asked for the lands three years later, they were told to show land titles or proofs of ownership. An entire Ayta family was then massacred. Fortunately, the perpetrators were caught and are now in prison.

Unable to recover his family's original sugar land from the SDA, Amado cultivated upland palay for home consumption and cassava, which he sold to vegetable dealers or flour mill operators from Mabalacat. Calumpang is known as the "vegetable basket" of Mabalacat and during good harvests can even supply Angeles City. Unlike San Vicente, it is not dependent on the SDA, and most residents get by on their own efforts. Besides, the barrio feels more affinity with the Mabalacat town hall than with the SDA office in San Vicente.

Amado reported that in 1985 then Pampanga Governor Mendoza visited Calumpang and said that he was going to make the village a model community. Nothing came of this promise.

CONCLUSION

The case of the Aytas under the government-initiated Sacobia IRD project typifies majority-minority relations in the Philippines. The disregard for and insensitivity to indigenous cultures have long been prevailing attitudes of the majority Indo-Malay population and government leaders. In recent years though, some positive developments have come about. The Philippine Constitution, promulgated after the February 1986 uprising, provides for the preservation and development of the cultures of ethnic communities, and government agencies have been established to protect and safeguard the rights of minorities. Also, two autonomous regional governments have been set up—one for the Muslims in the south and another for ethnic communities in the Cordillera area in northern Luzon. Although criticized for their gross inadequacies, these moves still constitute modest advances over previous state policies and programs.

For the most marginalized of the ethnic communities (i.e., the "Negritos"), however, no specific policies and programs compatible with their distinct cultures have been instituted. If not for the Mount Pinatubo eruptions, the situation of the Aytas may have gone unnoticed. Philippine and international media have highlighted the Aytas' case, and government resettlement areas for them seem to at least take into account their preference for the highlands.

The deeper issue, however, is the resolution of the conflict between two divergent cultures, which can initially come about when the dominant culture is able to use its control over economic and political resources to respond to the basic needs of minority populations without disrupting the cultural and spiritual bases on which their identity is based. In the long run, Ayta culture can best be safeguarded and developed by the Aytas themselves. In the political sense, this would imply granting them a measure of autonomy similar to that which Philippine law now recognizes for other minority ethnic communities.

CASE SUMMARY

- The Aytas "Negritos" are a minority hunting-gathering culture.
- The U.S. military occupied Aytas property, displacing them.
- The U.S. military came into conflict with nearby Aytas, who were seen as intruders and were shot.

- Aytas were relocated when the U.S. military moved out.
- Insurgent guerrillas recruited the Aytas and used their villages.
- The government tried to resettle the Aytas for its own purposes.
- Aytas were bitter about the rural development project but could not protest.
- The new villages were against their nomadic culture.
- After the Marcos regime ended, the project was divided up among those in power.
- The government investigated the Aytas' claims, but nothing was done.
- The eruption of Pinatubo further worsened the Aytas' plight.
- The Aytas were culturally disoriented by relocation and being mixed in with unfamiliar cultural groups.
- The safeguarding and development of the Ayta culture in attempts to find reconciliation is necessary and complementary to the granting of a measure of autonomy.

NOTES

1. BLISS stood for Bagong Lipunan (New Society) Sites and Services. When Marcos proclaimed martial law in 1972 and imposed authoritarian rule, he simultaneously declared the birth of a "New Society" for the Philippines. Thereafter, this term became a favorite stick-on for many martial law projects, including new currency notes.

2. With the exception of national personalities, all names of persons have been changed to protect their identities.

3. Expressing the Aytas' affinity with the Catholic saint, Castro said, "Kulot din iyon, eh" ("He is also curly haired, you know.").

25

Recent Attempt at Ethnic Conflict Resolution in Sri Lanka

JAYADEVA UYANGODA
Center for Policy Research and Analysis
University of Colombo, Sri Lanka

This case presents the history of ethnic conflict in Sri Lanka. Ethnic conflict grew rapidly after the island gained independence in 1948. In 1949, nearly 1 million "plantation Tamils," descendants of 19th-century indentured workers, lost Sri Lankan voting rights and citizenship on the basis of their actually being citizens of India. Many were repatriated to India. In 1956, Sinhala was made the country's official language, putting Tamil speakers at a disadvantage. Violence broke out in the early 1980s between Sinhalese-dominated armed forces and Tamil guerrillas. Language laws and other laws that may have precipitated the civil war have been scaled back and are not now perceived as major issues, whereas political rights and regional autonomy are.

The minority Tamil nationalists perceive the conflict as a just struggle. Sinhalese nationalist groups and the Sri Lankan government view it as terrorism to break up the state. Human rights groups view the conflict as political and requiring a political solution.

Sri Lanka lacks an institutional mechanism to mediate ethnic conflict and the government resists outside intervention in what is perceived as an internal problem. In its escalated state, the human and economic costs of the conflict have been enormous.

Sri Lanka is a multiethnic, multilingual and multireligious society. The Sinhalese are the ethnic majority; Tamils, Muslims, and Burghers constitute other ethnic groups. Buddhism is the majority religion, and all Buddhists are ethnically Sinhalese. Hinduism is the second largest religion, and all Hindus are ethnically Tamils. Christianity cuts across ethnic barriers: Small segments of Sinhalese and Tamil and all Burghers belong to various Christian denominations. Islam is practiced by the Muslim community.

Sri Lanka has three languages. Sinhalese, the language of the majority community, is the official language, with Tamil, which is spoken by both Tamil and Muslim communities, given the status of a national language. English is more or less the lingua franca among all ethnic communities.

Sri Lanka's political system is democratic, although authoritarian tendencies have emerged in the recent past. From 1947 to 1978, Sri Lanka's constitutional system had been designed according to the Westminster model. There was a major change in the constitution in 1978 when an executive president resembling the French system was introduced.

Although the Sri Lankan constitution is a unitary one, an important change occurred in 1987 when the constitution was amended to create a system of provincial councils. The objective of this change was to create a basis for a political settlement to the ethnic question through devolutionary measures.

Sri Lanka can also be described as a multiparty democracy. The United National Party, which has been in power since 1977, and the Freedom Party are the two main political parties. In the Tamil society, there are a number of political parties, and a Muslim party (Sri Lanka Muslim Congress) emerged in the early 1980s, indicating a tendency toward ethnic-centeredness in the party system in general. A number of left-wing parties also exist, although their electoral strength has been on the decline in recent years. Although Sri Lanka continues to have a multiparty system, a clear tendency in its politics is the bipolarization of the entire party system in electoral politics. Small parties tend to enter into electoral alliances with either of the two main parties.

NATURE OF THE CONFLICT

Sri Lanka's present conflict is an ethnic one between the majority Sinhalese and minority Tamil communities. In recent years, the conflict between Tamil and Muslim communities has also come to characterize the ethnic question.

The key actors in the current phase of the conflict are the Sri Lankan government and the Liberation Tigers of the Tamil (LTTE) *Eelam* (Tamil for homeland or nation), the latter being the dominant guerrilla organization among Tamil nationalist groups.

The conflict has a strong military character. Currently, the armed forces of the Sri Lankan government and the LTTE are the main participants in the war. In the early 1980s, a number of Tamil guerrilla groups were also involved on behalf of the Tamil community. The Indian army was also a major actor in the conflict from July 1987 to March 1990.

GENEALOGY OF THE CONFLICT

Political roots of Sri Lanka's ethnic conflict go as far back as the 1930s when Tamil political representatives demanded balanced representation for the majority and minority communities in the colonial legislature. Although this demand was not met, after political independence in 1948 the government instituted a series of policy measures that created a sense of alienation among minorities, particularly the Tamils:

- Denial of citizenship to nearly 1 million Tamil plantation workers of Indian origin under the Citizenship Act of 1948
- Disenfranchisement of more or less a similar number of Tamil plantation workers in 1949
- Making Sinhalese, the language of the majority Sinhalese community, Sri Lanka's official language in 1956
- Inauguration of land settlement and peasant colonization schemes in the eastern province for the Sinhalese peasantry in the southern parts of the country. This created a sense of insecurity among Tamils because they felt that the land policy was deliberately intended to alter the ethnic-demographic composition in traditionally Tamil-majority areas.
- Educational policies introduced in the 1970s, restricting opportunities for Tamil youths to enter the universities
- Continuous refusal by successive governments to introduce a system of decentralization that would enable the Tamil communities in the northern and eastern provinces to enjoy a measure of autonomy or self-rule

These and many other factors contributed to the emergence of Tamil nationalism in the postindependence years. However, in the early 1980s, Tamil nationalist politics entered a qualitatively new phase with the emergence of militant youth movements committed to an armed struggle. Two factors characterized this qualitative shift in Tamil politics:

The first was a severe breakdown of relations between the government and Tamil political parties in the 1970s: The traditional Tamil political leadership had been demanding a federal system since the early 1950s. When Sri Lanka adopted a new republican constitution in 1972, Tamil leaders again made a strong case for a federal government but without success. When the unitary system of government was reaffirmed in 1972, Tamil leaders led a protest campaign to which the government responded with hostility. In the context of tension, there was a series of anti-Tamil violence in 1976, 1977, and 1978.

The second was that, although ethnic relations were deteriorating, the Tamil United Liberation Front (TULF), the main Tamil political party, took part in the parliamentary election in 1977 on a separatist platform. When the TULF won the majority of seats in the northern and eastern provinces, that victory was interpreted by the Tamil leadership as a mandate to form a separate state. However, the traditional Tamil leadership could not go beyond that point. This created space for the politically mobilized Tamil youth to emerge as a militant alternative to the parliamentary politics of the TULF leadership.

ESCALATION OF THE CONFLICT

In the latter part of the 1970s and in the early 1980s, the United National Party government did not seem to give serious consideration to the emerging Tamil militant politics. When a system of decentralization was proposed by the government in 1980, it fell far short of Tamil demands for regional autonomy. Meanwhile, Tamil youth groups had decided to resort to an armed struggle. With the build up of clashes between Tamil guerrilla groups and Sri Lankan armed forces during this period, a major anti-Tamil riot broke out in July 1983. These riots quickly became a decisive turning point in Sinhala-Tamil relations. Very soon, the conflict turned into a full-scale military affair.

ROLE OF THE MEDIA

The media have played a mixed role in the conflict. The mainstream Sinhala and English press has primarily taken a pro-Sinhalese partisan view of the conflict, thereby contributing to the escalation of the crisis. During the past year, the media have been leading a campaign against any attempt at a negotiated political settlement. Meanwhile, there is a nonmainstream political press that has consistently argued for an early settlement and peace.

DIFFERENT PERCEPTIONS OF THE CONFLICT

At present, there are three main perceptions of the conflict:

1. The Tamil nationalists believe that theirs is a just struggle to realize the aspirations of the Tamil community.

2. The Sri Lankan government and Sinhalese nationalist groups are of the view that the conflict is merely a terrorist problem and that it is part of a larger conspiracy to break up Sri Lanka.
3. Human rights and democratic groups of the civil society argue that the conflict is primarily a political one with an ethnic character, and therefore a negotiated political settlement is necessary to resolve the problem.

THE PROTAGONISTS

The main cultural difference between the protagonists in the conflict is ethnicity. Unwillingness of parties to accommodate each other on ethnic interests and demands has contributed to the progressive escalation of the conflict.

There is, however, much common ground among disputants that has not yet been fully explored or made use of. Although the direct combatants may not want to stop the war, the civilian population of both ethnic groups desires peace and reconciliation. The desire of the protagonists has been to overplay political differences at the expense of common aspirations of the civilian communities.

THIRD PARTIES

The disputants have failed to resolve this conflict on their own initiatives.

A third-party mediation was once sought, but it further escalated the crisis. This was the Indian political and military intervention in 1987-1989. India has not been a neutral party, although it mediated in 1987. Up to that time, it supported the Tamil militants. Ironically, following direct intervention after July 1987, India waged an unsuccessful war against the LTTE.

Presently, there is very little space for a third-party mediation, be it a neutral country, a group of neutral countries, or the United Nations. The LTTE would prefer a United Nations mediation, but the Sri Lankan government has consistently opposed "outside intervention" on the premise that the conflict is purely an internal one.

LACK OF INSTITUTIONAL MECHANISMS

Sri Lanka lacks institutional mechanisms to mediate in the present ethnic conflict. These lacunae became explicitly clear on three recent occasions.

First, the Indian government mediated in July 1987 on the assumption that its military and diplomatic might could ensure an end to the conflict. In the absence of conflict resolution mechanisms, that mediation not only failed but contributed to the further aggravation of the conflict.

Second, President R. Premadasa and the LTTE initiated bilateral negotiation in May 1989. The informal talks continued until June 1990. Both sides did not appear to believe in the creation of and reliance on conflict resolution mechanisms, so the talks produced no positive results. The LTTE's unilateral violation of the ceasefire understanding in June 1990 marked the resumption of the military conflict.

Finally, in 1991-1992, the Sri Lankan Parliament appointed a select committee to propose a solution to the ethnic question. Only the political parties represented in Parliament were parties to these deliberations. Therefore, the LTTE, a most important party in the conflict, was not a participant in the process. Although the committee produced a report suggesting solutions, protagonists of the conflict have largely ignored it.

OUTCOME

The conflict has had far-reaching consequences for the entire country. Its human cost has been enormous in terms of people killed and maimed. The war-ravaged areas have not seen any development for more than 10 years. Massive displacement of populations, emigration, and refugee problem have added to the human tragedy of the conflict. Military expenditure has been rising. Militarization of political conflicts is a particularly disturbing development.

The conflict could have been managed without recourse to military confrontations. Space has always existed for political accommodation among Sinhala and Tamil communities, yet the state and militant groups who conduct the war do not appear to have much trust in political means of conflict management and resolution.

The primary lesson of this conflict is that ethnic and social conflicts should be managed at the initial and tractable phase, thus preventing them from transforming into militarized and intractable phases.

CASE SUMMARY

- Sri Lanka is multiethnic, multilingual, and multireligious.

- The constitution attempted to bring all groups together, but conflict between Sinhalese and Tamil continues.

- Government policy measures denied balanced representation and imposed policy measures favoring the Sinhalese.

- The Tamil went underground and joined guerrilla movements.

- The conflict escalated to a military conflict.

- The media have taken a pro-Sinhalese view, contributing to the conflict.

- The conflict is seen as a just revolution, a terrorist problem, and a human rights problem.

- The ethnic differences cannot be accommodated, but there is common ground for peace and reconciliation.

- There is no role for third-party mediation of this internal problem.

- The problem continues to escalate.

Conclusion

26

The Cultural Context of Mediation and Constructive Conflict Management

FRED E. JANDT and PAUL B. PEDERSEN

Conflict management strategies that are insensitive to each culture's unique context are not likely to succeed. The temptation to generalize conflict management strategies from Western to non-Western cultures or vice versa, regardless of the different cultural context, is a dangerous threat. Each cultural context has developed its own unique constraints and opportunities for constructive conflict management.

In the preceding chapters, 24 case studies from 13 different countries have demonstrated the diversity within the Asia-Pacific region. The contrast between Western and Asian styles of constructive conflict management is also apparent. Each case study presents a subjective and specific example of conflict management in its cultural context. From the perspective of the reader's contrasting cultural context, some case studies have no doubt seemed strange and presume unfamiliar assumptions. By attempting to understand each case example in its own cultural context, new alternative assumptions are tested for constructive conflict management not only for the Asia-Pacific region but also for other regions.

In the first chapter, we introduced two models for constructive conflict management. The first model emphasized the importance of cultural context, with some cultures putting a high emphasis on context and other cultures a lower emphasis on context. Conflict is managed differently in high-context cultures than in low-context cultures, and some of those contrasting patterns were identified. The second model emphasized the importance of separating expectations from behaviors between two groups or individuals in conflict with one another. Two individuals or groups may share the same positive common-ground expectations while behaving quite differently. Interpreting those different behaviors without regard for the similar positive expectations escalates the conflict unnecessarily. This concluding chapter applies both suggested models to the 24 case examples to test the usefulness of those models in constructive conflict management.

DO CULTURAL VALUES CONTROL THE PROCESS OF CONFLICT MANAGEMENT?

William Felstiner (1982) has observed that dispute resolution in any society is regulated by that culture's values, psychological imperatives, history, and economic, political, or social organization. The 24 case studies in this volume reflect both how cultural values define conflict and how cultural values regulate constructive conflict management. Perspectives of conflict management that put a "low" emphasis on context are less likely to be accurate than perspectives assuming a "high" context emphasis in the cases presented.

In "Han and Hui and a Shared Cooking Stove," Lu Guojiang describes a dispute between two families from two of China's many cultural groups. He acknowledges that each cultural group has its own language, religion, and custom. The mediation committee appealed to the disputants' shared membership in the larger family of the Chinese nation as taking a "parental" role, consistent with Confucian practice. The conflict over both parties' behaviors toward one another was diminished by separating that behavior from the shared, positive, common ground of national interest and Confucian belief in the family. The positive common-ground expectations provided a "context" in which to understand and adjust conflicting behaviors appropriately so that both parties would win and neither side lose.

Conflict and the means of managing that conflict are defined by cultural values in each different cultural context. For example, Shir-Shing Huang, in "The Reconciliation System of the Republic of China," attributes the widespread success of mediation in China to the traditional belief that "peace is best, lawsuit is the worst." The shared positive expectations for a peaceful—

or at least private—disposition of disputes has contributed to the majority of civil cases in China being settled by reconciliation. An effective conflict management strategy might be to prevent open conflict from ever occurring in the first place, emphasizing the role of prevention more than remediation.

As cultures change, the contextual rules of constructive conflict management change as well. Maraya de Jesus Chebat writes about "The Moral Recovery Program as a Political Tool for Social Transformation in the Philippines." She asserts that the traditional Asian worldview of wholeness and the interconnectedness of all things which had been the moral foundation of the Filipino society was lost during colonialism. Colonialism brought a contrasting cultural influence emphasizing materialism as a measure of success. The Moral Recovery Program in the Philippines is attempting to build peace and manage conflict by renewing traditional common-ground, historically rooted cultural values stressing common identity as interconnected beings regardless of race, creed, or background. In this case, the shared, positive, common-ground expectations being emphasized are historical perhaps more than contemporary but provide an important context for managing conflicts arising from the behavior of groups or individuals toward one another.

Cultural change also influences the context of Western countries as indicated by Michelle LeBaron's "Culture and Conflict in Canada: Tradition and Transition." This case points out the problems of managing conflict between individuals from two culturally different traditions. She ascribes the failure of mediating the conflict between Canadian-born Rajpal and her immigrant husband Balbir to their different interpretations of each other's behaviors. Rajpal accepted the individualistic and nuclear family model of dominant Canadian culture, whereas Balbir valued the extended family, high power distance, and women's deference to men. Balbir rejected the institutions for managing conflict available in the Canadian context and tried to apply traditional conflict management strategies from his back-home cultural context. The "foreign" conflict management strategies did not work in the Canadian context because there was no similar "village structure" and the role of women in the Canadian context was more "powerful." Shared, positive, common-ground expectations cannot be imposed from the outside to control one or both person's behaviors.

Another example of a wife and husband interpreting each other's behavior in ways that escalate the conflict was presented by Julie Foster Smith's case study, "The Effects of Tribal Wars on Personal and Family Disputes in Papua New Guinea." Norma's husband demanded his rights as husband under customary tribal law. Norma interpreted these rules as permitting the husband to rape her; consequently, she refused to conform to that role of woman and wife. The "context" was different for Norma than for her husband. When the cultural context allows behavior that outsiders consider wrong and hurtful it is difficult to avoid imposing judgment as outsiders on the way conflict is traditionally managed. Finding shared positive common-ground expectations among and between conflicting parties is sometimes more difficult than others.

Other cases also demonstrate how the cultural context regulates conflict management. For example, Ariya Rubasinghe, in "Mediation, an Effective Way of Conflict Resolution: Sri Lanka Experience," describes how a mediation board dealt with the effects of a Sinhalese woman marrying a Muslim. Because her marriage was not "approved" she was not able to carry out her responsibilities to her ill mother that are expected of a daughter in the Sinhalese customary context. Attempting to manage the conflict without regard to the complicated cultural context of this family would predictably result in escalation of the conflict.

Cultural values control the process of conflict management, and when the cultural values of the parties in conflict are different, the conflict will be particularly difficult to manage. Imposing a change of behaviors forcefully without regard for one or both cultures is not likely to succeed. Unless a new context of shared, positive, common-ground expectations can be derived from the larger context, the conflict is likely to escalate further.

DO AGE AND GENDER DESCRIBE SALIENT CULTURAL AFFILIATIONS?

Although the obvious cultural context is defined by nationality or ethnicity there are significant within-group differences that may become more salient than nationality and ethnicity in a particular time and place. Age and gender are two potentially salient and different within-group perspectives that might impose their own cultural context on a conflict between individuals or groups.

In 1990, the United Nations Development Program first used the Human Development Index (HDI) as a measure of purchasing power, health, and education. In its 1993 report, the U.N. reported separate HDI scores for women. The percentage of difference between overall HDI scores and women's HDI scores in Asia-Pacific countries showed that women's scores were significantly lower than the overall score for each country (see Table 26.1). The report concluded that in no country are women treated as well as men. In industrial countries, the differences are largely in employment and wages. In developing countries, health care, nutrition, and education are also factors. Many religions in the region emphasize the leadership of men and the

TABLE 26.1 HDI Scores for Women Compared to Overall Country Scores

New Zealand	–10.9
Australia	–12.3
Canada	–16.9
Japan	–22.4
Myanmar	–23.8
Sri Lanka	–24.7
Philippines	–25.2
Singapore	–31.1
Hong Kong	–32.3
South Korea	–36.4

SOURCE: United Nations Development Program (1993).

submissive role of the wife to the husband. In countries with a Confucian tradition, fathers transmit family honor and ancestral virtue to their sons through an unbroken line of male-linked kin. All authority is by metaphor paternal from the state to the family itself.

The relationship between culture and the role of women is most vividly demonstrated in Xue Wang's "Conflict Over the Role of Women in Contemporary China: Prospects for Liberation and Resolution." The case argues that women's liberation in China was a goal of the Chinese Communist Party (CCP) since its formation. However, women's equality has not yet been achieved because of the Chinese traditional morality that supports the power of men. The external context of "women's liberation" and the internal context of "male dominance" complicate the search for common ground and shared positive expectations in gender-related conflicts.

Constructive conflict management needs sensitivity to gender roles in each cultural context. Michelle LeBaron's "Culture and Conflict in Canada: Tradition and Transition" concludes that mediation is effective only when the process acknowledges the importance of gender roles. She argues that traditional Asian mediation strategies are male dominated and more likely to be effective in societies where male domination is accepted. Attempts to impose the values of male domination on societies valuing women's liberation are as unlikely to succeed as attempts to impose the values of women's liberation on societies valuing male domination unless a new context can be constructed.

Case studies of family conflict are most likely to involve gender issues. For example, in the Bangladesh case study "Khukumoni and Masud: Living Happily Now," the woman Khukumoni suffered physical and mental abuse because her marriage was not accepted by either her family or her husband's family. She was assisted not by family but by a social welfare organization that constructed a new context.

In "Rawshan Ara: The Victim of Polygamy," issues of arranged marriages, dowries, polygamy, verbal and physical abuse, and education are raised. In this case, Rawshan Ara suffered abuse from her husband's family, who did not value the need for an educated wife. Unless a new shared, positive context can be constructed the conflict will escalate.

In Julie Foster Smith's case study, "The Effects of Tribal Wars on Personal and Family Disputes in Papua New Guinea," the woman Norma experiences physical violence and emotional abuse and her daughter sexual abuse from the husband. Likewise in "Mediation, an Effective Way of Conflict Resolution: Sri Lanka Experience," a daughter's inheritance is accepted to be less than her brothers'. In still another case, the abuse of children in the carpet industry is described by Gauri Pradhan in "Child Labor in Nepal's Carpet Industries," where the working conditions are abusive and young girls are subject to sexual abuse. It is difficult, if not impossible, to understand these conflicts without first understanding the cultural context in which they occurred. The construction of a new context for constructive conflict management may well consider affiliations of age and gender to be legitimate and salient cultural groups as well as overlapping affiliations to nationality and ethnicity.

WHY DOES ETHNIC CONFLICT TEND TO BE ESPECIALLY EXPLOSIVE?

When two individuals or groups with different and contrasting ethnic affiliations experience a conflict of interest, the potential for escalation is increased to the extent that each party's assumptions are exclusively defined by their contrasting ethnic affiliations. Ethnicity is typically a strong, well-defined, and self-contained cultural category with clear and exclusive boundaries. To the extent that each ethnic group excludes members of other ethnic groups from membership, those boundaries defined by ethnicity frustrate attempts to find common ground. The conflict is enlarged beyond the individuals involved to include two competing ethnic affiliations in a win-lose struggle for superiority. Ethnic conflict involving ethnic minorities, where there is an unequal distribution of power, becomes particularly explosive.

Gauri Pradhan, in "Child Labor in Nepal's Carpet Industries," points out that the children recruited to work in the carpet industry come from poverty-stricken villages and many come from ethnic minority communities. The conflict was not just interpersonal but interethnic and difficult, if not impossible, to resolve. Lu Guojiang, in "Han and Hui and a Shared Cooking Stove," describes a conflict between families from the majority Han and the minority

Hui ethnicities involving the preparation of pork at a communal cooking stove. Although each ethnicity had its own language, religion, and customs, it was possible to find common ground in the shared positive expectations that both parties had in the larger national affiliation.

The problems of unequal power differences are described by Eduardo C. Tadem in "Philippine Rural Development and Indigenous Communities: Aytas and the Sacobia Project." The Aytas, a Filipino ethnic group, lost their ancestral land to U.S. Clark Air Base. When they also became victims of the Mount Pinatubo eruptions, the conflict turned into a crisis. Government officials perceived the Aytas as gullible people who could easily be "sweet-talked" into agreement. The Aytas felt they had no forum to address their complaints. If they resisted the more powerful government policies, the military could be used against them. Eduardo Tadem concludes that the history of disregard and insensitivity to indigenous cultures can only be improved by granting them the autonomy to develop and safeguard their own culture.

Another serious and costly ethnic conflict is described by Jayadeva Uyangoda in "Recent Attempt at Ethnic Conflict Resolution in Sri Lanka." Ethnic conflict between the majority Sinhalese and the minority Tamils has a long history. Plantation Tamils, Hindus, and descendents of 19th-century indentured workers lost Sri Lanka citizenship on the basis of their actually being citizens of India. The conflict has escalated because of official language laws and has resulted in terrorist military actions. The Sinhalese Buddhist nationalist groups view the conflict as requiring a political solution. Jayadeva Uyangoda points out that Sri Lanka lacks a mechanism to negotiate ethnic conflict and recommends that ethnic conflicts need to be addressed early before they escalate into armed confrontation.

Most ethnic boundaries are also defined by religious beliefs. Religion can become the basis of diversity as well as the foundation of common ground. Although the authors of "Nabin and Nasima: Conflict Engendered by Religious Prescriptions" point out that both the Hindu man Nabin and the Muslim woman Nasima share the culture of Bangladesh, Nabin belongs to the minority Hindus, who in Bangladesh normally keep a low profile. A similar issue is part of "Mediation, an Effective Way of Conflict Resolution: Sri Lanka Experience" in which a non-Muslim woman marries a Muslim and her family does not approve of the marriage.

Most ethnic groups are experiencing rapid social change due to modernization, industrialization, urbanization, and other contemporary pressures to change. In "The Effects of Tribal Wars on Personal and Family Disputes in Papua New Guinea," the husband behaves according to the guidelines in customary tribal law, whereas the wife behaves according to more urbanized and modernized guidelines through her professional affiliations. Rapid social change creates conflict between persons at different stages of change from traditional to more modernized guidelines. In "The Dumping of Industrial Waste in Teshima, Japan," Masaki Yokoyama identifies a conflict between urban, profit-oriented, and bureaucratic groups (including the TSKK, a processor of hazardous waste) and the rural, community-centered, and nonbureaucratic residents of Teshima island. The conflict of interest between these groups is predictable and can be avoided or prevented only through careful preparation ahead of time to construct common ground rather than wait for the inevitable conflict of interests brought about through modernization.

Most ethnic group boundaries are also defined by language. Language and dialect groups provide opportunities for misunderstanding and conflict in their diversity of meanings. Gurmit Singh, in "Toxic Waste Management in Malaysia," points out that the government must use a variety of languages and dialects to reach all the different ethnic groups to avoid misunderstandings leading to environmental conflicts.

Ethnic conflict is often the most explosive conflict between cultural groups because the issues of ethnic survival are almost always at stake and each group is reluctant to give up its well-defined boundaries in favor of common ground. Constructive conflict management of ethnic conflict is possible through anticipation and prevention of conflicts or by identifying superordinate identities that can provide shared positive expectations of common ground.

WHAT ARE THE CRITERIA FOR SUCCESSFUL MEDIATION ACROSS CULTURES?

Mediating multicultural conflict is a complex skill. Generalizing successful mediation strategies from one cultural context to another different context has often resulted in misunderstandings and failure. Although most of the literature on mediation and conflict management has been written in a Western, Euro-American context, assuming narrowly defined cultural values, there have been few attempts to modify those strategies to fit the cultural context of non-Western cultures. By reviewing the 24 examples of constructive conflict management in the Asia-Pacific region, we hope to identify alternative criteria for successful mediation in non-Western cultural contexts.

Lu Guojiang, in "China and Japan Dispute Copyright of 'Ultraman' Toys" describes court mediation in China. Court mediation is conducted by a judge, and the conciliation agreement has the same effect as a court judgment.

Mediation conducted by the 1 million mediation committees in China is voluntary, and the disputants retain the right to take the dispute to court if mediation fails. The mediation committees are composed of from 3 to 11 elected members. In rural areas, the mediation committees are village based. The model of establishing mediation agencies as formal institutions of society is gaining popularity in Western countries but is as yet not as well organized as it is in China.

Shir-Shing Huang, in "The Reconciliation System of the Republic of China," points out that traditional mediation in China was conducted by local gentry respected by their fellow townspeople. In Taiwan's formalized mediation process, mediators who are nominated by chiefs and mayors and approved by representatives of their villages and towns are respected and prestigious local people with some knowledge of the law. The formal institutions of mediation in Taiwan also require that at least one woman be on each local mediation committee. By incorporating mediation into local social institutions, the importance of each local cultural context is recognized.

The Bangladesh case, "Nabin and Nasima: Conflict Engendered by Religious Prescriptions," describes the local mediators as well-thought-of community members with knowledge of the local culture and with the ability to control the mediation process and negotiate deadlocks in the local cultural context. Rather than a single mediator, in Nabin and Nasima's conflict 14 mediators were involved—6 from each side and 2 from the Madaripur Legal Aid Association. The two mediators from the legal aid association also had knowledge of the law as applied to the local cultural context.

In "Khukumoni and Masud: Living Happily Now," the mediation committee of 10 persons was formed spontaneously with people from each party's side, from the social welfare organization Banchte Shekha which had legal experience, and from neutral individuals who knew the local culture. In "Ishaq Gets Back Land After 40 Years," 18 mediators, including representatives from both sides, were used. The pattern indicates local involvement, participation by all interested parties, linkage to the legal system and an ongoing established mediation process to reach a decision as well as to monitor the consequences of their decision over time. The objective of mediation is not just to fix blame but to reconcile all parties into a new superordinate context of social harmony.

In Sri Lanka, members of mediation boards are selected from nominations made by nonpolitical voluntary organizations, religious institutions, and government agencies. Their nomination reflects their acceptance by the community. The people selected receive five days' training in mediation as well as recognition and support from the community. In Nepal, the conflict resolution *Panchayat* was traditionally conducted by respected elders. Recently, elected public officials have also become involved in mediation, and Jagadish C. Pokharel, in "Manakamana Village's Demand for Drinking Water," notes that elected public officials may not hold the same values as the people in a local community and may not be as familiar with the context in which conflict occurs.

In the case from Thailand, "Vendetta and Buddhist Mediator in Southern Thailand," the mediator was a Buddhist monk who had worked for both of the disputing families before becoming a monk. He had a reputation for handling disputes between the people and bureaucrats. In this case, Prakru Kasem Dhammarangsri was acceptable as a mediator primarily because both disputing families knew, trusted, and respected him. He was thus able to incorporate their trust and his status as "a relative of both families" in defining common ground of shared positive expectations, mobilizing support of both families toward a mutually acceptable outcome. The model of detached neutrality more familiar to mediation in Western settings is perhaps less appropriate in this context.

The mediator or mediators need not act as individuals. Nongovernmental organizations (NGOs) can also act as mediators. In "Tiger Saves Taiga: Saving the Siberian Ecosystem From Hyundai's Logging Operations," Jae Hyun Yoo acted individually as a mediator but also depended on his association with the Citizens Coalition for Economic Justice (CCEJ), a Korean NGO, for legitimacy in the local context. Organizations are not always successful mediators. In the Japanese case study "The Dumping of Industrial Waste in Teshima, Japan," the prefectural government agency was expected to mediate pollution disputes, but it was unsuccessful and was finally seen as part of the problem rather than a problem-solving agency.

Several patterns emerge from these cases describing criteria for constructive conflict mediation. First, the mediators need to be part of the local community and thoroughly familiar with the context in which the conflict occurs. Second, the mediators need not be neutral but need to have credibility with the disputing parties. Third, mediation is seen as an ongoing nurturing process interested in long-term reconciliation of disputing parties and not merely fixing blame. Finally, there is an emphasis on the welfare of the social unit as being more important than the rights of individual members.

WHAT SHOULD A CONSTRUCTIVE CONFLICT MANAGER DO?

Constructive conflict management is complicated, and each cultural context imposes its own requirements on the mediator. What is done and what is not done by the mediator is interpreted as "meaningful," whether intended or not. The 24 case studies demonstrate skills that worked in these specific contexts, but one must be careful when generalizing from these specific cases.

Lu Guojiang describes court mediation in China in "China and Japan Dispute Copyright of 'Ultraman' Toys," where the mediator first finds out the facts and draws an independent judgment of right and wrong. The mediator then uses persuasion with the disputants, bringing them to accept "the common ground." In his case "Han and Hui and a Shared Cooking Stove," Lu Guojiang likewise follows the pattern of fact finding, investigation, and then persuasion with the disputants. The tendency to directly give advice and express an opinion through persuasion is in contrast with mediation procedures typical of Western cultures.

Shir-Shing Huang, in "The Reconciliation System of the Republic of China," calls attention to the mediator's role as a "persuader," who appeals to the disputants to reach a peaceful resolution, calling into play the culturally valued sense of community they both share.

In some cases, however, the mediator is clearly described as impartial and neutral. For example, Ariya Rubasinghe, in "Mediation, an Effective Way of Conflict Resolution: Sri Lanka Experience," makes it quite clear that the mediation boards in Sri Lanka strive to be impartial.

In the Bangladesh case "Nabin and Nasima: Conflict Engendered by Religious Prescriptions," the two mediators from the legal aid association had the role of organizing the meeting, presenting documents, and providing legal analysis. It is most important to note that the first mediation was arranged by locals and the second mediation was arranged by the Madaripur Legal Aid Association. The needs of the actual disputants were clearly secondary to the needs of the community for maintaining social harmony and discipline. The mediator then may be as much an agent of the community as an agent of either or both disputing parties.

Similarly, in "Khukumoni and Masud: Living Happily Now," the role of organizing the meeting was assumed by the social welfare organization Banchte Shekha. Banchte Shekha had multiple roles in this conflict. Members of the organization rescued Khukumoni from the street, tried to resolve the dispute through coordination among local influential people and elites, filed suit against Masud on Khukumoni's behalf, helped arrange the couple's remarriage, and arranged the mediation in which they also participated. The dispute between individuals is perceived as a community problem beyond the interests of either or both individuals.

In the Bangladesh case "Rawshan Ara: The Victim of Polygamy," the mediators are guided in their decision by Islamic law regarding polygamy.

In some cases, the best interests of the community might lead mediators to decisions that outsiders perceive as "unfair." In "Ishaq Gets Back Land After 40 Years," it was apparent that mediators had in the past favored powerful and wealthy landowners, who interpreted the best interests of the community in their own terms.

In the case from Thailand, "Vendetta and Buddhist Mediator in Southern Thailand," the Buddhist monk took on the role of mediator. The parties did not seek out a mediator nor see any end to their dispute in their attempts to solve the disagreement independently. Prakru Kasem dealt with both disputing families separately in their homes before bringing them together. The role of a successful mediator depends on credibility with all disputing parties and is less an "ascribed" than an "achieved" role.

The peacemaker described in these cases is not necessarily labeled a "mediator." In some cases, the peacemaker has quite different primary roles. In "The Effects of Tribal Wars on Personal and Family Disputes in Papua New Guinea," the peacemaker and author of the case acted as advisor and provided support to one of the disputants. In several cases, the dispute is decided by the mediators. In "Ishaq Gets Back Land After 40 Years," it was the mediators who reached a final decision for the disputants. In this case, the mediators were aware of property laws that the disputants themselves and the villagers did not know. Whatever persuasive skill or knowledge of the law the mediator has depends primarily on the mediator's own personal credibility in the community and awareness of the context in which a conflict occurs.

WHAT IS THE RELATIONSHIP BETWEEN MEDIATION AND THE COURTS?

It has been said that mediation is somehow more appropriate in some cultures than in others. The case studies in this volume show, first, how varied the process of mediation can be. Those variations reflect culture and demonstrate that there is no one way to conduct a mediation. Second, these case studies provide numerous examples of how mediation as a social institution can complement the legal system to the mutual advantage of both systems. Individuals chose to use either system, based on perceived advantages of honesty and cost. Models for constructive conflict management provide a parallel process with the courts for resolving disputes, but it is not necessary for either system to compete with the other.

Lu Guojiang, in "China and Japan Dispute Copyright of 'Ultraman' Toys," explains that in court mediation in China the conciliation agreement has the same effect as a court judgment. In "people's mediation," as illustrated by the case titled "Han and Hui and a Shared Cooking Stove," the disputants retain the right to take their dispute to the courts.

Shir-Shing Huang points out in "The Reconciliation System of the Republic of China" that the majority of civil cases are settled by reconciliation. In Taiwan's formalized mediation procedure, reconciliation agreements cannot be appealed in the courts, but the reconciliation memoranda are approved by the courts and thus can be enforced by judicial action. In Sri Lanka, mediation is perceived as a preliminary or supplementary device to courts of law. For example, the case "Mediation, an Effective Way of Conflict Resolution: Sri Lanka Experience" was referred by the courts to mediation because it was a dispute involving members of one family. In the Philippines, the traditional dispute resolution conducted by village headmen was institutionalized into a system for settling disputes on the *barangay,* or village, level. Disputants must first seek settlement at the barangay level before they can take a dispute to the courts.

Does some of the legitimacy of mediation derive from its relationship with the court? There is evidence supporting that in Michelle LeBaron's "Culture and Conflict in Canada: Tradition and Transition." She argues that immigrants perceive mediation as less legitimate than the courts. Contemporary mediation as practiced in Canada is informal, time and agreement driven, excludes members of the extended family, and is conducted by mediators who are neutral or impartial. With limited enforceability, mediation is perceived to have less authority than the courts.

In some cases, the courts are used as a strategy to encourage participation in mediation. For example, in the Bangladesh case "Khukumoni and Masud: Living Happily Now," Masud filed suit against his wife, and the social welfare organization Banchte Shekha filed suit against Masud on Khukumoni's behalf. The same authors cite the case of "Ishaq Gets Back Land After 40 Years," stating that if the mediation was not successful the dispute would be sent to the courts, which in Bangladesh are considered expensive.

In other cases, no conflict resolution mechanism exists to resolve certain disputes. Gurmit Singh points out in "Toxic Waste Management in Malaysia" that no mechanism existed to resolve environmental disputes outside the courts of law. Strategies for constructive conflict management have evolved out of necessity in local communities that seek to preserve harmony among their own people with a minimum of involvement by "outsiders" who may be expensive and whose involvement may even escalate the conflict. Constructive conflict management has emerged to fill a recognized need in each local cultural context and has been modified or adapted to meet the changing conditions as the local context changes.

WHAT IS UNIQUE ABOUT CONSTRUCTIVE CONFLICT MANAGEMENT?

Without doubt, the words mediation, arbitration, conciliation, conflict, and others are troublesome in that there is no consensus regarding their meaning. This is particularly true when we apply these words to the Asia-Pacific cultural context. For example, in the case studies in this volume alone, mediation is described as a process that ranges from the mediator being a spokesperson for one of the disputants, as in the Maori case study, to groups of respected elders—or in modern versions, elected mediators—who strive for compromise. In other examples, the cases speak of court mediation as a formal process.

History shows us that mediation has a long history. Some authors trace its origins to ancient Greek and Chinese traditions. We might more accurately contend that its origins were many. The history of mediation in Sri Lanka dates back to about 425 years before the Christian era, during which time clan chiefs acted as mediators to handle disputes. In China, mediation can be traced back to the Zhou Dynasty, 1,100 years before the Christian era.

Let's assume a purely hypothetical case. Let's take the descriptions of mediation presented in this volume and attempt to extrapolate back to what might have been the origins of the process.

If we assume a world of relatively small, isolated villages, it would be reasonable to assume that most conflicts that arose within that community dealt with the complexities of the relationships among village individuals. In Pakistan and Nepal, disputes among individuals were resolved by Panchayats, or groups of elders. In Bangladesh, the Shalish were village elders who mediated but also had the power of arbiters to make binding awards.

If we assume some degree of isolation, it is also reasonable to assume that the conflicts had repercussions throughout the community. With the shared objective of restoring harmony in relationships, the community turned to the wisdom and skills of trusted elders. Although the procedures the elders used may have varied, they most probably had the shared objective of healing and restoring the community hurt from the conflict. What we are describing as hypothetical may best be seen in the Hawaiian traditional dispute settlement technique known as *Ho'oponopono,* which continues to be practiced within Hawaii along with a Westernized court and legal system.

Traditionally, Ho'oponopono was a family conference led by a respected senior family member to "straighten out" problems through a process that includes prayer, a statement of the problem, discussion, confession of wrong-doing, restitution determined when necessary, forgiveness, and release of the problem (Shook, 1985).

Again, if we assume hypothetically population growth and increased contact among villages, it would be easy to assume that mediation was adapted to meet those changes. For example, in paternalistic societies with a strong king, such as Thailand for example, the administration of justice flowed from the king's authority. Courts became a manifestation of the king's administration of justice. A similar situation may have existed in Sri Lanka where the king "was" justice personified. It was the king who vested judicial authority in the *Gamsabhawas,* or village councils, and who met to amicably settle disputes.

With colonization, outside systems of justice from Western countries were introduced into the society. Treaties with Britain eroded the king's role in Thailand. Sri Lanka was expected to comply with Portuguese, Dutch, and British legal systems. The Philippines was introduced to the legal systems of Spain and the United States. In most cases, the foreign legal systems were slow, expensive, and difficult to comprehend when compared to indigenous alternatives.

To deal with the more interpersonal problems, customary law and forms of mediation coexisted with the court system. In the Malay speaking cultures, *adat* law was a highly developed and sophisticated legal system, and in Indonesia, for example, the local peoples were allowed to choose whether to be judged by Dutch law or adat law. In local community contexts, customary law and indigenous forms of mediation have survived in a variety of dynamic forms to meet the conditions of a rapidly changing social context.

Some countries have attempted to formally recognize the legitimacy of customary law and forms of mediation in their legal system. In the Philippines, a presidential commission drafted a decree establishing a system of resolving disputes at the barangay (village) level. This local system was at least partially based on historical accounts of conciliation that existed in precolonial days. In New Zealand, mediation has grown in part from the increased recognition of contributions by Maori traditions and processes to the national society.

Mediation and other forms of dispute resolution have become popular as alternative dispute resolution systems or alternatives to the formal legal/judicial system. Courts were the original alternative to customary law as a way of dealing with the demands of modernization, and now societies in the Asia-Pacific region are reexamining the viability or appropriateness of informal mediation alternatives in dispute resolution.

The strength of mediation has always been its capacity for stabilizing a community. Recently in the Philippines (as in the United States), the movement to revitalize the community-based traditional dispute resolution systems has been based on the shortcomings of an overburdened legal system. Civil disputes can take years to resolve and incur considerable expense going to trial. Perhaps an equally important motivation to seek indigenous strategies for constructive conflict management is the need to heal broken communities and reestablish systems that have worked to heal communities in the past.

CAN WE GENERALIZE FROM ASIA-PACIFIC EXAMPLES?

The case examples from the Asia-Pacific region seek to increase our body of knowledge about conflict. We have attempted to make explicit a series of situational patterns that occur in the case examples. A critical assessment of these specific cases might identify questions and insights about constructive conflict management that can be applied elsewhere.

The list of propositions from the case studies in this volume have been carefully selected from a long list of observations. Williams (1947) suggests three criteria for limiting propositions to a meaningful number: those of most probable validity, those that offer the most promise of fruitfully guiding empirical research, and those of potential importance for understanding social conflict or for application to policy problems.

The concept of high- and low-context cultures was popularized by Hall (1976). In low-context cultures, verbal messages are elaborate and specific and tend also to be detailed and redundant. Verbal abilities are highly valued. Logic and reasoning are expressed in verbal messages. Cultures commonly identified as low-context are Germany, the United States, Canada, and Switzerland, among others.

In high-context cultures, most of the information is either in the physical context or internalized in the person. High-context cultures decrease the perception of self as separate from the group. Very little is in the coded, explicit, transmitted part of the message. High-context cultures are more sensitive to nonverbal messages. Cultures commonly identified as high-context are China, Japan, and Korea, among others.

Bernstein (1964), before Hall, used the term "elaborated codes" and "restricted codes." Elaborated code cultures rely heavily on verbal communication. In restricted code cultures, nonverbal communication is critical for understanding.

For example, in comparisons of Japan and the United States, various researchers have identified differences on the basis of context. Ishii and Klopf (1976) found that Japanese spend considerably less time in verbal communication. Cambra, Ishii, and Klopf (1978) found that Japanese spoke less frequently and for shorter periods of time, were less likely to initiate and maintain conversations, and were less inclined to talk. Kunihiro (1976) concludes that language is *a* means of communication for the Japanese, whereas it is *the* means of communication in the United States. Kondo (1981) claims that the Japanese communicate primarily with their minds and not with spoken words. Ishii (1984) concludes that the Japanese place a positive value on silence and a negative value on speaking. Silence itself sends a message of positive emotions of serenity, harmony, and trustworthiness. In contrast, Wayne (1974) argues that in the United States, silence is related to negative emotions of grief, criticism, regret, and confusion.

There is a relationship between context and Hofstede's (1983) cultural dimensions of societies emphasizing group versus individualistic interests. High context requires a high degree of shared group awareness and identification, whereas low context may be more characteristic of highly heterogeneous societies.

The cultural dimension refers to how people define themselves and their relationships with others. Cultures characterized by collectivism emphasize relationships among people to a greater degree. Collectivist cultures stress interdependent activities and suppress individual aims for the group's welfare. Countries high in collectivism in the Asia-Pacific region are Taiwan, Thailand, Singapore, and Hong Kong, among others.

Hypotheses

The following list of hypotheses seek to generalize from the Asia-Pacific cases through "questions" that might be asked and tested against additional data. These hypotheses emerged as patterns from the case studies, but whether they can be generalized to other countries and cultural contexts is a subject for additional future research.

The first two deal with the labeling or acknowledgment that a conflict exists. No conflict exists until the participants acknowledge that there is a conflict. Behaviors that can appear to an outside observer as conflict behaviors may have a completely different meaning to the participants. The observer might not label as conflict behaviors those that in fact are significant conflict behaviors. Thus, it is important to understand who labels or acknowledges the existence of conflict.

This is very clear in Michelle LeBaron's "Culture and Conflict in Canada: Tradition and Transition." The Canadian-born Rajpal felt she had a conflict with her immigrant husband. She first addressed her feelings to family members. She received no acknowledgment of there being a conflict and nothing changed. In fact, Rajpal could find no one she felt would be acceptable as a mediator to both her and her husband and their family, except an elderly woman at the temple who was willing to sit and talk with both of them—but not to mediate. In one sense, Rajpal could get no one to even acknowledge that a conflict existed.

From this case from Canada, a relationship between context and the labeling of conflict becomes apparent and leads to the first hypothesis:

H1: In low-context cultures, individual participants must first accept and acknowledge that there is a conflict before resolution/mediation can begin.

Other cases from high-context cultures suggest a different relationship. In "Philippine Rural Development and Indigenous Communities: Aytas and the Sacobia Project," it can be concluded that no effective conflict management existed between the Filipino government and the marginalized Aytas. The government did not acknowledge that the Aytas had complaints and therefore did not acknowledge that conflict existed.

In Bangladesh, as in the case of "Nabin and Nasima: Conflict Engendered by Religious Prescriptions," mediation became a way of maintaining social discipline. The Hindu man Nabin had a relationship with the Muslim woman Nasima. The community felt this to be a social crime involving conflict and arranged for mediation. Nabin and Nasima did not ask for mediation; the local elites initiated mediation as an act of social purification and social discipline. In fact, Nabin was not even present at the mediation. The mediation was not so much for Nabin and Nasima as it was for the community.

In Bangladesh, in the case "Khukumoni and Masud: Living Happily Now," the woman Khukumoni suffered physical and mental abuse in silence. It was the social welfare organization Banchte Shekha that filed a lawsuit in her name and tried to resolve the dispute through mediation. Khukumoni was not able to get her problem addressed as an individual; she suffered in silence. In a similar way, it was the actions of Bangladesh's Madaripur Legal Aid Association in "Rawshan Ara: The Victim of Polygamy" that brought a transformation to Rawshan Ara's relationship to her husband Yousof.

The case "Ishaq Gets Back Land After 40 Years" also illustrates that conflict resolution cannot begin until the group acknowledges that a conflict exists. Ishaq's grandfather registered land in Ishaq's name, but his uncle claimed the land. Ishaq delayed asserting his demand for the land until his uncle, an influential man in the village, had died. While his uncle was alive, Ishaq knew that his claim would not be recognized. After the uncle's death, Ishaq believed his claim would more likely be heard by the village.

These cases lead to the second hypothesis:

H2: In high-context cultures, traditional groups must first accept and acknowledge that there is a conflict before resolution/mediation can begin.

The next two hypotheses deal with the public or private nature of mediation. In Michelle LeBaron's "Culture and Conflict in Canada: Tradition and

Transition," the Canadian-born Rajpal could get no one to acknowledge that a conflict existed between her and her husband Balbir. Rajpal did eventually find an elderly women intervenor at the temple to meet with them both. In low-context Canada, those meetings were held in the home with no other family members present. The next hypothesis is drawn from this case:

H3: In low-context cultures, conflict and the resolution/mediation process must often be kept private.

Other cases in this volume suggest something quite different. In Bangladesh, in "Nabin and Nasima: Conflict Engendered by Religious Prescriptions," because the mediation itself was serving a community interest rather than the interests of the parties, 100 observers were present at the mediation and were in fact participants. Also in Bangladesh, in "Ishaq Gets Back Land After 40 Years," 24 observers were present at the mediation, and in fact their participation was necessary for Ishaq to get his claim addressed.

The conflict described by Pauline Tangiora in New Zealand illustrates the importance the Maori place on a community meeting for talking through issues. Individual people voiced their feelings publicly. The public meeting itself was an expression of the Maori value of community. The person designated as spokesperson and mediator was chosen for knowledge of Maori community consensus decision making.

In "Child Labor in Nepal's Carpet Industries," Gauri Pradhan and the NGO Child Workers in Nepal Concerned Center (CWIN) made public an issue and became advocates for the children who had no voice. The CWIN called Nepal's attention to the issue of children's rights through research, surveys, and the film *Misery Behind the Looms.*

These sample cases lead to the fourth hypothesis:

H4: In high-context cultures, conflict is not private and must be made public before the resolution/mediation process can begin.

The next two hypotheses deal with conflict management skills—those of resolving conflicts and those of preventing conflicts from happening. As a generalization, it can be said that Western mediators are concerned that disputants are, in some way, "equally matched," that is, that neither disputant is harmed by a process they do not understand. Again, as a generalization, Western mediators value neutrality and, to avoid participating in the process as an advocate for a disputant, are concerned that individual disputants have the skills to participate as an equal in the mediation. The fifth hypothesis represents these generalizations:

H5: In low-context cultures, societal conflict management is most effective in preparing an individual's skill and teaching individuals how to negotiate/mediate or resolve conflict reactivity.

In several cases, the public nature of the mediation makes it clear that mediation serves a social purpose. In "Nabin and Nasima: Conflict Engendered by Religious Prescriptions," the public mediation served to reinforce the community's belief that Hindu men should not have relationships with Muslim women.

Central to the Moral Recovery Program in the Philippines, as Maraya de Jesus Chebat describes it, is its effect on future conflicts in society. She focuses on conflicts resulting from a disharmony among people in a society rather than on conflicts resulting from competitions over power. The Moral Recovery Program aims to transform Filipino society and reduce destructive competitive conflicts in the future by renewing Filipinos' common identity as interconnected beings.

In Malaysia, where no mechanism exists to resolve environmental disputes, Gurmit Singh, in "Toxic Waste Management in Malyasia," emphasizes the importance of the government being open with information and of all citizens becoming involved in environmental issues to avoid large conflicts.

The sixth hypothesis is suggested by these cases:

H6: In high-context cultures, social conflict management emphasizes preventive measures by monitoring or mediating stress in a more proactive manner.

Whereas Hypotheses 1 and 2 referred to the labeling of the existence of a conflict, the next two refer to defining the possible ways the conflict can be dealt with.

In "Culture and Conflict in Canada: Tradition and Transition," Michelle LeBaron argues that mediation in South Asia emphasizes acceptance over change and the integrative potential benefits of reconciliation. Thus in relationships with a power imbalance or high power distance, the high party participant frames the conflict as win-lose and thus limits conflict resolution procedures and outcomes. In the low-context Canadian culture, the husband's expectations of forbearance, nonconfrontation, face saving, and women's deference to men, limited how his wife's conflict with him could be resolved. There was no agency to force him to change his expectations and no traditional community ties to force Rajpal to comply. Thus, the individual, the husband Balbir, defined how conflict and conflict resolution would be defined. The seventh hypothesis was developed from this case in low-context Canada:

H7: In low-context cultures, resolution and mediation are individually defined by the individuals involved in conflict.

Other case studies in this volume suggest something different. In Pauline Tangiora's study of Maori conflict resolution, the tribe called upon the government's Ministry of Conservation and Environment. The intent was not to turn over the conflict to the government. In New Zealand's bicultural society, Maori traditions and processes are acknowledged. Thus, the Ministry directed that the developers must gain the consent of the tribal people as well as adhere to the Ministry's policies. In a real way, the Maori determined the conflict resolution process.

In the Bangladesh case study "Khukumoni and Masud: Living Happily Now," the woman Khukumoni suffered physical and mental abuse alone. Her marriage was not accepted by her or her husband's family. She had no way to deal with her situation until her cause was taken on by the social welfare organization Banchte Shekha. It was then Banchte Shekha's actions that transformed Khukumoni and Masud's marriage and relationship with their families.

In "The Effects of Tribal Wars on Personal and Family Disputes in Papua New Guinea," Norma had several options to address her dispute with her husband. Had she chosen to approach tribal elders, a likely outcome would have been tribal war, considered an accepted way to deal with conflicts that start on the family level. The tribal elders would not have likely dealt with the conflict on the one-on-one level between husband and wife.

The eighth hypothesis was developed from these cases from high-context cultures:

H8: In high-context cultures, conflict and its resolution/mediation are defined by the group or culture.

Given the characteristics of conflicts in high-context cultures, as have been suggested in the above hypotheses, it is reasonable to examine the role of outsiders in Asia-Pacific conflicts. The role of parties from outside the Asia-Pacific region can be seen in "Tiger Saves Taiga: Saving the Siberian Ecosystem From Hyundai's Logging Operations." International environmentalists, including Greenpeace, were threatening a worldwide boycott of Hyundai products. It would be easy to predict that such a boycott alone might have negative affects and unanticipated results. But the international environmentalists also made contact with a Korean NGO who could act as an intermediary and peacemaker. Both of these actions are important: They called world public attention to Hyundai's logging operations in Russia and also established a relationship with a potential mediator.

In "Philippine Rural Development and Indigenous Communities: Aytas and the Sacobia Project," international media called attention to the fate of the marginalized Aytas. The case author, Eduardo Tadem, believes that subsequent government actions seemed to have been influenced by that public attention.

However, the ethnic conflict in Sri Lanka does not yet show the positive outcome of public awareness. Jayadeva Uyangoda, in "Recent Attempt at Ethnic Conflict Resolution in Sri Lanka," argues that the Sri Lankan government resists any outside intervention as it perceives the conflict as an internal affair.

From these cases, the following hypothesis was developed to define the role of "outsiders" in conflicts in the Asia-Pacific region:

H9: The role of internationals and the media from low-context cultures is not to intervene in conflicts in high-context cultures but to call public attention to the situation so that resolution/mediation can take place on its own.

The next two hypotheses deal with the use of ritual and spirituality in the process of mediation in low- and high-context cultures. In one sense, a change in the conflict, a transformation, is its resolution, or what is labeled as a resolution is a transformation of the relationship between the parties. In the case presented by Michelle LeBaron, when Rajpal left her husband Balbir, the conflict was transformed. Nothing marked her leaving; the consequence was that her family no longer speaks to her. From this case, the 10th hypothesis was developed:

H10: In low-context cultures, settlements are usually devoid of ritual and spirituality.

Different authors do, however, refer to spiritual elements in their descriptions of conflicts and their resolutions. In her description of the Moral Recovery Program, Maraya de Jesus Chebat emphasized that among the relationships to be transformed was the relationship between individuals and the supreme spiritual force or principle governing the universe.

The settlement of a dispute itself may have more meaning than any tangible value the settlement may have. For example, in the Bangladesh case "Nabin and Nasima: Conflict Engendered by Religious Prescriptions," the woman's father asked the Madaripur Legal Aid Association for mediation in an attempt to regain social acceptance for his daughter. The outcome of the mediation, a fine assessed against the young man's father, was not legal, but it did allow the daughter to get married and purchase some land.

Lu Guojiang, in "China and Japan Dispute Copyright of 'Ultraman' Toys," describes the ceremony surrounding the signing of the conciliation agreement. An important part of that ceremony was an apology to the Japanese animation studio.

The most telling example of the importance of ritual is in Chalidaporn Songsamphan's "Vendetta and Buddhist Mediator in Southern Thailand." The disputing families had been through a year of gunfights, injury, and death. The Buddhist monk mediator first preached the Buddhist teaching that hatred could not be stopped by hatred but only by forgiveness. Then he had bullets, grenades, and knives put in a container of water, asked the members of both families to take an oath to stop killing each other, and had them drink from the container the *nam sabarn* ("sworn water"). Lao Tzu said in the 5th century B.C., "Ceremonies are the outward expressing of inner feelings."

From these cases from high-context cultures, the 11th hypothesis was developed:

H11: In high-context cultures, settlements are most often accompanied by ritual and spirituality.

One case examines the impacts of immigration from one culture to another. Michelle LeBaron's "Culture and Conflict in Canada: Tradition and Transition" best illustrates the consequences that immigration can have on conflict and conflict resolution. In a culture such as Canada, mediation is focused on an issue, is driven by time and the need to reach an agreement, and excludes all parties except the disputants. LeBaron argues that in South Asia traditional mediation emphasizes community and the extended family and thus values forbearance, nonconfrontation, face saving, and acceptance. The expectations that these immigrants have about mediation are not consistent with contemporary Canadian society. From this case, the 12th hypothesis was developed:

H12: New arrivals from high-context cultures will not be served best by conflict resolution/mediation strategies developed in low-context cultures.

Related to this are situations in which groups of individuals from high- and low-context cultures must work together. Such situations can occur, of course, in international conferences and in international organizations and businesses. The Maori case study addresses this question.

Because of their special role in New Zealand, the Maori could determine the conflict resolution process to be used. The government acted with the Maori to determine that the tribal community consensus decision-making process must deal with an "outsider" proposal for a development project. The

Maori had the power to determine how the dispute would be handled. From this case, the 13th hypothesis was developed:

H13: In groups combining high- and low-context cultures, the most powerful group's style of dispute resolution/mediation will predominate.

We can look at "The Effects of Tribal Wars on Personal and Family Disputes in Papua New Guinea" as contact between low context, as represented by Norma, and high context, as represented by Norma's husband. From the high context of customary tribal laws, Norma's husband had done no wrong nor had any reason to change. From the low context of her modernity, Norma could not deal with her husband as an individual disputant. In one sense, her husband was but a point of contact for the entire group he represented. For Norma to deal with him on his terms meant she would have to deal with the entire group and its traditions and values. From this case, the 14th hypothesis is suggested:

H14: Low-context organizations in high-context cultures will avoid "traditional" alternative dispute resolution strategies and prefer court settlements.

The next hypothesis deals with the relationship between mediation and the courts. Shir-Shing Huang, in "The Reconciliation System of the Republic of China," points out that the success of mediation in China is due to the traditional belief that lawsuits should be avoided in favor of peaceful dispositions of disputes. This is consistent with popular beliefs represented in the 15th hypothesis:

H15: Relying on courts to resolve/mediate conflict is regarded as a failure in high-context cultures.

Yet this is not universally true. For example, in China, as described by Lu Guojiang in "China and Japan Dispute Copyright of 'Ultraman' Toys," court-ordered mediation successfully handles the majority of disputes. Likewise in Japan, when mediation failed in the case "The Dumping of Industrial Waste in Teshima, Japan," the residents of Teshima Island then began to consider going to court.

However, it may be extrapolated from Michelle LeBaron's case study that the real issue is legitimacy and authority. South Asia immigrants in Canada demonstrate a preference for Canadian courts, whereas in South Asia, they may well have preferred traditional conflict resolution for the same issue. It may not be that relying on courts is regarded as a failure in societies with a strong traditional mediation process so much as it may be that the process with the most legitimacy and authority within the confines of a given culture are preferred.

Cost and delays of the court system are also an issue. In Sri Lanka, both mediation boards and the court system exist. Mediation is often chosen because the courts are costly and slow. For example in Bangladesh, the case study authors make it quite clear that the popularity of traditional village mediation by local elites had declined. Even though courts were expensive, traditional mediation declined because the people perceived that the mediators lacked neutrality and that mediation outcomes were determined by the mediators' opinions the disputants were compelled to accept.

The concept of "face," or the respect one has in the eyes of one's reference group, is mentioned in several case studies in this book. Chalidaporn Songsamphan, in "Vendetta and Buddhist Mediator in Southern Thailand," describes how the mediator Prakru Kasem met with both parties separately before the mediation so that neither side would lose face.

And in "Tiger Saves Taiga," Jae Hyun Yoo describes the importance of face. His role as the intermediary and his presentations to Joo Young Chung, chairman of Hyundai, demonstrate his skill in avoiding what could have developed into an international incident.

These cases lead to the final two hypotheses:

H16: Low-context cultures prefer dispute resolution/mediation to be face-to-face.

H17: High-context cultures prefer to do dispute resolution/mediation through intermediaries.

FINAL REMARKS

This chapter has attempted to synthesize what we have learned from studying the 24 cases of conflict management in the Asia-Pacific region. We have attempted to demonstrate the importance of context, differentiating between high-context and low-context cultures. Generally, these Asia-Pacific cases demonstrated a high-context perspective that made quite different assumptions than are typical of a low-context perspective demonstrated in most of the literature about mediation and conflict management in the Euro-American context. We have also tried to demonstrate the importance of interpreting behaviors in the context of the expectations and intentions of the person displaying those behaviors. The separation of behaviors from expectations prevents our interpreting the behaviors outside their cultural context, which can result in misinterpretation.

We have addressed several important issues in constructive conflict management. First, do cultural values control the process of conflicit management? We conclude that cultural values have at least a strong influence on the way that conflict is managed and the success or failure of that management. Second, do age and gender describe salient cultural affiliations? We conclude that affiliations of age and/or gender may at times be more salient than nationality and/or ethnicity in a particular conflict. Third, why does ethnic conflict tend to be especially explosive? We conclude that the stronger the two cultural groups each are, the more explosive a conflict is likely to be between those two groups who see the outcome as a win-lose alternative. Fourth, what are the criteria of successful mediation across cultures? We conclude that the criteria used in the 24 Asia-Pacific cases are often quite different from those used in the Euro-American context. Fifth, what should a constructive conflict manager do? We conclude that the task of constructive conflict management is a complicated one with no easy or simple set of guidelines. Sixth, what is the relationship between mediation and the courts? We conclude that in instances where mediation was linked to the court system in a harmonious way it provided an economical and efficient supplementary service. Seventh, what is unique about constructive conflict management? We conclude that there are features that are clearly unique. Eighth, can we generalize from the Asia-Pacific examples? We have offered 17 hypotheses that could be researched to determine the generalizability of patterns emerging from these 24 case examples.

The task of constructive conflict management is complicated and is defined quite differently in each cultural context. This analysis of selected case studies from the Asia-Pacific region is an attempt to sharpen the questions we might ask as we seek to increase the efficency and effectiveness of constructive conflict management in the global context.

REFERENCES

Bernstein, B. (1964). Elaborated and restricted codes: Their social origins and some consequences. *American Anthropologist, 60,* 55-69.

Cambra, R., Ishii, S., & Klopf, D. (1978). *Four studies of Japanese speech characteristics.* Paper presented at the annual meeting of the International Communication Association, Tokyo, Japan.

Felstiner, W. F. (1982). *Influences of social organization on dispute processing in neighborhood justice: An assessment of an emerging idea.* New York and London: Longman.

Hall, E. T. (1976). *Beyond culture.* New York: Anchor.

Hofstede, G. (1983). Dimensions of national cultures in fifty countries and three regions. In J. B. Deregowski, S. Dziurawiec, & R. C. Annis (Eds.), *Expectations in cross-cultural psychology* (pp. 335-355). Lisse, The Netherlands: Swets & Zeitlinger.

Ishii, S. (1984). Enryo-Sasshi communication: A key to understanding Japanese interpersonal relations. *Cross Currents, 11,* 49-58.

Ishii, S., & Klopf, D. (1976). A comparison of communication activities of Japanese and American adults. *ELEC Bulletin, 53,* 22-26.

Kondo, M. (1981). *Karucha shock no shinri* [The psychology of culture shock]. Osaka: Sogensha.

Kunihiro, M. (1976, Winter). The Japanese language and intercultural communication. *The Japanese Interpreter,* pp. 267-283.

Shook, E. V. (1985). Ho'oponopono: Contemporary uses of a Hawaiian problem-solving process. Honolulu: University of Hawaii Press.

United Nations Development Program. (1993). *Human development report.* New York: Author.

Wayne, M. (1974). The meaning of silence in conversations in three cultures. In ICU Communication Student Group (Ed.), *Patterns of communication in and out of Japan* (pp. 127-130). Tokyo: ICU Communication Department.

Williams, R. M., Jr. (1947). *The reduction of intergroup tensions.* New York: Social Science Research Council.

Index

About the Editors

Fred E. Jandt received his doctoral degree in communication. He has been a professor of communication and director of faculty development and research at State University of New York, College at Brockport, and founding chair and professor of communication at California State University, San Bernardino. His research interest is the overlap of culture and conflict studies. His publications include *Intercultural Communication: An Introduction* (1995) and *Win-Win Negotiating: Turning Conflict Into Agreement* (1985), which is available in seven languages. He has consulted in the establishment of a community-based mediation service and developed a training program for the California Department of Transportation based on his model of negotiation and conflict. He has extensive experience in organizational training in the areas of intercultural communication and diversity, negotiation and mediation, and other aspects of communication.

Paul B. Pedersen is a professor in the Department of Human Studies at the University of Alabama, Birmingham. Prior to this appointment, he was a professor at Syracuse University in the departments of Counseling and Human Services and of International Relations. He taught at universities in Indonesia and Malaysia and studied Mandarin one year in Taiwan. He holds an M.A. in American studies and an M.S. in educational psychology from the University of Minnesota. He has been on the faculty at both the University of Minnesota and the University of Hawaii where he was also director of a NIMH training grant to develop interculturally skilled counselors. He is a Fellow in three divisions of the American Psychological Association and was president of the Society for Intercultural Education Training and Research. He has published 26 books, 44 chapters, 76 articles, and 19 other monograph-length documents.

About the Contributors

Maraya de Jesus Chebat is a depth and transpersonal psychologist, a human development specialist, and a process consultant. She founded the Center for the Management of Core Energy and the Tahanan Wholistic Health Center in the 1980s. She conducts workshops on human development and organizational transformation through body-mind and spiritual integration that leads to wholeness and has authored two books, *Core Energy: A Primer on Body-Mind Integration* and *Core Energy as a Stress Management Program.* She was facilitator for the NGO's Earth Summit Conference in Brazil in 1992. Currently, she is a training director for the Propagation of Moral Recovery, a program aimed at mobilizing all Filipinos for nation building through the practical exercise of human values. She and her team conduct transformational leadership training workshops for government officials and for NGO leaders to awaken all to their powers and potential in bringing about a just, humane, and prosperous society, espousing the national goals of a leadership and citizenry that are concerned with love for people, country, environment, and God.

Julie Foster Smith is of Australian Aborigine and Papua New Guinean descent and has lived and worked among her own people in both countries. She has taught at the University of Sydney and presently teaches inmates in Sydney's Long Bay jail. Through her work she has researched social problems of alcohol, drug abuse, and prisoner rehabilitation. As a member of the Morata Community Development Foundation she has come in contact with women victims of domestic violence and sexual assault.

Lu Guojiang holds a bachelor's degree in law from Fudan (Branch) University and a master's degree in law from Shanghai Academy of Social Sciences. In 1987, he was appointed Judge of Shanghai High People's Court. In 1992, he was appointed the same court's Deputy Chief Director of Research Department and in 1994 was appointed its Deputy Chief Judge, Division for Intellectual Property.

Shir-Shing Huang attended the National Taiwan University from 1978 to 1982 and the Graduate School of East Asian Studies at National Chengchi University, was a junior staff member of the Board of Foreign Trade and a specialist in, and currently a section chief of, the Ministry of Justice.

Michelle LeBaron received her training in law and counseling psychology and teaches at the Institute for Conflict Analysis and Resolution at George Mason University. She directed an extensive study from 1990 to 1993 called "Multiculturalism and Dispute Resolution" at the University of Victoria, Canada. She lectures internationally on multicultural, environmental, and public policy conflict resolution and is an experienced mediator and trainer in family, commercial, public policy, and diversity-related disputes. She is author of numerous publications, including *Conflict and Culture: A Literature Review and Bibliography* (1993), *Conflict Analysis and Resolution as Education: Culturally Sensitive Processes for Conflict Resolution* (1994), *Conflict Resolution for Educators* (1994), a chapter titled "The Quest for Qualifications: A Quick Trip Without a Good Map" in *Qualifications for Dispute Resolution: Perspectives on the Debate,* edited by Catherine Morris and Andrew Pirie (1994), and a coauthored article, with Jim Potts, titled "Story and Legend: Powerful Tools for Conflict Resolution" (1993).

Madaripur Legal Aid Association was formally founded in 1978 from a small group of volunteer lawyers and social workers who had been offering free legal assistance to the poor in Madaripur. The organization now has a permanent staff and law library and training center. Its objectives include settling disputes through mediation as an alternative to litigation, educating workers about their rights under labor law, protecting women against torture and arbitrary divorce proceedings, educating citizens about their fundamental human rights, and working to reform the law and legal system in Bangladesh. The association provides free legal assistance to the disadvantaged for land, matrimonial, and oppression-type criminal cases and makes every effort to assist helpless women and orphans by providing free legal assistance and access to justice. Its women's welfare project provides economic assistance and loans to divorced, abandoned, widowed, and other poor female clients for small income-generating projects such as making handicrafts and tailoring and raising poultry. A major effort of the association is its Training and Resource Center, which works with mediators, paralegals, legal aid lawyers, human rights workers, and students and teachers in schools and colleges.

Wan Halim Othman is executive director of HITEC Management, a human resources/mediation consulting group. He received his B.A. from Monash University in Victoria, Australia, and his M.Sc. and doctorate from the University of Bristol in England. He was Dean of Social Sciences and Director of the Centre for Policy Research at the Universiti Sains Malaysia. He has been a research or training consultant for UNICEF, The Asia Foundation, the Konrad Adenauer Foundation, and Malaysia's Department of National Unity for more than 10 years. His publications include *Perkembangan Awal Kanak-Kanak: Panduan Bagi Pengasuh* [Early Child Development: A Guide for Caregivers], *Pendidikan Sivik Untuk Belia* [Civil Education for Youths], and *Asas Bimbingan Individu dan Keluarga* [The Basics of Individual and Family Counseling].

Jagadish C. Pokharel is president of the Center for Alternative Dispute Resolution (CADR), a nongovernmental organization based in Kathmandu, Nepal. He holds a master's degree in urban and regional planning from the University of Hawaii and a doctorate from the Massachusetts Institute of Technology. He has taught at the Tribhuban University Institute of Engineering in Kathmandu. He was a senior advisor to the United Nations Development Program's decentralization support project in Nepal. He has been senior advisor to the Water and Energy Commission, Ministry of Water Resources, HMG/Nepal. He has published numerous articles on natural resource management, conflict, and security issues, including "Population Displacement and Compensation Planning in Kulekhani Hydroelectric Project" in *Development, Displacement, and Resettlement: Focus on Asian Experiments* (1995) and *Environmental Resource Negotiation Between Unequal Powers: Power Sources of Weaker Nations* (1995). His research interests include the role of power in natural resource conflicts at the community and national level. He is currently working on environmental and natural resource management in an interjurisdictional context and particularly the problems along the international borders in the South Asian countries.

Gauri Pradhan is the founder and president of Child Workers in Nepal Concerned Center (CWIN). He received both his bachelor's degree in commerce and his MBA from Tribhuvan University in Nepal. He is also president of the Defense for Children International—Nepal (DCI) and of the Children at Risk Networking Group (CAR-NWG) and convener of the South Asian regional forum on the rights of children. He is a member of the National Council of Women and Children, the Forum for Protection of Human Rights (FOPHUR), and South Asian Coalition Against Child Servitude. He was writer and resource person for the publications *Misery Behind the Looms, Child Labour in Nepal,* and *Trafficking in Young Girls in Nepal* and continues to work for the rights of children and women.

Ariya Rubasinghe is a senior officer in the Sri Lanka Administrative Service. Prior to his present assignment, he served as secretary to the Mediation Boards Commission and initiated the establishment of 211 mediation boards in the country as an effective system of conflict resolution in the community. Presently, he is director of the Government Information Department and a member of the National Mediation Boards Commission appointed by the president of Sri Lanka.

Gurmit Singh is an environmentalist, social activist, and engineer. He received his B.E. (electrical) degree from the University of Malaya in 1970 and has been a registered professional engineer and member of the Institution of Engineers, Malaysia since 1974. He has held or holds the positions of executive director of the Centre for Environment, Technology & Development, Malaysia; president of and advisor for the Environmental Protection Society, Malaysia; secretary-general of the National Human Rights Society; member of the Environmental Quality Council, Malaysia; Steering Committee member of Climate Action Network, Southeast Asia; and coordinator for the Malaysian Climate Core Group. In 1993, he received the Langkawi Award from the Malaysian government.

Chalidaporn Songsamphan is a lecturer on the Faculty of Political Science at Thammasat University, Bangkok, Thailand. Research interests include conflict resolution, feminism, culture, and the military and politics.

Eduardo C. Tadem is currently coordinator of the Asian Regional Exchange for New Alternatives, a regional forum of concerned Asian scholars for the promotion of alternative paradigms of development to benefit the continent's vast majority of marginalized populations. He is presently on leave as Assistant Professor of Development Studies at the University of the Philippines, Manila. Over the years, he has published extensively and conducted numerous research projects on, among others, rural development, agrarian reform, peasant movements, plantation economies, foreign aid and investments, development theories, and Philippine-Japan relations.

Pauline Tangiora has worked for over 40 years with both Maori and Pakeha on issues of peace, justice, and women. Her tribal affiliations are to Rongomiwahine and Kahungunu. As a tribal elder she has taken a leading role in Maori issues concerning the environment, health, education, land rights, and foreign affairs. She is a member of the Earth Council, Nobel Peace Laureate Rigoberta Menchu Tum's Committee on Indigenous Initiate for Peace, World Council for Indigenous Peoples, Women's International League for Peace and Freedom, and the Maori Women's Welfare League. She has represented Aotearoa at many international gatherings, including the World Conference on Human Rights and the United Nations Year of Indigenous Peoples, and has published or spoken on Maori perspectives, on conflict resolution, mediation, and negotiation, and on the environment.

Jayadeva Uyangoda is a human rights and peace activist. He received his B.A. in political science in 1980 and his doctorate in political science in 1986. He is a senior lecturer in political science at the University of Colombo, Sri Lanka; director of the Center for Policy Research and Analysis, University of Colombo; and currently chair of the Sri Lanka Foundation, Colombo. He was a founding member of Movement for Inter-Racial Justice and Equality, Sri Lanka, and a founding member of Information Monitoring in Human Rights, Sri Lanka. He is actively involved in the campaign for peace and democracy in Sri Lanka.

Xue Wang was a lecturer in the Department of Social Science of Northeast University of Technology (now known as Northeast University) in Shenyang, northeastern China, before leaving for Australia in 1991 to begin doctoral studies in the Department of Government and Public Administration. Current research focuses on the social role of Chinese women in contemporary China after 1978.

Nacha Worawattanamateekul is chief of the Personnel Division in the Office of Judicial Affairs in Thailand. Formerly, she was an assistant general service/general administration officer on the National Economic and Social Development Board in the Office of the Prime Minister of Thailand.

Masaki Yokoyama is Professor of Asian and Environmental Studies in the Department of Sociology at Shikoku Gakuin University, Kagawa, Japan. He received a B.S. degree in physics and his master's and doctoral degrees in economics from Rikkyo University, Tokyo. He served as coordinator of the open lecture forum of the Anti-Pollution Citizens' Movement at Tokyo University (Jishu-Koza) and as publication coordinator of *KOGAI—Newsletter From Polluted Japan.* In 1991, he was a visiting research scholar in the Political Science Department, University of Canterbury, New Zealand and a visiting research fellow at Third World Studies Center, University of the Philippines in 1991-1992. His publications include *Japan, Inc. in Asia: A Documentation of Its Operations Through the Philippine Polity,* coedited with Akashi Shoten (1992), *Shiminrentairon to Shiteno Daisan Sekai* [A Theory of Citizens' Solidarity With the Third World], coathored with Jun Kubota and others (1993), and *Kankyo Hakai: Shakai Shokagaku No Oto* [Environmental Destruction: A Response From the Social Sciences], coauthored with Jun Ui and others (1995). He has been a governing board member of the Peace Studies Association of Japan since 1989.

Jae Hyun Yoo has a B.S. and M.S. in architecture from Seoul National University and a M.S. and doctorate in urban planning from Columbia University. He taught architecture at Ulsan University, was a research fellow at Columbia, and a housing policy analyst at the Department of Housing Preservation and Development in New York City. From 1988 to 1992, he was director of Hanssam Housing and Environment Research Institute. Currently, he is general secretary of the Citizen's Coalition for Economic Justice (CCEJ), which he helped found in 1989. CCEJ is working for social reform and development of citizens' movement through rational criticism and presentation of concrete policy alternatives, based on the participation of citizens from all sectors and classes. He previously served as executive director of Korea Economic Justice Institute and as chief executive officer of the Center for Environment and Development of CCEJ.